CW00406918

DOES INDIA NEED A DICTATOR

Bill K Koul

Vitasta

LET KNOWLEDGE SPREAD

Published by
Renu Kaul Verma
Vitasta Publishing Pvt Ltd
2/15, Ansari Road, Daryaganj
New Delhi - 110 002
info@vitastapublishing.com

ISBN 978-93-86473-33-2
© Bill K Koul
MRP ₹595
First Edition 2018

Editor Veena Batra
Cover and layout by Somesh Kumar Mishra
Printed by Vikas Computer and Printers

To India

&

My mother, Rani

And to those struggling millions in India, who suffer daily, feel helpless, have no voice, crave for positive changes in the country, pray to God and hope for miracles that can transform their country into a happy and habitable place.

People of accomplishment rarely sit back and let things happen to them. They go out and happen to things.

—Elinor Smith

This book

This book should be of interest to the policymakers in India and all those readers who are interested in political science and legislation, education and education system, environment and sustainability, Kashmir, and all well-wishers and friends of India.

This book is about India and India alone, and not about religion. It has been written with intent to provoke a debate across the country.

This book has been driven by heart; it will need a heart to understand its core message. It is an expression of the author's feelings, personal observations and deep concerns about India's sustainability in all areas of life. It is based on the obvious.

Kashmir, being the geographical head of the country, has a special coverage in this book. A peaceful Kashmir is vital for India's health, and vice versa. Without Kashmir, the country will disintegrate. Kashmir must be peacefully and earnestly integrated into the union of India.

The author is a professional engineer and deals with engineering work for foundations that support the civil and mining infrastructure. This book is an extrapolation of the author's concerns about the integrity of the foundations of India as a country. It has been written and compiled as a desperate attempt to save the country. It does not claim to be a scholarly work.

The author is not affiliated with any political party in India or abroad.

He is inspired by John Stuart Mill (1806-1873), the most influential English philosopher, naturalist, utilitarian and liberal of the nineteenth century.

The author is also inspired by Kees Boeke (1884-1966), a Dutch reformist, educator, Quaker missionary and pacifist, who originally put sociocracy into action at his school in the Netherlands; and Gerard Endenburg (born 1933), a Dutch electrical engineer and entrepreneur, who has run his organisation based on the sociocratic principles and has been a champion of sociocracy in the Netherlands since the seventies.

HOW?

How can a country achieve good health when its leaders, howsoever dynamic and visionary, fear the prospect of losing the general elections once they talk about a dire need to eliminate the sources of its diseases via the introduction of a stringent population control and the imposition of uniform civil law?

How can a country claim to be secular and democratic when it gobbles up, just within a space of 28 years, half a million indigenous Kashmiri Pandits who were forced to leave their home and hearth in 1990 to save their lives and honour from foreign sponsored Islamic terrorists in Kashmir?

How can a country survive when its army looks mainly outward to defend the country's borders from foreign enemies, whilst turning a blind eye towards much bigger enemies who lurk inside the country disguised as politicians, political activists, human right activists, journalists and the media personnel, constantly striving to tear the country apart?

How can a country survive self-annihilation when its people look at one another as material things and exploit them for personal gains—by using, abusing and misusing them as consumables and commodities?

How can a country get rid of corruption and immorality if its citizens believe in making donations and offerings to gods and temples with an expectation of not only washing away their sins but also receiving greater wealth and success as return gifts?

How can a country attain happiness when it focusses mainly on its economic growth, and not on the education of its poor masses and the health of its people—both internal (spiritual and mental) and physical health?

How can a country be sustainable when it consciously replaces its traditional simplistic and spiritual lifestyle with a materialistic lifestyle driven by consumption and consumerism, with least awareness and respect for the environmental health?

How can a country survive fragmentation and strife when its people identify themselves first with their religions, castes and ethnicities, and then with India, if at all? How can it survive where even colours are divided along religious lines; saffron associated with Hindus, yellow with Sikhs and green with Muslims?

How can a country call itself progressive when women, that comprise half of its population, are not regarded as equal to men; if its educated classes form opinions based on polarising rhetoric by the media, rather than the obvious; and mindlessly show off their status in grand social weddings?

Acknowledgement

I wish to acknowledge all those hundreds of students, taxi drivers, porters, rickshaw pullers, street vendors, working class citizens and professionals across India with whom I have interacted during my several visits to the country between October 2016 and August 2018.

Support from my family in Perth, in particular my wife, Dr Rekha Bhan Koul, is also sincerely acknowledged during the writing phase of the book—for initial proofreading of the manuscript, discussions about the Indian education system and for putting up with the long hours of my absence.

I wish to thank wholeheartedly and acknowledge the input of a number of authors whose articles, published in various newspapers in India and abroad, have been referenced and included in this book solely in the context of the book and to supplement my independent thoughts about the current state of the country.

I also wish to thank and acknowledge my friend Rakesh Misri from Mumbai, as well as Dale Hartley (Blue Wheelers Applecross), for their input into our discussions about the subject matter. I also wish to thank my colleagues Nick Lowe and Payam Sadeghi for their inputs to our numerous lunch-time heated discussions on several serious matters of life and liveability. Nick is also acknowledged for his assistance with formatting of the first draft of the manuscript. My very sincere thanks to Ella Fitriani and Farzad Beyghi for their respective key roles in my writing journey thus far.

This book would not have been possible without continued support from my publisher, Vitasta Publishing Pvt Ltd, New Delhi. I, therefore, wish to acknowledge that support and sincerely thank the Managing Director of Vitasta, Renu Kaul Verma, for bringing this important book to the people of India and overseas, and my editor, Veena Batra, for her excellent editing work.

Vitasta has previously published my following three books:

- *22 Years—a Kashmir Story*

- *My life does not have to be unhappy*

- *Issues White-anting India.*

Bill K Koul
Perth, Western Australia
6 August 2018

Contents

Introduction

Why this book?

India gained independence from the British rulers seven decades ago, but not from the Indian rulers. The erstwhile kings and princes were simply replaced by modern day, self-aggrandising politicians who operate mainly for their own personal interests under the guise of a tweaked and flawed Indian democratic system, and by throwing dust in the eyes of millions of Indians. Nepotism is the order of the day.

How is 2018 different to 1947? What has changed? Same politicians, albeit with different names and faces, and party ideologies! Same electoral system! Same ignorance and backwardness! The country still practises the same Indian version of democracy, with numerous big question marks on it. If the system has not worked for the masses all these decades, except for the politicians and the wealthy, how can one hope that it will work for the poor masses and the country's environmental sustainability in the future—just because the politicians promise it will?

The country's Happiness Index is low, far below that of its neighbours. This is a country where females, who comprise half of the population, are not considered as equal to the males; their rapes are an everyday affair; even one year olds are not spared. Female foeticide is practised and females are disproportionately disempowered in many communities. This is a country where army jawans and farmers commit suicide on a regular basis, albeit for different reasons. The army and their military missions are imprudently politicised by the politicians and the media.

Since 1947, the country has become four times more populated. It has also become much more polluted, corrupt and divided. New states have been created in the past decade to address some inherent divisions within the country. Kashmir has constantly been on the boil and the Khalistan movement has not died out. North-East and the south of India have a mind of their own.

In 2018, India continues to be backward and poor, with a very low level of education across the country. One can imagine the levels of backwardness and education in the country from the current campaign against defecation in the open and why people should use a lavatory with a closed door. Paradoxically, this country boasts of being a leader in space technology.

The environment and liveability in the cities have been constantly dwindling; cities are fast becoming inhabitable, with ever rising pollution, insecurity, traffic woes and disease. One does not know what one is breathing, drinking and eating. The trust factor between the individuals is all but gone. Individual survival has become the utmost priority, breeding several selfish generations in the country. Without connections and, of course, bribes, no work can be accomplished; corruption is entrenched in the Indian DNA. Insecurity is so high in the country that students are now provided with tracking devices and are constantly monitored by surveillance cameras and CCTVs in some schools. What can be the future of a country where the medical and law & order systems are known to be amongst the highest corrupted?

This is a country where the Opposition and a section of the media term the current Prime Minister a 'dictator'. Obviously, they have no idea what the term 'dictator' means because they have not seen one yet; they were born mostly after 1947! One would only wish the current Prime Minister had much freer hands to nip the core issues facing the country in the bud once and for all, and not working with his hands tied with the ropes of democracy and the Constitution! His situation is not much different to the jawans in Kashmir who share a similar feeling—fighting the enemies of the nation with one hand tied at the back!

Interestingly, this is also a country where the Leader of the Opposition is branded as a 'fool', without any obvious political leadership qualities or any great educational qualifications to boast of. He seems to be hiding behind an inherited famous family name, an obvious product of the age old practice of nepotism in the country. Undoubtedly, he must be sympathised with for the legacy he is carrying. At a young age, he saw the blood of his father and grandmother being violently spilled on the ground. Numerous greedy people in the Opposition exploit his family name and prop him up as the party's face and hide behind him, but only for their own selfish gains. On a regular basis, hilarious video clips showing what the Leader of the Opposition says at public gatherings and media interviews circulate on the social media as free entertainment at the end of a tiring work day. At the same time, one wonders what would be the fate of the country if the current Prime Minister loses in the next general elections! It would be a big circus show! The founding fathers of the country's independence must be rolling in their graves as we speak.

A big circus but who is paying? The country is paying and will pay dearly if the current system of governance is allowed to continue; it will keep throwing the country in the hands of criminals, buffoons, looters, exploiters and impotent people.

The Indian subcontinent had never seen anything like democracy prior to 1947. India has seen the Indian version of democracy in the past seventy years since her independence. Given the current sad state of environment and liveability, with more than 70 per cent of population poor and uneducated, and an alarmingly rising population, Indian democracy does not seem to have served the country as well as it ought to have, not because of democracy itself but mostly because of the gross exploitation, misuse and abuse of the democratic principles by generations of corrupt and selfish politicians.

Only a small percentage of Indians, mainly from urban areas, apparently have benefited from Indian democracy and that too very disproportionately. Wealth and education have not been spread uniformly across the country. In comparison, one could take a look at China and the progress that country has made by leaps and bounds despite having more population than India. Even by Happiness Index, the Chinese people are about 40 places above (happier) than the Indians.

For a healthy democracy to thrive, voters must be educated and well-informed, which is not the case in India, mainly due to the poor state of education especially amongst the 70 per cent that live in the villages. Most importantly, for a healthy democracy, the electoral system must be transparent, sans cronyism, nepotism and corruption, which is also not what one sees in India.

Democracy, based on a majority vote tends to exclude the interest of the minority vote. India being a flawed democracy, with different laws for different faiths and a policy of reservations does not treat all its citizens equally. The country is perceived differently by different people, with different levels of sense of belonging, or no sense at all. Currently, the Indian community is seen to be divided along regional, religious and caste lines, pulling in different directions, and potentially ripping the country apart. The Indian democracy has sowed deep-seated elements of discontent and discord, marginalisation, and apprehensions within many communities. Furthermore, decision-making by the majority vote has encouraged widespread malicious practices of social and political bullying. It has also seen growth in corrupt practices, such as selling and buying of votes at the village-head level, booth capturing by political parties, fake votes, coercion, fudging of numbers etc. all of which thwart the very concept of democracy and undermine its foundation.

As such, Indian democracy is not deemed fit for the country and, therefore, must be scrapped at the earliest before it causes any further damage to the nation. India must change its course before it is too late. Indians deserve an effective and decisive form of governance to quickly turn things around. Why should the country live with a system that has seemingly failed its masses? It is not too late to change it for good. A period of seventy years is not a very long time in the history of a massively populous nation such as India, where it is a matter of 1.35 billion people at present, and potentially 1.7 billion lives in the next 30 years or so. It should not matter who is at the helm or which party is ruling. Instead, what is more important is that the country must be given a sustainable and healthy system of governance to serve all her people regardless of who is ruling and from which political party.

As an alternative to democracy, a governing system based on the sociocratic principles is most suited for India—a multi-faith, multi-racial and multi-ethnic nation—one which is also divided along the caste and regional lines. Sociocracy truly serves to meet the basic noble objectives of democracy sans the shortcomings of democracy, as seen in India and other countries around the world. Sociocracy provides a system of inclusiveness amongst the citizens, builds trust between the communities and creates an environment of harmony in the country. Decision-making is undertaken by consensus by the elected (educated and level-headed) representatives of the people. Because decisions are taken only by consensus, and not by the majority vote, all decision-makers are on board with the decisions taken and no one person feels left out to sulk and plan disruptive political moves, as is seen in the current Indian democracy.

The decision process in sociocracy has potential to be transparent, honest and based on rationale, not just based on whims and the self-interest of the members. A sociocratic organisation also has the potential to build mutual trust between the members. As such, people operate in an environment of harmony and, consequently, the overall productivity of the organisation increases.

But as sociocracy cannot be implemented overnight, a transitional system of governance will be required to move the country from one system to another over a period of time. Sociocracy will need all citizens to be formally educated to at least the Matriculation level, and not being merely literate (defined by one's ability to sign one's name in an Indian language). It will take time to educate the country as a whole and rid her of her current corrupt and corrosive culture. The current educational infrastructure is currently in dire straits and will need complete revamping which will also take time. While all this is happening, the country cannot be left to corrupt politicians to undermine her further and deeper.

As a solution, although very difficult to accept but completely unavoidable, like bitter quinine in malaria or chemotherapy in cancer treatment, a benevolent dictatorship in the country, for at least a generation, is required to provide a transitional system of governance and prepare the country for sociocracy. Unfortunately, India seems to have lost all other options. It is a race against time.

Ironically, most people who dread the terms 'dictator' and 'dictatorship' don't realise or want to admit that most Indian homes, private businesses, armed forces, schools and government organisations run as dictatorships in varied forms and to varied extents, with varied levels of benevolence. Interestingly, strong opponents of dictatorship themselves act as dictators when they are at the helm—in their homes or in organisations. So, it is only the term 'dictator' that may be scary. In practical terms, however, it is not expected to be such a disaster. At the ground level, people will see distinct and rapid positive changes and the country will move forward at a much faster pace to make up for the last 70 years.

On the surface, following a traditional thought, 'benevolent dictatorship' appears to be an oxymoronic expression. But if necessary checks and balances are introduced in the system of governance, common apprehensions against dictatorship can be addressed. In India, benevolent dictatorship will need a benevolent, strong and visionary ruler, such as Lee Kuan Yew of Singapore, to govern her for at least 25 years and bring about a generational positive change in the country and eventually lead it seamlessly into sociocracy, which should be the permanent solution to the problem.

Objectively, the interim governance by a benevolent dictator must prepare the country for sociocracy by directly addressing the issues that have been undermining the country. (Refer to *Issues White-anting India*, 2017, by the author).

The interim administration must see the past wrongs being righted through a firmer and decisive form of governance, one that does not have to face disruptions, as commonly seen nowadays, due to party and vote bank politics which impede the rate and extent of development of the country and her people. The decision-making process and implementation of the decisions must be for the country's greater good, timely and effective; otherwise dictatorship will quickly lose its validity. If the country has to make a sacrifice in the form of introducing a dictatorship, it must bear fruit for all Indians, and not plunge the nation from the 'frying pan into the fire'.

A transitional rule by a visionary and benevolent dictator must strive to bind the country as one entity where every in-dividual calls himself and herself first an Indian and then any-thing else; where males and females are considered as equals;

where religion is a private and personal affair for every individual and people are not discriminated based on their religion, region and caste; where every child receives minimum education up to Class 10 absolutely free; where every citizen renders two years of national service before receiving a voter's card; where people are happier and enjoy a sense of belonging to the country and the world; where people have high environmental and ecological awareness.

It does not matter if the country's economic growth slows down initially. Once all above conditions are met, the economy will naturally rebound as the people's productivity and happiness improves. The country will prosper in both spiritual and materialistic domains based on the inclusiveness that a sociocratic system of governance will provide. Indians will experience a much-needed sense of ownership of the country and develop a national character. The country will undoubtedly flourish and march ahead happily, with good health and prosperity, into the 22nd century, and possibly into the 30th century and beyond!

Many educated Indians will ask, 'Why do we need dictatorship, albeit benevolent, or something called sociocracy? Why can't India get rid of her issues through the current democratic process? All we need is a good and strong leader who can get rid of corruption and spread education across the country!'

To the above people, a plausible answer is, 'Yes, it is possible to get rid of corruption and spread education in the country but only if good, honest and strong persons are allowed to function as the country's leaders'.

Most Indians, through centuries of poverty and illiteracy

are currently hungry for wealth and prosperity. To make things worse, after gaining independence in 1947, the country has seen a four-fold increase in its population. There is increasing aggressive competition as a consequence of the population issue and people have learnt to live, survive and prosper by getting things done through smart shortcuts and ingenious corrupt practices, by hook or by crook.

Over time, therefore, through several generations, Indians have become materialistic, selfish, whimsical and uncertain. Any leader who tries to get rid of the corrupt practices in the country will not be allowed to function with ease without crossing massive disruptive hurdles. The leader will sooner or later be voted out. People will vote for another person, get disillusioned and vote out that person also. All this will result in a revolving-door practice of changing leadership and the country will not make much progress; time will be wasted in party politics and elections. In the meanwhile, the white-ants will keep undermining the country, surreptitiously.

The main problem with India is that its people don't know what they want. There is a wide gap between people's personal needs/expectations and the country's needs/expectations. Many people want the country's needs to align with their personal needs; they want the country to work for them, instead of them working for the country.

For a democracy to be fair and thriving, all citizens must be educated and well-informed about (a) the election process; (b) the background and track record of political candidates; (c) manifesto of the political parties; and (d) the current and potential issues facing their nation and the country's immediate and future requirements. There must be clear and honest levels of communication between the candidates and the voters, about people's expectations and promises by politicians. The politicians must be visibly and legally held accountable for their past performance before standing again for elections. As none of these conditions can be met in India at the moment, the so-called Indian democracy can be deemed as not the right system of governance for the country. In such a situation, is there any other solution other than what has been proposed in this book?

To alleviate concerns about an authoritative rule or dictatorship, albeit benevolent, the following analogy is deemed to be very pertinent. If a country is considered to be analogous to a human body, every citizen could be considered as a cell. For practical reasons though, a family could be considered as the smallest functional unit of the country. It is reasonable to assume that most family-oriented people of reason will support an argument that a family unit is generally happy when the head of a family—mother or father—is benevolent and strong. The word 'strong' generally means 'a little authoritative, confident, unselfish, decisive, wise, prudent, rational, considerate, bold, brave and fair, reasonable and accountable, with other known and proven leadership acumen.' When the head of the family demonstrates such leadership qualities, the family members are seen to be generally more reassured, settled, responsible, happy and progressive, which is not the case if the head of the family is weak, soft or confused. Similarly, a country is happier if the leadership is firm, decisive, benevolent and a little authoritative. For example, China is indicated to be much happier than India on the Happiness Index.

Man is a herd animal, a social beast. Every herd needs a

leader who must be strong and caring for the herd. There's nothing wrong with being authoritative. As long as you are benevolent and good, people will not mind your authoritarian rule. Only when people feel directionless due to a weak leader, they also feel less assured, fearful and uncertain; and then they go in different ways and try to find alternatives or, what has happened in India, just ignore the country and selfishly look after themselves. People generally like to follow benevolent and authoritarian rulers, as illustrated by the following example:

Dr Mahathir bin Mohamad (born 10 July 1925), a medical doctor by training, is a Malaysian politician whose political career spans more than 70 years.

After his retirement from active politics in 2003, Mahathir became a harsh critic of his hand-picked successor, Abdullah Badawi, in 2006, and then Najib Razak in in 2015. Earlier this year, he came out of retirement and fought a general election against his previous political party, UMNO, following strong resentment against widespread corruption in the country during the rule of Prime Minister Najib Razak, who is himself facing a major corruption case.

Following the results on 10 May 2018, Mahathir claimed victory in the general elections held on 9 May 2018. Despite numerous disruptive tricks and tactics adopted by Razak's government to thwart Mahathir's election campaign. Malaysian people turned out in large numbers and successfully voted Razak out in favour of Mahathir. At 92, Mahathir is now the oldest living Prime Minister of Malaysia and the world's oldest head of state. Earlier, as a dominant political figure in his country, he won five consecutive general elections, from 1981 to 2003, when he served Malaysia as its fourth Prime Minister, which made him the longest-serving Prime Minister in his country. During his time, Malaysia witnessed over two decades of rapid economic growth and modernisation through a series of bold infrastructure projects initiated by his government. He was also an advocate of third-world development and a prominent international activist as Prime Minster.

Mahathir's earlier tenure of 22 years as Prime Minister has been widely judged as an authoritarian rule. His accumulation of power impacted on the independence of the judiciary and the traditional powers and privileges enjoyed by the Malaysian royalty. He introduced the controversial Internal Security Act (ISA) to detain activists, non-mainstream religious figures and his political opponents, including the then Deputy Prime Minister, Anwar Ibrahim, whom he fired in 1998. Mahathir's record of curbing civil liberties and his antagonism towards the western interests and economic policy deeply strained his relationships with a number of western countries, including the US, the UK and Australia.

Despite Mahathir's authoritarian history, Malaysian people have brought him back. He fulfilled his election promise immediately. On his recommendation, Anwar received the royal pardon and was released from jail on 16 May 2018. Mahathir has promised to install him as his successor within the next two years.

Author's note

The idea of this book was born on the early morning of 14 November 2017, soon after the author's earlier book launch in a formal ceremony at the NCERT's Regional Institute of Education (RIE) at Bhopal, India, on 13 November 2017.

After the completion of a number of formal chores during the launch ceremony, many RIE teachers and students interacted with the author during an interesting hour-long Question & Answer session. Towards the end, as he was beginning to feel a little tired but immensely satisfied with his response to numerous questions asked by the audience— about Kashmir, growing mental sickness and unhappiness in the youth, and white-anting issues in India—a young student stood up and asked him a question that shook him to his core. The question was in regard to an urgent need to improve the liveability in the country. The student, speaking mainly in Hindi and occasionally using some English words, asked him gently, but with deep sadness, frustration and hopelessness in his voice, 'Sir, I fully agree with all that you have said today in this auditorium. But what can we do to improve the liveability in our country? Who will listen to us? The two main political parties are mainly engaged with mudslinging on each other, what do we do?'

The author was not prepared for the question; he had no ready answer for it. He replied, 'I am sorry for your hopelessness and share your frustration. Honestly speaking, I have no solution to the issues raised by you. But can I suggest that you also do what I am doing—discuss all serious issues that, in your view and reasonable opinion, are undermining the country with your fellow students in debates and seminars. Raise your voice and write in the newspapers and magazines. Let all Indian youth and students create a movement across the country and send a clear message to the government that *"enough is enough; we want to live in a healthy country; please govern this country properly and make it a better place to live"*. Your youth movement across India should be able to give the government a clear mandate to do the needful; otherwise, due to the vote bank politics, and the known defects in India's democracy, no leader in India will take the initiative to touch the liveability and population issues. There is a reason why no politician in India dares to talk about the monster of population issue.'

That night, in his hotel room, the author cried. He was deeply overwhelmed by the level of helplessness and desperation of that student, as also by a painful realisation of his own helplessness to make any positive changes in the country. A small fry like him, who lived mainly overseas, is a virtual nonentity. This massive country—a world of its own kind, with such a great inertia could gobble up millions like him in no time.

After some serious thinking, he decided to write this book. The book was, thus, conceived on that day. Incidentally,

14 November is celebrated in India every year as Children's Day, being the birthday of the first Prime Minister of independent India, Jawaharlal Nehru, also known as *Chacha Nehru*. Perhaps that was a sign.

It is tragic that the country seems to have forgotten the slogan of India's ex-Prime Minister, Lal Bahadur Shastri— *Jai Jawan, Jai Kissan*—which literally means 'hail the soldier, hail the farmer'. Sadly, Indian newspapers on a regular basis report tragic deaths of Indian soldiers and Indian farmers, due to suicide, which is extremely heartrending. Does the nation not support the hands that toil in challenging conditions to produce food for the nation? Does the country not honour those *jawans* who defend it and don't sleep on the border so that the nation can sleep peacefully?

Soldiers work in extremely harsh environments defending the country's borders, for extended periods of time far away from their homes and families, to render their selfless service towards the country. What must they be thinking when they see politicians and bureaucrats, proven to be corrupt, travelling in air-conditioned cars and sitting in air-conditioned offices, enjoying disproportionate wealth and authority, under the safety provided by their personal Indian security personnel? The author has met many current and ex-Indian army personnel in India and in Perth, and none seemed to be happy. In July 2016, on his return from Srinagar on 10 July, after Burhan Wani's death, he met many Indian soldiers at Srinagar airport, who fumed with anger and showed extreme disappointment in the civil administration of the country. They felt they had been directed to virtually fight against the foreign sponsored militancy in Kashmir with one hand only, with the other hand tied at their back. They suffer from fatigue, anger, helplessness and frustration. They feel dejected and disappointed.

Not everything is hunky-dory with the soldiers! Just because they don't vent their feelings in the media or on the public forum does not mean they harbour no bad feelings or grievances against the civilians. Has the country not let them down?

Farmers, like soldiers, physically toil extremely hard in harsh and challenging conditions, braving the sun, unpredictable monsoons, floods, difficult ground conditions and, of course, the greedy middlemen, who steal their hard-earned and rightful earnings. Why do they commit suicide? Because they borrow money from greedy money lenders at unreasonable borrowing rates, (as depicted in numerous movies in India of the 40s to 60s), or from the banks, but then find themselves in a difficult position where they can't repay their loans within the specified time period!

In addition to the reasons underlying their defaulted repayments, another major reason could be a dual effect of: (a) urbanisation of rural areas, which has seen conversion of traditional agricultural land for residential and commercial use; and (b) growing families (due to population growth), which lead to subdivisions of their ancestral agricultural land and, therefore, a perpetual shrinkage of their share of the land, resulting in poorer returns on their investments, which does not suffice their needs.

It is paradoxical that, on one hand, the country seems to boast a decent economic growth, albeit accompanied with an epidemic increase in the obesity and associated affluent life-style diseases in the upper socio-economic community.

On the other hand, however, the food producers of the nation are malnourished, poor and skinny. Like *jawans*, has the country let its farmers down too?

The country urgently needs a complete overhaul of its governing structure to address a number of sustainability and existential issues facing the country, as well as properly look after her *jawans* and *kissans*, as her own children. It is very sad that, for achieving a fast economic growth, the country's governments have been sacrificing the country's ecology and environment, which shows the extent to which the country's leaders are blinded to the currently fast deteriorating living conditions in the cities across India, as well as their lack of imagination about the country's living conditions and sustainability in the future.

On 27 March 2018, the author was invited to attend a panel discussion in Perth on 'India: Challenges & Opportunities', at the University of Western Australia, organised by the Australian Institute of International Affairs for Western Australia. The panel members were the Indian Consul General to Perth, Mr Amit Kumar Mishra, Professor Anu Rammohan (Associate Dean (International) for the Faculty of Arts, Business, Law and Education (UWA), Mr Michael Carter (President of the Australia India Business Council) and Mr Tom Calder (WA State Director of Austrade). The theme of the panel discussion was:

'While many developed nations face the problems of an ageing population, a vibrant and youthful demographic is emerging in India. This large, young population, along with extraordinary economic advancements such as the 160 million people lifted out of extreme poverty between 2004 and 2012, provide hope for a broader prosperity as this fiercely independent nation seeks to take a prominent place on the world stage. How will India capitalise on the opportunities ahead while striving to overcome the considerable obstacles it faces, as environmental issues, skills shortages and public health challenges threaten to slow its progress?'

The panel discussion was very interesting. In particular, Mr Mishra impressed the audience with his speech, data about India's recent progress in various areas, and his answers in the Q & A session. However, at no stage did anyone speak about the challenges the country is facing in terms of the dwindling human happiness, growing rate of mental sickness in the Indian youth, poor implementation of the Right to Education, dwindling liveability of Indian cities, growing population, environmental pollution and corruption. It was mostly about the country's progress in the areas of military, IT and the economy, and what needs to be done to sustain a high economic growth.

Indians seek what is important to them. A middle class Indian family spends its weekend in a mall, whereas a typical Aussie family spends its weekend in the natural environment —picnics, trekking etc. In the process of their fight for survival and under spell of materialism, Indians show scant care for the environment around them. The environmental consciousness and overall conscientiousness have fast disappeared as greed and corruption—material and moral—have bedded at the core of the Indian mind. Survival has become paramount, at any cost and *sub chalta hai* is how Indians go about their daily lives.

The country's focus needs a drastic readjustment—a shift from the material development to the human development—

with emphasis on clean air, clean drinking water, authentic food and medicines, honour, dignity and safety of all people; good quality—free but compulsory—school education for all young citizens with the provision of the necessary educational infrastructure; compulsory national service for all students for national character building, and drastic measures for population control.

If nothing is done soon, what is going to happen? The country will take its natural recourse to correct the current economic and social imbalances. In the author's reasonable opinion, before long, the country will undergo environmental failure, quickly followed by economic and social failures. It will potentially land in a state of anarchy and witness widespread civil disorder between the haves and have-nots—between the people belonging to the two largest religious communities—between the people from various castes etc. After widespread destruction and loss of millions of human lives, it will attain a position of equilibrium, either as one integrated nation or as a disintegrated country. As a person of Indian origin, such a potential state of mess and mayhem is not acceptable to the author or anyone who cares for the country. It is an extremely serious matter for the people of India. But, unfortunately, people watch too much television and spend a significant amount of time on the social media, which distracts them from visualising an existential threat looming on the horizon. Prudence requires that they should instead sit down, see the situation with their very own eyes and seriously think and imagine how it is going to be in the future; coordinate with one another to help themselves and get the country out of a serious rut and a potential anarchical scenario in the future.

But that requires a national character and an unselfish mindset. Unfortunately, however, both of which are holidaying overseas!

So what are the alternatives? Can it be a dictatorship or a sociocratic system of governance? That word 'dictatorship' sounds very alarming and can run a shiver down anyone's spine. No one wants dictatorship. How about a 'benevolent' dictatorship then? Well, the word 'benevolent' may douse the alarm about the word 'dictatorship' to some extent but not fully. The issue is with the word 'dictatorship' itself. People are afraid of the term in the same way as they are afraid of the term 'surgery'. Little do people realise that every parent and every school teacher is practically a dictator for young children, be it in terms of enforcing discipline, rules and regulations; or infusing their religion, faith and values into the child.

Elders punish the children one way or the other if the child does not heed their instructions. The child knows there are consequences for nonconformities. So, when they grow up, why don't people fear the law? Because they can avoid the consequences by corrupting the law enforcers! Sad and unfortunate!

Many readers will challenge the author's credibility for writing a book on this relatively sensitive topic, with such an alarming and contentious title. The author is neither an expert on Constitutional Law (or Indian politics) nor a professor of Political Science. A simple answer from the author could be: 'If alleged lawbreakers and criminals can run for office in India, sit in the country's Parliament and be allowed to work as lawmakers by the country's constitution and the political system, why can't an educated, experienced, responsible, professional engineer of international standing write on the subject. The issues discussed in this book affect not only the lives of 1.35 billion humans in India, but also the entire world, considering India is home to about one-fifth of the world population, and any problem in India has the potential to be a problem for entire humanity on the planet, and that includes Australia, where the author lives. The world is a global village and if we live in it, India is everyone's problem.

In his defence, the author also throws a counter challenge and argues: 'Is the language used to write the Constitution of India and its Preamble so ambiguous or difficult to be understood in plain English by a common person? Is the interpretation of the Constitution and its Preamble only within the jurisdiction of experts on Constitutional Law or Indian politics, and not within the domain of the common person? Should a common person not touch the subject matter?'

If the answer to any or all the above questions is 'yes', then one could argue: 'What was the purpose of promising something to the people (in the form of the Constitution), which they were not expected to understand in plain English? Was it a sham i.e. promising something which can't be understood? Has 'Indian democracy' been a myth?'

A 'no' answer, however, provides the author with a window of opportunity to write on the subject matter. The author is emboldened by the fact that most Members of Parliament (MPs) and the Civil Servants (IAS), who administer on behalf of the Ministers, are not Constitutional Law experts or Political Science graduates. Also, it is understood that about one-third of the MPs in India have criminal records. Given that only about four per cent Indians are understood to be university graduates, one can expect that a considerable number of MPs will also not be university graduates.

So one does not need to be an expert on Constitutional Law or a Political Science graduate to write on the subject matter. Any person who can follow simple English with average reading and writing skills, and capability to think rationally should be able to touch this contentious topic.

The readers must note that this book presents the author's personal ideas, based on his interaction with numerous Indian citizens—from a wide socio-economic cross-section, belonging to several ethnicities, faiths, castes and regions. His observations and experience are supported by the published data and literature and the thoughts of many people.

One can wonder how long will an average hardworking, honest, and educated Indian wait before raising his/her voice, which will be loud enough for whole world to hear—a voice that will change India for the better? *Mahabharata*, the great epic, painfully reminds one about many learned and brave men, including the invincible *Bhishma*, well known for his vow of celibacy, who remained passive witnesses to many wrongs being done by others. Their sworn blind loyalty to the king, rather than the country, cost them not only their own lives but many other precious lives. The country lost as a whole and nobody won. India has many great intellectuals and patriots even in this day and age. Will they follow Bhishma or Lord Krishna?

Millions of Indians, awakened and having the capability to think and to foresee the looming issues on the horizon, wish and pray to God to improve the liveability in the country. But God does not do anything without human thought and human endeavour, be it in the fields of medicine, agriculture, engineering, transportation, mass communication etc.

Likewise, in the areas of social engineering and the environmental sustainability of the country, some visionary humans, as God's representatives, must stand up and urgently act to fulfil the wishes of millions of sufferers in India and their future generations—work wholeheartedly to bring the derailed Indian train back on the rails.

Many people have advised the author, 'Why are you so concerned about India? You left that country about a quarter of a century back. Leave India and the Indians alone; they have got what they deserve.'

Some well-meaning friends may rightfully call this book a 'cry of anguish'. The author does not blame or contradict them for calling it so, as he perceives them as true citizens of India and wishes every Indian citizen is like them and learns from them. These friends are also intrinsically optimistic in nature; they are quite hardworking and highly responsible citizens too. Importantly, these friends are directly involved in the implementation of a number of noble schemes that the current government of India has launched to uplift the masses, especially in villages, to ease lives through such projects as electrification of villages, supply of cooking gas etc. They have first hand information and hard-core statistics about the progress that the country has made in the recent years in numerous areas which the media is not highlighting because these achievements don't comprise the social gossip.

The author would not hesitate to share the optimism of his friends on the proviso that the population of India was low and stable, with a much lower rate of population growth; the education level was high and evenly spread across the nation;

and, most importantly, corruption in almost all walks of life was at negligible levels. In that case, this book was not required at all. But, unfortunately, that is not the case. When one looks at the bigger picture, logically, it appears that whatever good is being done in the country, or possibly will be done in the future is likely to fall short, as the country welcomes nearly 85,000 new citizens every day. This fact together with prevalent corruption at all levels in the country throws all optimism out of the window. To the author, being optimistic is healthy but, unfortunately, in this context may be considered to be similar to burying one's head in the sand, like an ostrich.

It is not the time to be optimistic and do nothing to address the core issues that are destabilising the country. A massive country, that currently contains nearly one-fifth of the humanity, is like a runaway bull. It is the time to act and act firmly and decisively and hold the bull by its horns and control it once and for all. It is the time to look into the eyes of the bull and show it who is in control. The bull needs to be tamed, calmed and nourished.

Author's dream

To realise a fully integrated, healthy, happy and prosperous India, which will survive and thrive through the next 80 years or so, and finally move into the 22nd century like a well-oiled, well lubricated, German machine; where all people live and work responsibly and in complete coherence with one another towards a common ambition—ambition to make their country a habitable nation with a sustainable environment.

The author wishes to hear the following typical response, in that order, from an average Indian citizen, coming from any nook or corner of the country, to a question about one's identity. *Who are you?*:

- I am a human, a world citizen.
- I am an Indian.
- I am a teacher, a carpenter, an engineer etc.
- I am a woman; I am a man.
- I am a mother, a father, a brother, a sister etc.

Identifying oneself first or solely with one's ethnicity (Punjabi, Tamil, Kashmiri etc.), or with one's religion (Muslim, Sikh, Buddhist, Hindu, Christian etc.), or with one's caste (Dalit Yadav, Kshatriya, Brahmin etc.), or one's region (south Indian, north Indian etc.), practically impedes the development of a national character. Such personal identifications are potentially toxic for the integrity of the country and must, therefore, be discouraged at all costs. If that is not possible, then the country should be renamed as '*the United States of India (USI)*', where each state will be practically autonomous except in terms of national defence, currency, common law, educational standards, infrastructure, and environmental regulations.

Currently some states in India, such as Uttar Pradesh, Bihar and Madhya Pradesh, have disproportionate representation in the country's parliament because of their large population and the population density. Such large states drive the overall direction—rather hijack the country—and contribute to the inertia of the country due to their large masses, which is not fair to other smaller, relatively more progressive and responsible states.

There are also some states, such as Jammu & Kashmir, which don't contribute much to the revenue of the country, but on the contrary are pampered and high maintenance, and practically black holes in the country's economy.

The current system allows some (irresponsible) states to feed on other (more responsible) states.

In the USI, therefore, each state must be made to look after itself and be responsible for its own economy and the civil infrastructural development. In doing so:

- The federal government should comprise equal number of representatives from all states, and not in proportion to their respective populations.

- All states should receive equal share of the federal resources, and not in proportion to their respective populations.

- Due to autonomy, each state must manage its own budget and reserves; generate and manage its own revenue; manage its law and order, intra-state immigration; and its natural resources.

If the above can be easily achieved by the current 'Indian democratic' governmental structure, the readers may stop reading this book at this point; however, if it is not possible to achieve the above objectives, the readers are encouraged to continue reading this book...

Why Dictatorship?

Failure of democracy in India

India claims to be practising a western parliamentary democracy. One can reasonably question if the Indian version of democracy, whatsoever, has been fit for the purpose, considering the various types of the people and the living conditions in the country. India seems to be going nowhere in so far as her dwindling liveability is concerned. People have been breeding to alarming and unsustainable levels. At this rate, it is hard to see her marching confidently into the 22nd century. She needs a complete overhaul of her system of governance, or a miracle, sooner than later.

The Indian democracy certainly does not seem to have improved the condition of the Indian cities, which see people and vehicles everywhere, with breathing and movement of life increasingly becoming more and more difficult. Nor has it looked after the general health and the level of education of the people, in particular, the backward and poorer communities. Nor has it bonded the people as Indians first, then anything else! The national character has not developed in the last 70 years. The country remains divided, lacks true nationalism. Kashmir remains a significant nagging distraction, affecting India's relationship with her neighbours. Regionalism plays a major part in the country's politics with reservations and representation in sports.

The Indian democracy is all about vote-bank. If you form the vote-bank, you are in. You will be wooed and pampered by the politicians. If you are considered not important for vote-bank, you will be left to fend for yourself. The case of Kashmiri Pandits is a classic example to illustrate the vote-bank politics. Indian democracy has not been fair; it has not served the poor well. The socio-economic divide has been widening. Such is the disparity in the distribution of wealth that currently about one per cent Indians disproportionately own about 73 per cent of the country's wealth. India lives in several ages at the same time; a significant portion lives in the bullock-cart age, some in the cycle-rickshaw age, some in the auto-rickshaw age, some in the black & yellow taxi age and some in the current Ola and Uber age. Of course, a small percentage of Indians are jet-fliers and some wealthy Indians take their personal chopper to go to work and move around on a daily basis.

India has been growing economically, as has its population. Due to economic disparity, the lower socio-economic community comprises more than half of its population.

One needs to visualise what it means to add nearly 55,000 people to the population every day and nearly 50,000 vehicles to roads every day. This is a country where about one-third of the population lives on less than a dollar a day. Any person of common sense can say, if things are not turned around soon, some kind of revolution or uprising is not very far away. But that is common sense, which, unfortunately, is not very common.

Materialism has gripped India, accompanied with a rapid erosion of the traditional Indian spiritual mindset. It is taking a massive toll on the country's liveability and traditional values, mental and physical health of the people, and the family life. The definition of 'life' has changed over time. Time is the most precious commodity and the wealth that a living being is gifted with. What is the meaning of life if people have no time to live it? In their endeavour to survive, gain wealth and become richer, most Indians living in the cities are fast becoming extremely *time-poor* despite leading a richer lifestyle than their ancestors.

The industrial development and economic growth in India during the past half a century or so has seen a steady increase in the country's population and clogging of her streets and roads with parked vehicles and mixed traffic on the roads that comprise pedestrians, bullock carts, bicycles, rickshaws and motorised vehicles. The travelling distances, in cites at least, are measured by the time to commute and not by the actual distances. The commuting time over the past quarter of a century or so has increased by 2 to 3 times. For covering a distance of 15 km in an Indian city such as Delhi it normally takes about 1.0 to 1.5 hours to commute in a relatively freer flowing traffic, but sometimes up to 2 hours or more if the traffic worsens.

The present deteriorating conditions especially in the Indian urban areas, which are fast turning into gas chambers, warrant drastic and urgent measures, such as a compulsory population control (eg One-child policy), immediate ban on immigration from rural to urban areas, crackdown on everything that pollutes air and drinking water, compulsory schooling of all children across the country, quick and harsh punitive measures to deal with all lawbreakers. But the existing governing system will not allow any such measures to be undertaken on several grounds, eg human rights and the basic principles of (western) democracy.

This is a country where the current government is on a campaign to promote the use of closed-door toilets for reasons of hygiene, environment and the security of female defecators against rapes. This is a country where girl children as young as one-year-old get raped.

India, therefore, urgently needs to move completely from the current 'flawed' democracy to a benevolent dictatorship, even a military dictatorship, for at least the next twenty-five years, or a complete change of governance, such as sociocracy or the Chinese form of government for achieving all the above.

Due to the urban sprawl, as the commuting distances have increased, the commuting time has also increased correspondingly which results in:

- Increase in the fuel consumption and the carbon emissions, exacerbating the air pollution;

- Wastage of time, the most precious gift of any human and, therefore, the human resources from an economic point of view;

- Reduced family and social time;

- Increase in the stress level due to ever increasing frustration on the roads due to traffic, leading to chronic impatience, mental anxiety, and road rage, which have the potential to develop into mental illness and suicide; and

- Reduced work efficiency and productivity at the workplace.

The above list illustrates some of the tangible costs but, most importantly, the intangible costs that Indians pay for their uncontrolled population growth, urban migration and industrial development are immensely significant as they potentially erode the basic survival of human life in India.

On average, people may be living a little longer in India and the lifestyle of some of them may have improved over time, but a big question arises, *'Are they also happier and physically healthier and fitter now?'* Based on common observations, most people seem to be rushing, whether on foot, or riding a bicycle, or seated inside a vehicle, with unhappy expressions on their faces. Richer people have generally become overweight and obese, and live with diseases that are commonly associated with an affluent lifestyle, such as diabetes, hypertension etc. Undoubtedly, the current lifestyle has undermined the mental and physical health of many people living in the cities. It is not uncommon to see that many people have simply no time to improve their personal well-being and physical fitness; they are either chasing wealth or trying to survive.

Indian people must individually decide if they want to live a relatively happier, less diseased, contented and simpler life.

Should wealth or attainment of health and contentment be the ultimate target of their lives? The answer to that question is a no brainer!

The country's focus indeed needs a drastic readjustment—a shift from the material development to the human development—with emphasis on clean air, clean drinking water, authentic food and medicines, honour, dignity and safety of all people, good quality—free but compulsory—school education for all young citizens with the provision of the necessary educational infrastructure; compulsory national service for all students for national character building, and drastic measures for population control.

With the current 'Indian democracy', it is inconceivable that in the face of the following, the country will ever come out of her chronic issues within one generation or even a few generations, if at all:

- A fast growing population
- Rampant corruption at all levels
- The Kashmir issue
- Unfriendly neighbours

All above issues will continue to keep the administrators embroiled in distractions without maintaining any focus on the improvement of the basic liveability in the country. It will not be wrong to doubt if, in the face of the above factors, the country will ever come out of poverty—material and character both. The disease of capitalism has truly gripped the country and the exploitation of the poor and backward by the rich and the politicians will continue unabated.

It will be eventually up to the people of India to decide

how they would like to be governed. They will have to decide if they would like to continue with the current system of governance—a system that has seen a significant number of people with criminal background, some very serious, to represent them in the Parliament—a system where the people's votes are auctioned by their village chief, a system where the parliamentarians are constantly busy with mudslinging on each other, a system which has allowed the population to grow mindlessly and where one-third of the population lives on less than a dollar per day and a significant number of children don't have access to good or any school education, a system in which all Indians have not been looked after well, a system where the poor continue to remain poor and illiterate, only to be exploited by politicians, the rich and affluent.

In the engineering world, if a structure is too dilapidated, too unsafe for use, or too inadequate, and can't be practically repaired and made habitable or functional, it is razed to the ground and the site is cleared. Thereafter, new foundations are laid which are fit for the purpose—adequate and deep enough—and a new structure is constructed to meet its objectives and the future demands. In my reasonable opinion, like a dilapidated unsafe structure, Indian governance system also needs a complete overhaul, as it is not serving the country well and is grossly inadequate to meet her future demands.

India's living and political conditions can also be likened to a diseased, cancer stricken person. When a person is diagnosed with cancer, what do doctors do? Depending upon the organ involved and the stage of cancer, as well as the age and general state of health of the patient, together with a range of complexities and parameters known to the medical sciences, it is generally seen the person may be subject to a range of treatments available, such as chemotherapy, surgery, radiotherapy, immunotherapy etc. In many cases, it may start with chemotherapy to contain the cancer to the affected part of the body, followed by the surgical removal of the cancer-affected part. For precautionary purposes, depending upon the severity of the cancer, the patient may be subject to further rounds of chemotherapy or radiotherapy or both. While that is happening and the person is recuperating, emphasis is laid on the strengthening of the patient's body and mind.

Similar to the above, several drastic measures, including a complete replacement of the current so-called (flawed) democratic system will be required to rid the country of several chronic problems, while the country's poor and backward are taken care of as the country's own children (and not God-forsaken children), in terms of their education, health and overall human development.

Many people may argue that we need patience to deal with the situation and should instead focus on the economic prosperity of the country. It is akin to saying that strengthening of a sick person's body will get rid of the person's cancer. No, it will not. On the contrary the cancer will keep growing. So, a complete change in the system of governance is warranted.

Democracy is beautiful in theory; in practice it is a fallacy.
—Benito Mussolini

Dictatorship comes naturally to Indians

Historically, Indians have never seen anything like democracy. Most are blissfully still oblivious to the concept of democracy, which works in favour of corrupt politicians. They are traditionally used to being lorded over by others. The concept of equality between all humans is an alien concept to most Indians. Most people still don't believe in equality, which is reflected in their actions, behaviour and treatment of the people belonging to lower socio-economy strata. Employees have been, and are still called *naukars* (servants) and employment is called *naukri* (servitude). And women are traditionally marginalised in every community.

In India, parents behave as dictators, so do the teachers with students, employers with employees, and bosses with their subordinates. Respect is generally only the birthright of people in power and with authority.

Before gaining independence on 15 August 1947, in all its history with more than 550 princely states and kingdoms, Indians were used to following the whims and wishes of kings and princes who ruled over them. As per Wikipedia˙: 'At the time of the British withdrawal, 565 princely states were officially recognised in the Indian subcontinent, apart from thousands of *taluqars*, *zamindaris* and *jagirs*...The era of the princely states effectively ended with Indian independence in 1947...The Indian Government formally derecognised the princely families in 1971...'

The following excerpt from Wikipedia illustrates how the present Indian subcontinent was ruled just 70 years ago and how the rulers perceived themselves.

'The Indian rulers bore various titles—including Chhatrapati (emperor), Maharaja or Raja (king), Sultan, Raje,

---

˙ https://en.wikipedia.org/wiki/Princely_state

Nizam, Wadiyar, Agniraj Maharaj, Nawab (governor), Nayak, Wāli, Inamdar, Saranjamdar and many others. Whatever the literal meaning and traditional prestige of the ruler's actual title, the British government translated them all as "prince," to avoid the implication that the native rulers could be "kings" with status equal to that of the British monarch. The most prestigious Hindu rulers usually had the prefix "maha" (great) in their titles, as in Maharaja, Maharana, Maharao, etc....'

Prostrating before deities and symbols and people of power—spiritual, political, wealth, influence, authority is in the DNA of most Indians. They love to follow and bow before power and powerful people in return for favours (blessings and grace) from them. Seventy years after independence from the British, Indians still love to use the titles 'sir' and 'sahib' in most formal and informal introductions. Indians have historically created a deep hierarchal social system, which differentiates people based on their religion, caste and wealth. Nepotism is an acceptable and normal way of life in India, as is seen in the Indian political system and political parties. Princes and kings have been replaced by Ministers.

It is unfortunate that, after the British exit, powerful and wealthy Indians have misused the democratic form of governance to their personal advantage and to further their influence and control of the country's wealth, instead of working for the benefit of the country at large. At micro-level in most Indian societies—homes, schools and workplaces—democracy does not exist. The powerful and the wealthy have the resources and know-how to get any job done, by hook or by crook. Money does talk in India and Goddess Lakshmi, who is worshipped as the goddess of wealth and prosperity, is very popular with most Indians.

Now that the noble objectives of democracy have not been met by Indian democracy, can those objectives be attained through benevolent dictatorship, or sociocracy, or even Chinese form of socialism? The objectives of 'democracy' are indeed noble—ensure the well-being of the people—but so are the objectives of 'sociocracy' or a 'benevolent dictatorship'.

It can be concluded that, at the time of her independence from the British monarchy in 1947, India seemingly was not ready to embrace the concept of democracy. The reasons could be:

- Traditional monarchies and religions which have genetically inculcated a characteristic habit in the Indian people of prostrating before authority and powerful people.

- Social hierarchy and a vibrant caste system, which has traditionally promoted deep inequality between people and also exacerbated the prostrating practice. People are treated based on the nature of their jobs and their position in the society.

- Low levels of literacy and education across the country where most people lived and still live, in villages, with very poor educational infrastructure.

Note that the terms 'literacy' and 'education' don't carry the same meaning, especially in the Indian context where literacy means just being able to write one's name in any one Indian language. It is, therefore, hard to imagine if more than 10% Indians even understand the concept and meaning of the word 'democracy'. For them, the Indian Prime Minister is like an Emperor. Minsters, bureaucrats and senior government servants are generally addressed as '*mai-baap*' (mother-father) by the people belonging to the lower 50 per cent of the socio-economic strata. Over time, a phenomenal population growth, accompanied by an ever-increasing 'demand to supply' ratio, has steadily eroded the democratic principles in India. People's thinking and their general behaviour has shifted from 'civil, patient and courteous' mode to a more 'aggressive, impatient and discourteous' mode, mainly due to their animal survival instincts taking over, which makes them feel insecure and, in turn, think and behave selfishly and aggressively. So, when the generally behaviour of people shifts from a more 'human' mode to a more 'animal' mode, democracy fails to deliver. People work mainly for themselves. For that very reason, no police or army in the world can afford to practice democracy; it has be an authoritarian chain of command, albeit within the defined rules of engagement.

Democracy is not suitable for societies like India where a predominant section constantly struggles to survive and feed itself, to serve a more privileged section of the society which lords over them, exploits them and uses (rather misuses) them. People in such a populated nation must fear the rule of law, which is not the case presently. The only way they will mind themselves and work for the nation is through dictatorship. And Indians are well suited for dictatorship. This marriage will work.

In practical terms, when the country is taken over by a benevolent dictator, half of the Indian population belonging to the lower socio-economic strata will not notice any difference in terms of any harshness in the governing system. On the contrary, their lives will improve immediately; they will feel more reassured and looked after. The middle income earners, comprising about 40% of the population, will immediately notice the difference; their lives will be more streamlined and regulated, and they will not feel marginalised or neglected. It will be mainly the upper 10% of the population, and the press, that will not be happy initially—albeit only temporarily. After a while, all people will get used to a new system of governance, feel accountable and responsible towards their country, follow the supreme leader and march in unison in the same direction. Vote bank politics will go out of the window, and so will numerous distractions associated with everyday political gimmicks that slow the country down from moving ahead with the rest of the world.

One must note that, in India, as also in the rest of the world, corruption is driven mainly by the wealthy and powerful, who know how to manipulate the system and exploit the human weakness to their advantage. A benevolent dictatorship will put a full-stop to the common corrupt practices.

The proposed change in the system of governance in India has to be a generational change, perhaps over two generations, as the supreme leader will need to oversee the implementation of his/her vision through to its fruition. Thereafter, unless and until India does not completely get rid of its caste system, gender and social inequality, bring down the 'demand to supply' ratio to more manageable numbers—by a strict state-administrated population control, development and expansion of its infrastructure (civil, educational, health) and increase its resources—and compulsorily educate all its population, democracy must not be allowed to return to India.

The author believes it is imperative to take a look at the definitions of some important terms being discussed in this book, as understood by the author, to address any potential ambiguities up front.

Dictator

Dictionary[1] defines the term 'dictator' as '*someone who has absolute power—or who at least behaves as if they do by bossing others around.*' It goes on to add: 'In government, a dictator is a ruler who has total control over a country, with no checks or balances to prevent abuse of power. Dictator can also describe someone who acts like that on a smaller scale. When you get married and your mom makes you order roses instead of lilies for the table arrangement and yells at you for addressing the invitations too slowly and insists that all of her co-workers be invited, she's acting like a dictator.'

Wikipedia[2] defines the term 'dictatorship' as: 'Dictatorship is a form of government in which a country or a group of countries is ruled by one person or by a polity and power is exercised through various mechanisms to ensure that the entity's power remains strong...a type of authoritarianism in which politicians regulate nearly every aspect of the public and private behaviour of citizens. Dictatorship and totalitarian societies generally employ political propaganda to decrease the influence of proponents of alternative governing systems.'

Benevolent Dictatorship

What does the term 'benevolent dictator' mean? Expectedly, it will carry different meaning for different people. Therefore,

---

1 https://www.vocabulary.com/dictionary/dictator
2 https://en.wikipedia.org/wiki/Dictatorship

let us first look for the meaning of the word 'benevolent'. As per Dictionary[3], some adjectives are: 'intending or showing goodwill, kindly, friendly, doing good or giving aid to others, charitable...' The following terms are considered to be its synonyms: Good, kind, humane, generous, liberal, benign, philanthropic, and altruistic.

As per Wikipedia[4], a 'benevolent dictatorship' is a form of government which enables an authoritarian leader, solely for the benefit of the entire population, to exercise absolute political power over the state. The dictator may, through public referenda or in consultation with elected representatives, albeit with limited power, allow for some economic liberalisation or democratic decision-making process to exist in the governance, as well as make preparations for a transition to democracy during or after the term(s).

John Emerich Edward Dalberg-Acton[5], 1st Baron Acton, KCVO DL (10 January 1834-19 June 1902) was an English Catholic historian, politician, and writer. He is known for the remark in a letter to an Anglican bishop, *'Power tends to corrupt, and absolute power corrupts absolutely. Great men are almost always bad men...'*

Benevolent dictators are not born or created; they are a product of circumstances and chaotic situation in the country when the system is ridden with corruption and nothing else seems to be working. They are born out of turmoil, helplessness and anarchy, and they want to fix things at the earliest. There is always a potential that 'absolute power can potentially corrupt

---

3 http://www.dictionary.com/browse/benevoient
4 https://en.wikipedia.org/wiki/Benevolent_dictatorship
5 https://en.wikipedia.org/wiki/John_Dalberg-Acton,_1st_Baron_Acton

absolutely'. Therefore, despite assurances about benevolence, people will always remain nervous about being ruled by a dictator unless and until there are checks and balances in place to monitor and manage the authority of a 'benevolent dictator'.

Some illustrious examples of 'benevolent dictators' are: Mustafa Kemal Atatürk (Turkey), Charles de Gaulle (France), Josip Broz Tito (Yugoslavia), Lee Kuan Yew (Singapore), Abdullah II (Jordan), Paul Kagame (Rwanda), France-Albert René (Seychelles), and Qaboos bin Said al Said (Oman).

History has also seen two more benevolent dictators—Rafael Trujillo in Dominican Republic and Thomas Sankara in Burkino Faso, who are not so widely known as the above figures. They were both assassinated.

Rafael Trujillo (24 Oct 1891-30 May 1961) was the dictator of Dominican Republic. He seized power in a military revolt in 1930 and served as president from 1930 to 1938 and again from 1942 to 1952. He was assassinated in 1961. He brought an unprecedented degree of peace and prosperity to his country through his competence in business and administration, and ruthlessness in politics.

Thomas Isidore Noël Sankara (21 December 1949-15 October 1987), a charismatic and iconic figure, is commonly referred to as Africa's Che Guevara. His revolutionary programmes for African self-reliance made him an icon to many of Africa's poor. He said, 'Our country produces enough to feed us all. Alas, for lack of organisation, we are forced to beg for food aid. It's this aid that instils in our spirits the attitude of beggars'. He also said, 'Our revolution in Burkina Faso draws on the totality of man's experiences since the first breath of humanity. We wish to be the heirs of all the revolutions of the world, of all the liberation struggles of the peoples of the Third World. We draw the lessons of the American Revolution. The French Revolution taught us the rights of man. The great October Revolution brought victory to the proletariat and made possible the realization of the Paris Commune's dreams of justice.' Upholding women's rights and equality, he is reported have said, 'The revolution and women's liberation go together. We do not talk of women's emancipation as an act of charity or because of a surge of human compassion. It is a basic necessity for the triumph of the revolution. Women hold up the other half of the sky.'

Common man's views on present conditions in India

Readers must be wondering why an author who does not live in India is feeling so jittery about India, especially when people living in India don't complain. Suhail (name changed), a fellow Australian of Indian origin, who is also concerned about India like most Indians overseas, amply answers that question, 'If a frog falls into hot water, it will immediately jump out to save itself. But if it lives in lukewarm water and then the water is heated slowly, it will get used to the heat. A stage will arrive when it will feel the need to jump out but, by then, it will be too late and it will be cooked.'

During the author's numerous social interactions with people of Indian origin in Perth, and the Indian citizens in India, he has received a common whinge from most people about the worsening conditions in India. When asked about the possible solutions, most people generally respond as follows:

- 'Modi Ji will fix everything, don't worry. Give him time. He is very capable. If he remains in power, he knows what are the issues facing the country and he will address them one by one. The only problem is that all opposition political parties, in collusion with the proven enemies of India, are out to get him. Pray to God that he prevails upon them and leads the country to glory.'

These people are diehard Modi followers. The reasons these people see him as their only ray of hope are bedded in their suffering from yesteryears under the Congress rule, which, according to them, continued the *'divide and rule'* policy of the British after the country's independence, indulged in the appeasement policy, encouraged corruption etc.

One must understand that under the present system of governance, the country's Prime Minister, with all his dynamic leadership, noble intentions and an unprecedented two-hundred per cent commitment towards the country will not be practically able to make much impact on the serious issues that are undermining the country—the alarming population growth and the regional/religious/caste divisions that are pulling the country apart. The reason being the ruling party can't afford to touch such issues, as they will potentially lose the next election; all opposition parties and religious groups will gang and pounce on them in such a situation.

As far as Mr Modi is concerned, he has the capability to address all serious issues confronting the nation in a timely manner, but for doing that, he will need to take over as the country's absolute dictator.

With their disruptive politics and unruly tactics, the Opposition does not allow him to function normally to the extent he had to go on fast on 12 April 2018 in protest against the recent budget session washout, during which the parliament was not allowed to work for little more than three weeks. The Indian taxpayer pays millions of rupees every month to these irresponsible and disruptive MPs, as their monthly salary and facilities—bungalows, amenities, travel, support staff, security, subsidised food etc.

Interestingly, as a pre-emptive action, some members of the Opposition had observed a laughable '5-hour fast' on 9 April 2018! Was it a fast or a joke, considering most people don't normally eat anything during the time period between the meals, which can extend much beyond five hours? But these are Indian politicians; five hours is a long time for them to go without food, unlike Mr Modi, who is known to actually fast for days, even when he was a Guest of Honour at the White House, US.

Livemint's[6] Gyan Verma wrote on 10 April 2018: *Narendra Modi, BJP MPs to observe fast to protest budget session washout.*

Some interesting excerpts of Gyan's news report are as follows:

Prime Minister Narendra Modi will observe a day-long fast on Thursday…to protest against the recent washout of the second half of the budget session of Parliament…The

---

[6] https://www.livemint.com/Politics/WBaddN4Esm5OBn1FPjBHVL/Modi-to-observe-fast-on-12-April-protesting-Parliament-washo.html

budget session was the worst session in terms of productivity in the last 18 years.

Speaking at the centenary celebrations of Mahatma Gandhi's fast at Champaran in Bihar on Tuesday, Modi alleged that opposition parties were creating hurdles for the NDA while it was working for the upliftment of financially weaker sections.

'*From the streets to Parliament, roadblocks are being created in the government's work. While the government is working towards uniting people and their hearts, some opponents are working towards breaking up society,*' said Modi.

Without naming any political party, Modi said there are people who don't want any improvement in the condition of the poor as they feel it would become difficult to mislead financially weaker sections if the government succeeds in its efforts to uplift the poor.

'*We have to eradicate the problems affecting our society which are weakening the country. We have to build a new India which is free from corruption, caste differences and religious divide. The entire country is one big family, we have to work together, only then we would be able to pay respects to the people who fought for the independence of the country,*' Modi said.

Michael Safi of *The Guardian* wrote on 11 April 2018: *Hunger games: Modi to lead tit-for-tat fast in row with opposition.*

Some interesting excerpts of Michael's news report are reproduced below:

The rival protests are part of growing showdown between Modi's ruling nationalist Bharatiya Janata Party (BJP) and the Congress party before national elections.

The Congress organised a five-hour hunger strike on Monday in a pre-emptive move against a BJP plan for a fast on Thursday. But the party was left embarrassed after photos circulated on social media showing senior leaders tucking into chickpeas and fried roti shortly before the fast. Congress faced sarcastic comments on Twitter, while the BJP called their protest a 'joke'.

Modi will fast to expose Congress's 'undemocratic style of functioning and pursuing divisive politics and [an] anti-development agenda'.

A strictly observant Hindu and teetotal vegetarian, Modi fasts every year for the Navratri festival—a nine-day ritual when he consumes only liquids during daylight hours. In a 2012 blog, Modi called his annual fast an act of self-purification. Fasts in Indian politics were pioneered by Mahatma Gandhi as a moral weapon against the British empire as well as his compatriots. He also fasted as a means of penance when he felt he or the freedom movement had erred.

The British regarded the high-profile fasts as political blackmail but feared riotous consequences if Gandhi were ever to die during one.

The tradition continued after independence, and in 1952 the south Indian political activist Potti Sriramulu died after fasting for 58 days to campaign for the creation of the state of Andhra Pradesh.

The activist Anna Hazare catalysed a national anti-corruption movement in 2011 by fasting in Delhi. Critics continue to argue the tactic is coercive and a form of blackmail at best, and often a cheap political stunt.

It seems the people of India, including politicians, have learnt nothing else from Mahatma Gandhi, the Father of the Nation, other than fasting.

In India, as in the rest of the countries—underdeveloped, developing and developed countries alike—many politicians feed and thrive on the illiterate /uneducated/ignorant masses. So, the more the population, the better it is. It works for them. Also, as more and more people in India are taking to politics as their career choice, not because they love their country or wish to serve her people, but because politics offers them the prospects of power and money, the competition between the politicians is also on the rise.

Therefore, not many politicians will support a firm state control on the population growth, such as the *One-child* policy.

And, why should the politicians support getting rid of those numerous social divisions based on the sickening regional, religious, and caste divisive politics and strive to introduce a uniform civil law across the country to unify the country? They exploit such divisions to their advantage. They have learnt the good old '*divide and rule*' policy from the past masters of the Indian political school.

- '*God will do something; Nature will play its role in controlling population, such as earthquakes, floods, disease, nuclear war outbreak etc.*'
  These people seem to have given up on the politicians and the governments. They see no hope in the way the country has been run. Their daily struggles make them wish for Nature's interference.

- '*Don't worry. Modern India is a young country. She is just coming out of centuries of slavery. She was left poor by the British. As the country defeats poverty, liveability in India will also improve. The country needs education to eliminate poverty and all her issues.*'

These people see India's poverty as the core reason for her current state of affairs and see hope in her economic prosperity.

- *'Population growth is not an issue. Population is actually India's strength and a massive resource. We need more people so that we can take on the world. We have suffered for long but now it is our time to be a superpower. The world must listen to us. We'll spread across the world.'*

For these people, India has a score to settle. Rather than coexistence with the rest of the world, they wish India to play a dominant role and dictate terms to her contemporaries and enemies.

- *'Arre yaar, sub chalta hai. India is a great country. You can make the system work for you there, all you need is to have money. Everyone has a price and can be bought … if you have the enough cash, you can make anyone work for you, and that is literary anyone … IAS officers do a fantastic job in running the country; they are so sharp and have so much knowledge … I plan to retire there one day. One can also afford so many facilities at home, such as domestic help, which is not possible overseas.'*

The above words are from a person of Indian origin, from Punjab, in his late fifties. He is not the first one to utter such words. These people are street-smart and know how to use (or misuse) the system; they know how to acclimatise with the country's political and corrupt environment. They feed and exacerbate her corrupt culture.

- *'India needs a dictator—a benevolent dictator—to improve the liveability in the country; control population,*

> *pollution, corruption; tame the enemies of the state—*
> *within the country and outside the country; and lead the*
> *country to strength and respectability.'*

These people seem to have lost patience and want something to be done quickly. They don't see the current system of governance in the country working—considering the country's hybrid and evolving culture, people's lack of national character and true nationalism, despite the best intentions of her leaders. They believe, in a complex country like India it is impossible to make people move from point A to point B unless they are dictated right from the top, and at every level (or rather herded) through an effective, firm and just 'law and order' infrastructure.

An Australian friend, Gerry, who is a businessman, travels very often to China in connection with his business. During a recent dinner meeting, he said that he has been travelling to China for over 20 years now, roughly every 3 to 4 months and, interestingly, with each visit, he has been observing a constant improvement in the life and living conditions as seen on the country's roads and streets, and in his dealings with the local people. On the contrary, the author's experiences of India's liveability, based on his observations during his frequent visits to the country, are not similar to Gerry's.

Another friend, Rachel, who was recently on a maiden visit to India on a work assignment and lived in 5-star hotels in two cities, was so overwhelmed by the living conditions on the roads that she vowed never to return to India. Interestingly, her parents who had visited India about 15 years ago, had also left the country with a similar (sick) feeling. A visitor to a country will always judge that country and its liveability based on the quality and ease of his/her life during a visit to that country.

A close friend in India, Rakesh, a top executive in the corporate sector, refused to accept that India is sliding. He said, '*It is true that India lags far behind the developed countries in many areas, but it is not correct to say that India is sliding.*' He added, '*Look, the lifestyle of people has definitely improved over time; we eat and wear much better than our forefathers. Our affordability has also greatly increased over time, as salary increases have been much more than the inflation.*' On education and overall condition of the country, he stated, '*The Prime Minister is doing a lot of work for the country ... in many areas. Literacy has increased over time ... more budget is being allocated to help the (poor) people living in the rural and backward areas ...*'

It seemed that Rakesh, like many other people, did not readily differentiate between the terms 'lifestyle/affordability' and 'liveability'; the latter term being judged based on a number of basic life essentials: quality of air; authenticity of food, fruits, vegetables, dairy, drinking water; security of women; movement on the roads and streets, traffic jams; happiness and mental health etc. Also, his view on improved 'lifestyle and affordability' could hold good for only the upper 50% of the population, considering about one-third of the population earns less than a dollar a day.

An optimist will always categorise a 'marginal' improvement as a 'significant' improvement although, in itself, a 'marginal' improvement over a long period of time may not mean much on the ground, given that population is growing uncontrollably.

When Rakesh was asked if the country is heading for some kind of people's revolution in the future (such as the Oct

1917 Revolution in Russia), he conceded, 'If the literacy of the youth increases and the country's economy also increases correspondingly, then there are no chances of any revolution. However, if the economy does not keep up with the literacy and education of the youth, leading to joblessness and frustration, then certainly there are chances of a people's revolution in the next 15 to 20 years. The probability of the revolution increases with a growing disparity of wealth between the rich and the poor, given that the top one per cent of the Indian population owns around 70 per cent of the country's wealth, as against the US where the top one per cent owns about 40 per cent of the country's wealth. A fast growing population is also likely to exacerbate the disparity in the wealth across the country—the rich becoming richer and the poor becoming poorer—and the middle class caught up between the two extremes—struggling to maintain and hang-on to its precarious position, stretching in the process and thinning out.'

The coming times look a little ominous for the educated Indian youth as their popular destination countries (the US, the UK, Australia, and many other European countries) are gradually turning screws on their immigration intake. Brexit is a warning about times to come. Indian youth will be forced to look more and more for jobs within the country as the international squeeze tightens. The changing global paradigm will turn out to be a major issue for India if the country is not able to sustain an economy which will employ its youth.

Like their counterparts in more developed parts of the word, all Indian citizens deserve a much healthier lifestyle. The question is how long more the significant lower half of the economic strata has to wait till they stand tall and proud, alongside the more affluent and educated citizens of the country, or should they be left to be exploited by the upper half. Justice delayed is justice denied.

The author discussed the possible forms of alternative systems of governance to improve India's liveability with his daughter, Deeksha Ladakhi Koul, who has two first class honours' Bachelor's degrees—in law and in engineering from University of Western Australia (UWA, which is one of the world's top 100 universities).

Deeksha challenged the author, '*India has already a strong system of governance—executive, legislative and judiciary; why should she require any other form of governance? Dictatorship will bring along tyranny. Dictatorship is terrible. Why do you want the country to slip backwards? Give her time. She needs a soft and gentle approach, through education. By the way, the world has not known any benevolent dictator.*'

In response to her immediate alarming reaction, the author also provided Deeksha with some examples of 'benevolent dictators', but she was not convinced. Perhaps because she has not visited the country in the past four years and, therefore, has no idea how the country's liveability has slipped with each passing day since her last visit.

Incidentally, Deeksha's law honours thesis, in 2016, is titled, *Our Founding Fetters—Re-imagining constitutional pre-commitment's aspirations within a democratic order.*

The thesis reviews the philosophy underlying Australian Constitution and comments on the extent of freedom the constitution provides. Deeksha says people generally believe they enjoy absolute freedom in a democratic country without realising that they have been made to commit to the constitution of the country even before they were born, so the founding fetters. The Australian Constitution was drafted at a series of constitutional conventions held in the 1890s, and was passed by the British Parliament as part of the Commonwealth of Australia Constitution Act 1900. It took effect on 1 January 1901. The Constitution is the legal framework for how Australia is governed and it can only be changed by referendum.

Many young people react immediately when they see 'democracy' being theoretically threatened or invaded by 'dictatorship'; they are just paranoid about the word 'democracy'. They don't realise that the world has changed significantly since the time democracy was first introduced in the world. The demands of the world and social order have constantly been in a flux. Once must keep one's mind and eyes open and not get fixated or blinded with a concept, which does not exactly meet the demands of the present time. The extent to which the world has changed in the last 117 years, in practically all walks of life, is obvious in the manner we live, eat, move, communicate in 2018. Since the introduction of Australian Constitution in 1901, the world saw two world wars, nuclear bombs, space missions, several gulf wars, Islamic militancy, rise of Asia, internet, smart phones and same-sex marriage. The world population also more than doubled in this period and so did the life expectancy in many countries of the world, including India. The issues that the world faces in 2018 are not the same it faced way back in 1901. These days, the Australian Parliament witnesses debates on novel issues such as legalisation of same-sex marriage, right to euthanasia, human-driven global warming, clean energy versus coal based energy, the Australian republic movement, and dual citizenship of the members of parliament. In 1901, these issues did not exist and, therefore, there are provisions in the Constitution to cover these issues of the present time. To bring about any changes in the Constitution, both Houses of the Parliament must sit down and pass them unequivocally, otherwise referenda are carried out. Australian Constitution requires a referendum in order to change it.

For example, in 2017, a referendum was carried out in Australia about legalisation of the same sex marriage. In the US, several amendments were made in the American Constitution to meet the demands of the time. Such amendments are not practically possible in Australia. Very recently, President Trump of the US was quoted as asking if America should emulate China and consider indefinite term for the American President, similar to what the Chinese government announced recently in favour of President Xi Jinping.

How sad it is that people, who have long been exploited, have finally come to realise 70 years after the country's independence that no government or politician will really listen to them and effectively improve the liveability in the country.

The country has never been so divided along caste and religious lines as it is now. Many people belonging to the two major religions are constantly running a scare campaign through the social media, driven by their respective religious organisations. They are also competing with each other in so far as their respective population is concerned, which, in turn, is potentially choking the country. Many Hindus believe that the country will become an Islamic entity in a few years given the relatively much higher 'birth to death' ratio of the Muslim community across the country. The latest Census is reported to indicate a drop in the percentage of the Hindus and increase in the percentage of the Muslims.

To prevent the country from having more than 50 per cent of its population as Muslims, many Hindu leaders and organisations are exhorting the Hindu community to produce more children. If you ask them to stop breeding, they ask, 'Why don't you first ask the Muslims community to do so?' Many Hindus are bitter about the partition of the country that took place in 1947 on religious grounds. If you ask the Muslims to check their birth rate, they say their religion forbids them to adopt any birth control measures. Interestingly, about 28 years ago, soon after their exodus from Kashmir, a female gynaecologist at AIIMS, Delhi, encouraged a Kashmiri Pandit migrant to produce at least four children to counter the corresponding increase in the population of the Muslims in the country. That advice shocked that Kashmiri Pandit, as she had never thought along those lines in Kashmir. Demography was never an area of interest for Kashmiri Pandits. After 1980, Kashmiri Pandit couples rarely produce more than two children.

Most people pray to God for a better tomorrow. Many people hope the present government leadership does something miraculous. Some people wish for natural disasters for her population control. But no one is prepared to do anything other than talk.

Instead of focusing on more important and pressing issues of their country, people are distracted by petty politics and made to waste their energies on relatively trivial matters, such as protests against movies like *Padmavati (renamed Padmavat)*, loud speakers from religious places, demands for further reservations etc.

The phrase, *justice delayed is justice denied*, is often used as a rallying cry by legal activists who find courts or governments acting too slowly in resolving legal issues, partly because the system is too complex or overburdened, or because the issue or party in question lacks political favour. Is this phrase applicable to the 'denial of basic rights' of a large section of the population to have access to basic education, healthcare and security?

It is alarming that many people believe no government can fulfil its primary function to serve them without bias or prejudice, as promised by the country's Constitution? The current system of governance clearly lacks the cutting edge and effectiveness required to improve the conditions in the country. An alternative system is urgently required. Can it be 'benevolent dictatorship?'

In early February 2018, at a graduation ceremony at Curtin University in Perth, a Singaporean academic, in his mid to late sixties, asked the author, 'How would you tackle corruption in India? Corruption is in the DNA of Indians.'

The author replied, 'A benevolent dictator would first take a good look at the whole country at one glance, then identify all factors causing or contributing to corruption at all levels, let social scientists work out solutions, identify consequences and whet them through lawmakers, anti-corruption squads, with necessary checks and balances in place.' The Singaporean gentleman asked the author, 'How long do you think it will take to weed out the corruption in such a massive country?'

The author replied, 'At least one generation—25 years.'

Thereupon, the gentleman provided the author with the following advice:

- The leader (benevolent dictator) of the country must be able to control the population of the country, as China did. He must also have the vision to take the country into the future like Lee Kuan Yew.

- In a country like India, the leader must get rid of all social divides. The leader himself/herself must be far above the religious or ethnic divides, and must work for the country's greater good like Lee Kuan Yew did. He transformed the country from a dirt poor state to a developed state with his vision.

- The country will need a Master Plan for everything worked out to the minutest details and not the kind of bastardy that is commonly seen now. For example, it is not uncommon to see, due to a total lack of coordination between various departments, one department contracts a road and after a while other departments dig it out one by one to install their facilities—water supply pipes, telephone cables, gas pipes, electricity cables, Fibre optic cables etc. The Master Plan must carry the leader's vision of the requirements of the future world.

- The leader needs to be in control for at least one generation to oversee the Master Plan being implemented. Lee Kuan Yew led the country for 25 years.

Suddenly he asked, 'Who do you think can be eligible to be the (benevolent) dictator in India?'

The author replied, 'None other than the current Prime Minster, Mr Modi. All we need from him is to transcend all current religious and ethnic divides. He will need to see and treat every Indian as an Indian only, nothing less and nothing more. He has the good intent to serve the country selflessly and he has the vision for the future. Being a practitioner of yoga and a vegetarian, he should be expected to maintain good physical and mental health, with sharp faculties and last for the next 25 years to see the Master Plan through its complete implementation. The current so-called parliamentary democratic system will not let him address the core issues that are undermining the country. And, if Mr Modi does not take the full reins in his hands now and assume the supreme leadership of the country, the frustrated common man on the street will do so in a few years from now and bring about a revolution similar to the 1917 Bolshevik Revolution in Russia.'

In late February 2018, at a health-related seminar in Perth, a young doctor of Indian origin in his late forties, born and brought up in Delhi, swore that he would never return to Delhi. On his smart phone, using a weather App, he compared Delhi's (sick) grey sky at that time with the (healthy) deep blue sky in Perth. Then suddenly turning towards his wife, he said, 'I have been telling her that India needs a dictator if things have to be improved there.'

Author's India visit—March 2018

In March 2018, the author visited India after a gap of about three months during which he visited Delhi, Jammu and Srinagar and made the following observations:

- The traffic conditions in New Delhi appeared to have worsened and so had the air quality. However, at Jammu, thanks to a newly appointed strict Inspector

General of (Traffic) Police, traffic conditions seemed to have improved. Public vehicles without permits were being confiscated.

It is said many private bus owners in Jammu have been operating up to five or six vehicles for public transportation based on single permit from the local transport authorities, thanks to their 'connections' and assistance from 'brokers'. As a relief, uncharacteristically though, illegally parked vehicles along the roadside were being craned away by the police. Due to all this, the privately owned public transport drivers and conductors were on the alert and very careful. There was a rumour that the privately owned public transport operators were soon going to organise mass protests—*jaloos* and *dharna*—and try to put pressure on the government for immediate transfer of the new IG police.

The above change illustrates how an upstanding and responsible police officer of integrity can lead his police force and help bring about a positive change in the country. The country needs every police officer to follow his example. Needless to say the said police officer will have to surmount significant opposition, not only from the corrupt stakeholders, public figures and members of the public, but also from within his own police force for doing something which has not been done in years. He will be summoned by the concerned minister(s) to explain, as the government does not want to have any issues with the public. The author won't be surprised if the officer is transferred from his current position on the pretext of something related or even unrelated, which is tantamount to being punished (rather rewarded) for doing one's job. The author hopes the officer prevails over all obstacles in the course of his work.

On the other side, the impending reaction by the emboldened bus operators illustrates the extent to which they can think of daring the system and challenging the authorities via a mechanism of resistance taught by the Father of the Nation, Mahatma Gandhi, albeit for wrong reasons. Sitting for *dharna*, taking out *jaloos* (procession) of resistance and doing *nare-baazi* (shouting slogans) is common in India; most participants get paid for staging these by mischief mongers.

- Many people appeared to be suffering from viral fever in all three cities, with prolonged periods of cough and cold, possibly due to polluted air—aerosols, dust and smoke particles being carriers of air-borne bugs, drug-resistant strains due a common gross misuse of antibiotics (being sold over the counter) and birth of new strains of viruses, exacerbated by ineffective and spurious medicines. (The readers are referred to the author's book, *Issues White-anting India*, for some details about spurious drugs in India.)

- Eighty per cent of people whom the author met in the three cities this time, similar to the people he met during his earlier visits in 2016 and 2017, favoured and wished for some form of dictatorship to improve the conditions in the country and to instil fear of law in the public so that corruption could be eliminated. It is a common view amongst the general public that Indians don't have any fear of the law, unlike people living in countries like Singapore or China, and they can get away with anything if they have money in their pocket. The reason they give is the widespread corruption by the people who are responsible for upholding the law and order in the country.

• Early morning on 3 March 2018, around 6.30 to 7.00 am, a dull sun appeared on the horizon on the east behind a veil of smog and the visibility on Delhi streets was not more than 200 metres. The traffic seemed to be heavy even at that time. On the same evening, around 7 to 7.30 pm, a key link road leading from ITO to New Delhi railway station was closed by the Delhi traffic police because the ruling party (BJP) had just shifted to their new headquarters located on that road, which BJP followers were reported to be visiting in large numbers. Possibly so-called VIPs were also using that road. One can imagine the level of inconvenience for Delhi commuters who had to take detours and search for alternative routes in the cover of darkness. But, this is India; who cares for general public? VIPs are most important; they are the 'princes' and 'kings' of the modern 'democratic' India.

• On the afternoon of 9 March 2108, upon his return from Jammu, the author's taxi after coming out of the airport was immediately caught in a traffic jam due to the presence of a VIP in the area for whom a road was closed by the traffic police. Somehow, his taxi driver, Nathu Lal, in his late fifties, originally from Rajasthan but having lived in Delhi for nearly three decades, managed to take a U-turn and take a detour, but only to find the taxi crawling at snail's pace for the next five to six kilometres. Nathu Lal was full of disgust and anger at the way things have been shaping in Delhi. He sounded very critical of Delhi traffic police officers and their impotence in managing traffic. He claimed they had their bank accounts full. He anticipated that Delhi could choke itself in the next five years or so due to traffic woes, which tallied with the assessment of most other taxi drivers in Delhi and other cities of India.

- In Kashmir, the author visited his uncle Abujan, who had been admitted to Sher-I-Kashmir Institute of Medical Sciences (SKIMS), for all four days of his brief stay in Kashmir. Abujan's story is very interesting and well within the domain of this book. It provides a snapshot of how ordinary citizens in India suffer due to lack of proper health care at the hospitals and the adverse effects of spurious drugs on people's health and risk to their lives.

Abujan suffered from a tooth ailment in early Feb 2018. A couple of his teeth needed extraction but, due to tooth infection, the dentist put him first on antibiotics. Initially there was no change in his condition, so the antibiotic was changed. As soon as he took the new antibiotic, his body reacted. His felt extremely weak and his joints swelled up. He could not sit or walk and became extremely sensitive to human touch. As soon as that happened, he was admitted to the Government hospital at Jammu. The facilities in the hospital were apparently poor and basic but despite that he was provided with the best the hospital could provide. Since he was suffering from severe body pain, his family replaced the stiff hospital mattress with a couple of softer mattresses from home. Doctors in the hospital tried to do what they could but his condition did not improve. His body fluids were sent to a lab in Mumbai and the results came back as negative, much to his relief, but his physical condition kept him virtually paralysed. After staying in the hospital for about a week, he was released without any improvement in his condition. Within that week his infected teeth were extracted.

The family was not happy with the way things were going, seeing him slip from a bad to a worse condition, without a clue why that was happening. Abujan's all four daughters, and their husbands are doctors. After conferring with one another across the globe—the UK, the US, Saudi Arabia and Kashmir—his children decided that he must be either moved to a better hospital at New Delhi or at Srinagar for a detailed investigation and treatment. However, as he could not even sit, air travel was ruled out immediately. He had to be transported by road; of the two, Srinagar being nearer was accordingly chosen. After a painful search, the family found a private ambulance provider in Janipur, Jammu, who asked for a hefty fee of Rupees 35,000 for transporting him to Srinagar. The ambulance came with a technician. Abujan's daughter and son-in-law sat with him in the ambulance.

The facilities, hygiene, doctor's care and other

miscellaneous allied services at Sher-i-Kashmir Institute were impressive and far superior to the Government Hospital at Jammu. Abujan remained in the hospital for over two weeks and his condition improved with each passing day. He was very happy with the way he was treated by the doctors. All tests returned negative. Eventually, it appeared to be a case of his body reacting adversely to a fake or spurious drug. India is well known for spurious drugs. This case history illustrates what can happen in India to ordinary citizens. Thanks to his quick thinking children, all doctors, Abujan could be revived. In Abujan's own words, 'Imagine what must have happened to all those Kashmiri Pandit migrants in Jammu, where many people died in the past 28 years, some very young, possibly due to a paucity of good hospital care and facilities.'

• In general, the author felt a sense of deep belonging to the valley where he was born and where he grew up, and all her people. Three young men, Adil Shah (23), an engineering graduate but helping his family with business, Manzoor Ahmad (39) and his younger brother (who drove his chartered car) won his heart with their warmth and politeness, a reminder of traditional Kashmiriyat, and what it means to be a Kashmiri. Credit goes to the parents and families of these young men for bringing them up well and immunising them against the enemies of peace and all corrosive elements of the community, and without developing any hate or ill will towards the Pandits. Such bright young men strengthen a hope that sense and conscience lives on in the valley.

- Lastly, the author's recent Kashmir diary will not be complete without an interesting vignette about his interaction with a bright matriculation student of Delhi Public School, Srinagar. The student desperately tried to convince the author, for nearly three hours, providing all kinds of supporting arguments, that the earth is a disk shaped planet, as written in the religious books, and not a sphere. The student is understood to be highly influenced by a school teacher who believes in the Flat Earth theory and has been campaigning for it. The student said that the scientific community from the western world had been deliberately misleading humanity, as a well-knitted global conspiracy, about the shape of the earth in order to weaken the contents of religious books regarding the Creation and the earth. She also claimed there is no space, it is all a lie. The student's parents, both science graduates and professionals, are also understood to be on board with the Flat Earth concept. How strange that all this is happening in 2018, when the world community is trying to explore Mars for possible migration of the human species to the planet in the future!

Elsewhere in India, people's stories of helplessness and complaints against the system of governance, in March 2018, were similar to complaints from most other people whom the author met and spoke with during his earlier visits to the country. Most people urgently want dictatorship as the form of governance in the country and the rule of law. But most people don't know how that is going to happen, so they just give up thinking about it.

A question arises: 'How long will they simmer inside and keep watching?' It is only a matter of time before someone stands up and leads a people's army to bring about a total revolution in the country! The dormant volcano may erupt someday and cause widespread violence across the country and loss of numerous lives if nothing is done by the politicians and the government, when the country still has the time to genuinely address the people's issues.

The Constitutional Promise

Preamble to the Constitution of India[1]

A Constitution is a set of rules by which a country or a state is run. The USA, Australia and India have written constitutions. Some countries, such as New Zealand and Israel do not have formal written constitutions; their constitutional rules are derived from a number of sources. Britain's constitution is from a number of important statutes, or laws, as well as principles decided in legal cases and conventions. Other countries have formal written constitutions in which the structure of government is defined and the respective powers of

---

[1] https://en.wikipedia.org/wiki/Preamble_to_the_Constitution_of_India

the nation, and its states, are written in one single document. These systems may also include unwritten conventions and constitutional law, which can inform how the constitution is interpreted. Some constitutions may be amended without any special procedure, for example, the documents that make up New Zealand Constitution may be amended by simply a majority vote of its Parliament. In other countries, a special procedure must be followed before their constitution can be amended, for example, Australia requires a referendum to amend its constitution.

Preamble to the Constitution of India, as its heart and soul, provides a brief introductory statement that sets out the guiding purpose and principles of the Constitution, and it indicates the source from which the document derives its authority—the people. The hopes and aspirations of the Indian people as well as the ideals before the nation are described in the preamble.

The Preamble states:

'WE, THE PEOPLE OF INDIA, having solemnly resolved to constitute India into a SOVEREIGN SOCIALIST SECULAR DEMOCRATIC REPUBLIC and to secure to all its citizens:

JUSTICE, social, economic and political;

LIBERTY of thought, expression, belief, faith and worship;

EQUALITY of status and of opportunity; and to promote among them all

FRATERNITY assuring the dignity of the individual and the unity and integrity of the Nation;

IN OUR CONSTITUENT ASSEMBLY this twenty-sixth day of November, 1949, do HEREBY ADOPT, ENACT AND GIVE TO OURSELVES THIS CONSTITUTION.'

The preamble was drafted and moved in the Constituent Assembly on 13 December 1946. Thereafter, it was adopted on 26 November 1949 by the Constituent Assembly and came into effect on 26 January 1950. The preamble has been amended only once, in 1976, during the Emergency in India. On 18 December 1976, the then government carried out the Forty-second Amendment of the Constitution, through which the words *socialist* and *secular* were added between the words *sovereign* and *democratic* and the words 'unity of the Nation' were replaced by 'unity and integrity of the Nation.'

About the preamble, BR Ambedkar[2] said: 'It was, indeed, a way of life, which recognises liberty, equality, and fraternity as the principles of life and which cannot be divorced from each other. Liberty cannot be divorced from equality; equality cannot be divorced from liberty. Nor can liberty and equality be divorced from fraternity. Without equality, liberty would produce the supremacy of the few over the many. Equality without liberty would kill individual initiative. Without fraternity, liberty and equality could not become a natural course of things.'

It is very important to note the wording:...*Liberty cannot be divorced from equality...Without equality, liberty would produce the supremacy of the few over the many...*One can easily question if during the past 70 years of independence, the country's successive governments have been able to address this objective. On ground, citizens are divided into numerous categories

---

[2] https://en.wikipedia.org/wiki/Preamble_to_the_Constitution_of_India an jurist, economist, politician and social reformer. He campaigned against social discrimination against untouchables. He also supported the rights of women and labour. He was a founding father of the Republic of India. After independence, he was India's first law minster, as well as the principal architect of the Constitution of India.

based on where they live, their religion, their caste, their socio-economic background; many of them face marginalisation. In practice, no two individuals eg a bureaucrat and a street cleaner (sweeper) are considered as equals. They have unequal privileges and rights. Opportunities are also highly variable depending upon who you are! So, no two citizens are equal.

Also, due to downside of capitalisation, society finds itself at a wide range of socio-economic levels—with variable access to opportunities to receive education and move upward on the ladder of prosperity. The emergence of unequal societies, coupled with constantly dwindling liveability in the country is a stark reminder that something is amiss in the current system. Can one say, therefore, that the spirit of the preamble, and therefore the Constitution, has not been fully satisfied? Has democracy, in its present form and practice, really helped the masses in India?

Let us now analyse the meaning of some terms: Sovereign, Socialist, Secular, Democratic and Republic.

Sovereignty

India became a sovereign country on 26 January 1950, yet she voluntarily chose to be a member of the United Nations Organisation (UNO) and the Commonwealth of Nations. The memberships do not affect her sovereignty to any extent and she is free to cut off these associations at her will.

Sovereignty means the independent authority of a country. It has two aspects—internal and external.

Internal sovereignty relates to the internal and domestic affairs of a country and is divided into four branches—the executive, the legislature, the judiciary and the administrative. It refers to the relationship between the states and the individuals within its territory. External sovereignty relates to the independence of a country, of the will of other states, in her conduct with other states in the comity of nations. It also means that it can acquire foreign territory and also cede any part of her territory, however, subject to limitations (if any) imposed by the Constitution.

Socialist

Socialist state means the wealth is generated socially and should be shared equally by society through distributive justice, and not be concentrated in the hands of a few. Democratic socialism means achievement of socialistic goals through democratic, evolutionary and non-violent means. Government should regulate the ownership of land and industry to reduce socio-economic inequalities. The term was added in the Preamble in 1976, through the 42nd Amendment.

Author's Comment: Has the country succeeded in meeting the intent embedded in the wording '...wealth is generated socially and should be shared equally by society through distributive justice. It shall not be concentrated in the hands of few...?' The answer would be 'no', given the capitalist nature of the country, with a significant portion of the population 'poor' in all sense of the term, and a major portion of the country's wealth in the hands and control of a minority.

Secular

It means the relationship between the government and the people as determined according to the Constitution and law. In essence, it means all religions will be equally respected and there will be no state religion. All the citizens of India will be allowed to profess, practise and propagate any religion. This term was also introduced in the Preamble in 1976, through the 42nd Amendment.

Author's Comment: Following the mass exodus of Kashmiri Pandits from the valley, on and after 19 Jan 1990, who were a minority in a Muslim majority state, a question arises about the failure of the country in ensuring secularism in all her parts and the safety of the people in areas where they are in minority. There is also a strong perception that the union governments of the past have consistently followed a policy of appeasement, rather than equality between the religions, and annoyed many people from the majority community.

Democratic

This gives every citizen of India, 18 years of age and above, and not otherwise debarred by law, a right to vote. The word 'democratic' refers to political, social and economic democracy.

Author's Comment: It does not mean the voter should be educated and informed about the background and the merit of political candidates standing in the election. It also does not provide safety/security to the voter during the process of voting. Booth capturing used to be a common affair in Kashmir and some parts of India, which sowed seeds of distrust in the whole voting process and triggered the start of a politico-religious uprising in Kashmir in 1988.

Republic

This means the head of the state is an elected person for a fixed tenure and not a monarch, and a government in which no one person holds public power as proprietary right.

Author's Comment: The cronyism, nepotism and dynastical leadership, as seen in the country at various state and national levels clearly undermine the republic status of the country. It seems the country moved from the British monarchy to the modern-day, self-aggrandising, political maharajahs, who rule for a while and then hand over power to their next of kin.

Justice

The Constitution of India promises social, economic and political justice for her people.

Author's Comment: Once again, numerus questions can be asked about whether the country has served justice to all social, educational, environment and political causes. The plight of Kashmiri Pandits serves as a fine example of social and political injustice to the community. Similarly, lack of educational infrastructure in the villages, leading to low or no education amongst the villagers and the poor, and the country's poverty speak for themselves.

Social Justice

It means the absence of socially privileged classes in the society and no discrimination against any citizen on grounds of caste, creed, colour, religion, sex or place of birth, and elimination of any forms of exploitation from the society.

Author's Comment: The ground reality, however, contradicts the aforementioned promise in many areas of the statement. The country has different laws for different religions and different genders.

Reservations in the schools/colleges/university admissions, job appointments and promotions for the candidates that belong to certain castes and categories can be deemed to be tantamount to discrimination against the people belonging to the mainstream. It makes it so much easier for a person belonging to a certain caste/category, with much lesser merit or qualifications, to win a job or get a promotion or job despite being a child of a 2nd or 3rd generation bureaucrat or a professional. Ideally, as soon as the first generation of a SC/ST family moves up the socio-economic ladder and into the mainstream—through the country's reservation system (in admission to tertiary education and/or government appointment), the family should no longer be entitled to benefits from the reservation system.

For equality and fairness, the country's 'reservation system' should be based on the socio-economic standing of a person (and family) regardless of the person's religion, caste, class etc.

Economic Justice

It means economic equality—decentralisation of economic resources, equitable distribution of wealth without anyone's monopoly over means of production and distribution, and provisions of adequate opportunities to all people to earn their living. Importantly, it means no discrimination between man and woman on the basis of their income, wealth and/or economic status, whatsoever.

Author's Comment: The current unlimited 'reservation policy' in the country and capitalism undermines economic justice.

Political Justice

It means equal, free and fair opportunities to all people to participate in the political process. It provides equal political rights to all people without any discrimination.

Author's Comment: Widespread practice of nepotism, favouritism and political hooliganism undermine political justice in the country. For half a million Kashmir Pandits, who were forced to leave their home and hearth, it has been a case of justice delayed is justice denied.

No Indian government since 1990 has been able to create political conditions conducive to their safe and dignified return to their home in Kashmir. It is matter of time before the exiled community will lose its culture and identity in their continued struggle to assimilate with numerous local communities across the world. History will in time forget why Kashmiri Pandits had to become refugees in their own country and why the country could not help them to go back.

Liberty

Liberty refers to freedom of activities of the citizens so that there are no unreasonable restrictions on them in terms of what they think or their expressions or the way they wish to follow up their thoughts in action.

Liberty does not mean having freedom to do anything that can cause harm—physically or emotionally—to other people or the country and, therefore, must be exercised within the constitutional limits.

Equality

Equality means all people are equal before law in its all three dimensions—political, economic and civic. It means no section of the society enjoys special privileges and that individuals are provided with adequate opportunities without any discrimination.

Author's Comment: The law has been divided on the basis of the religion—Hindu law, Muslim law etc. and castes. This means all Indians are not treated by the Constitution as one people. Furthermore, the reservation policy, albeit with a noble intent to uplift the backward class, unfairly marginalises and discriminates against the people that belong to the mainstream general category, as it continues to extend the privileges down the generations of families from backward categories.

As a classic example, a case involving two IAS candidates has recently come to the attention of the people, on the television as well as through the social media. One candidate belongs to the mainstream General category and the other to the Dalit category. Reportedly, the General category candidate, scoring 230 marks in the preliminary assessment, was declared as 'failed', whereas the Dalit category candidate, who scored 195 marks, was declared as 'passed'. When questioned, the examining body confirmed the marks and, to support their argument and decision to disqualify the higher marks holder in favour of the lower marks holder, said the latter had the right to use her constitutional privileges.

One could accept this 'policy' decision, albeit with a grain of salt, if the winning candidate would have been the first educated person from her family and her family would have been really backward—illiterate, poor and underprivileged. However, that is not the case. Interestingly, but not surprisingly though, her parents are reported to be educated and professionals, both in engineering services.

The issue here is not about extending the constitutional privileges to the downtrodden backward class; in fact, it is the duty of the state, as a noble cause, to uplift the people from the lower socio-economic strata. But the constitutional privileges must be limited to only one generation unless that generation fails to capitalise on the opportunity. Thereafter, the privileges (reservation) must be assessed based on the family income. It is not morally or ethically fair, or a democratic treatment of all citizens equally based on merit, that the privileges are extended down the generations. Such a policy is not a sign of democracy in its purest form. What does it do except harming the nation?

- It sends a wrong message to the public that the constitution is not fair to all;

- It results in an overall drop in the quality of the work. People from the privileged (ie Reserved) category can qualify and enjoy privileges without having to put in the same quantum of effort as the people from the General category;

- It encourages many people from the mainstream community to fraudulently obtain documents that support their (false) claims that they too belong to a backward community, in order to enjoy the constitutional privileges.

- It demoralises relatively much brighter candidates belonging to the mainstream and General category. Their competition increases significantly due to a high 'demand to supply' ratio because of a growing population. The probability of their anxiety and mental depression also increases considerably, making the nation unhappier in the process. Finally, when they get the opportunity, they leave the country, causing brain-drain.

So, what is the solution? Free and compulsory education of good quality must be provided by the State to all children from all communities in the country, under the RTE, to at least the Matriculation level for children from mainstream and up to the Secondary education level for children from backward categories, so that all children have equal opportunities to compete at the Tertiary education levels. Thereafter, only one generation (the first) from the backward category must receive benefits and constitutional privileges under the country's reservation policy.

Can this dream change be accomplished in India under the present system of governance, which at best can be considered to be a flawed version of Indian democracy? No, as the people who have benefited from it, or are benefitting from it, or will potentially benefit from the current system will not let that happen; they will be up in arms if any changes are even hinted and the country will come to a standstill. On the other hand, yes, undoubtedly it can happen but only if the country is run by a well-intentioned, firm, decisive, and visionary form of governance.

Fraternity

This refers to a feeling of brotherhood and a sense of belonging with the country among the citizens of the country. It encompasses psychological and territorial dimensions of National Integration, whilst leaving no room for regionalism, communalism, casteism etc.

The Preamble declares that fraternity has to assure: (a) the dignity of the individual; and (b) the unity and *integrity* of the nation. The word 'integrity' was added to the Preamble by the 42nd Constitutional Amendment in 1976.

Author's Comment: Has the country been truly integrated? The divisions in the country—social, regional, religious, caste—have been kept well and truly alive by the system. The politicians have exploited people and all those divisions to their maximum benefit. In the last seven decades, the country has allowed formation of some new states. Uttar Pradesh and erstwhile Andhra Pradesh have given birth to those new states. Kashmir has constantly been seeing strife and the Khalistan movement has not completely died down. The North-East is a different world and the young people from the North-East get physically assaulted in the national capital. The South does not see eye to eye with the North. The national language is Hindi but it has not enjoyed popularity in the country's border states, especially the South. Dalits are up in arms against the government and raise fingers towards the higher caste people. Brahmins also allege discrimination and marginalisation against them. Reservations have sown deep seeds of hatred amongst the people coming from various castes.

India must follow Bangladesh and abolish reservations. On 12 April 2018, News18.com,[3] announced: *Bangladesh Ends Reservation in Govt. Jobs as PM Sheikh Hasina Gives in to Protesting Students.*

Some excerpts from the news clip are reproduced below:

Bangladesh Prime Minister Sheikh Hasina on Wednesday said she has decided to scrap the quota system in government services…Police were deployed to the Dhaka University where clashes in recent days left more than 100 students injured by tear gas and rubber bullets…

'The quota system will be abolished as the students do not want it,' she said in a statement in Parliament. An apparently annoyed premier added that, 'They have demonstrated enough

---

[3] https://www.news18.com/news/world/bangladesh-ends-reservation-in-govt-jobs-as-prime-minister-sheikh-hasina-gives-in-to-protesting-students-1715723.html.

protests, now let them return home.'

She said the government could make special arrangements for jobs for the people with disabilities and the backward ethnic minority. The premier, however, said those who attacked the vice-chancellor's house were not 'eligible to be students' and promised to punish the guilty. According to police, more than 5,000 protesters rallied at the Dhaka University campus alone while the private universities joined the public ones across the country to mount pressure on the government to abolish the system, meant for freedom fighters' descendants, ethnic minority groups and women. The protests also drew a number of girl students demanding they be made eligible to compete for the public services on merit basis. 'They (girls) said that they will get job through (appearing) examinations … it's a good word and I'm very happy … as they don't want quota. What is the necessity of it?' Hasina said.

This development shows a high level of awareness of the Bangladeshi people and an example of decisive governance, unlike their Indian counterparts. This is not the first time Bangladesh is taking a lead in important matters. It has a successful family planning programme, despite being an Islamic country. Bangladesh also ranks much above India on the Happiness Index.

The Current system of Governance

The Government Structure[1]

The Republic of India has a quasi-federal form of government called the Central or Union government, with officials elected at the Central, State and local levels. India is currently the largest democracy in the world, with around 834 million eligible voters, as of 2014.

India follows the Westminster system of governance, where the Central government consists of three branches: executive, legislative and judiciary. The individual State governments also comprise a similar governmental structure.

---

[1] https://en.wikipedia.org/wiki/Government_of_India

The division of power into separate branches of government—executive, legislative and judiciary—is central to the republican idea of the separation of powers.

The President is the Head of State and the Supreme Commander of the Indian Armed Forces.

The Prime Minister is the head of Central government and is appointed by the President from amongst the party which wins the majority seats in the Lok Sabha.

The Constitution of India vests all powers in the Parliament, the Prime Minister and the Supreme Court of India.

The **Legislative** exercises its powers through the Parliament, which comprises two houses: The Lok Sabha (lower house or the House of the People) and the Rajya Sabha (upper house or the Council of States).

- The Lok Sabha is a temporary house. It can be dissolved only when the ruling party loses the support of the majority of the house. The members of the Lok Sabha are directly elected for five-year terms by universal adult suffrage through first-past-the-post voting system.

- The Rajya Sabha is a permanent house. All members of Rajya Sabha (except 12 members who are nominated by the President) are elected by the members of State legislative assemblies and territorial legislatures by proportional representation for a six-year term.

- The Cabinet, comprising the Council of Ministers headed by the Prime Minister, is responsible to the Lok Sabha. The members are chosen from Parliament. They can also be elected within six months of assuming office.

- Parliament does not have absolute control over the government or any sovereignty. Its laws are subject to judicial review by the Supreme Court. However, it does exercise some control over the executive branch.

The **Executive** has sole authority and responsibility for the day-to-day administration of the State bureaucracy. The Prime Minister acts as its chief executive and is responsible for running the Central government.

The **Judiciary** comprises the Supreme Court, the highest court in the country, which is supported by lower courts that include 24 High Courts and numerous District Courts.

- The civil and criminal laws are set down in major parliamentary legislation, such as the Civil Procedure Code, the Indian Penal Code and the Criminal Procedure Code.
- The legal system, applicable to both the Central and State governments is based on the English Common and Statutory Law.

The President

Article 53 (1) of the Constitution of India vests the executive power in the President. Despite having all constitutional powers and authority to exercise them directly or indirectly through his subordinate officers, the President is required to act in accordance with assistance and advice provided by the Prime Minister.

In theory, the Cabinet can remain in power during the 'pleasure' of the President; however, in practice, it cannot be dismissed by the President as long as it holds the support of a majority in the Lok Sabha. A constitutional crisis can trigger if a Cabinet is dismissed by the President without receiving the advice from the Cabinet.

On the recommendations of the Cabinet, the President is responsible for appointing the President's Officer, the Cabinet Secretary, the Ambassadors and High Commissioners to other countries, the Governors of the states, the Chief Justice, other judges of the Supreme Court and High Courts of India (on the advice of other judges), the Attorney General, Comptroller and Auditor General, the Chief Election Commissioner and other Election Commissioners, the Chairman and other Members of the Union Public Service Commission.

The President receives the credentials of Ambassadors from other countries.

The President can grant a pardon to a convicted person, or reduce the sentence, particularly in cases of death sentence. Although such decisions can be independent of the Prime Minister's opinion or the Lok Sabha majority, the President generally exercises executive powers on the advice of the Prime Minister.

The Vice-President

After the President, the Vice-President is the next highest constitutional head of the state. The Vice-President takes charge as acting President in the absence of the President or an incident of impeachment or resignation of the President. The Vice-President acts as the Chairman of the Rajya Sabha and is elected by the members of both Houses of Parliament in accordance with the system of Proportional Representation via a single transferable vote, conducted by secret ballot by the Election Commission.

The Prime Minister

The Prime minister is appointed by the President for administering the affairs of the executive. He is also the chief adviser to the President.

Being the chief executive, and responsible for running the Central government, the Prime Minister is the head of the government and the Cabinet, as well as the leader of the majority party in the parliament.

The Prime Minister selects the other members of the Cabinet, and can dismiss them, if required. The Cabinet is dissolved upon the resignation or death of the Prime Minister. The Prime Minister allocates portfolios to members of the Government and is responsible for bringing a proposal of legislation.

The Cabinet

The Cabinet includes the Prime Minister and Cabinet Ministers. The Prime Minister heads the Cabinet and is advised by the Cabinet Secretary who also acts as the head of the Indian Administrative Service (IAS).

Other than Union Cabinet Ministers, other ministers are: Ministers of State or Junior Ministers of State.

Each Minister must be a member of one of the Houses of Parliament. Every Minister has the right to speak and to take part in the proceedings of either House, any joint sitting of the Houses, and any committee of Parliament of which she/he may be named a member, but shall not be entitled to a vote in the House where he is not a member.

Civil Services

The Civil Services (IAS) comprise the bureaucracy to assist the ministers carry out their role. The ultimate responsibility for running the administration rests with the ministers who are the elected representatives of the people. Due to practical constraints, as the ministers cannot personally involve themselves with the day-to-day administration, they lay down the policy and require the civil servants to enforce it.

Cabinet Secretariat

The Cabinet Secretariat is operated under the leadership of the Prime Minister and its administration is carried out by the Cabinet Secretary, the senior most civil servant.

The Cabinet Secretariat is responsible for the administration of the government and assists in decision-making by ensuring Inter-Ministerial co-ordination, ironing out differences between Ministries and evolving consensus through the *instrumentality of the standing* or ad-hoc Committees of Secretaries. Management of major crisis situations in the country is also one of its functions.

The Cabinet Secretariat must ensure that the President, the Vice-President and the ministers are kept informed of the major activities of all government departments via a monthly summary report on their activities.

Judiciary

India's judicial system resembles those of Anglo-Saxon countries. The Indian system of justice consists of a unitary system at both Central and State levels, unlike the US system.

The Supreme Court of India is the highest court in the country. It is supported by 24 High Courts at state levels, which, in turn, are supported by District Courts and Session Courts at District level.

The Supreme Court consists of a Chief Justice and

30 Associate Justices. On the advice of the Chief Justice of India, all judges are appointed by the President.

The Supreme Court of India has the power of original, appellate and advisory jurisdiction. Its exclusive jurisdiction extends to any dispute between the Government of India and one or more states, or between the Government of India and any state or states on one side and one or more states on the other, or between two or more states, if and insofar as the dispute involves any question (whether of law or of fact) on which the existence or extent of a legal right depends.

What does Democracy mean?

Origin

The word 'democracy[1]' which has originated from the Greek language is a combination of two words:

- *demos*: It refers to 'all' citizens living within a particular city or state; and
- *kratos*: It refers to the power or rule.

In short, 'democracy' refers to people's rule over their country.

Anecdotally, Abraham Lincoln, the legendary US President, uttered the famous words, '*government of the people,*

---

[1] Museum of Australian Democracy https://www.moadoph.gov.au/democracy/defining-democracy/

by the people, for the people', in his famous Gettysburg Address on 19 November 1863, during the American Civil War at the Soldiers' National Cemetery in Gettysburg, Pennsylvania— about four months after the Union armies defeated the Confederacy armies at the Battle of Gettysburg. In his speech, which is widely considered as one of the best-known speeches in the American history, Lincoln lauded the sacrifices of soldiers who laid down their lives defending the founding principles of Declaration of Independence 87 years earlier. Urging his audience to continue the struggle for the survival of democracy in the country, Lincoln is reported to have said, *'that these dead shall not have died in vain—that this nation, under God, shall have a new birth of freedom—and that government of the people, by the people, for the people, shall not perish from the earth.'*

Historically, it is believed that in 1384 in the prologue to his translation of the Bible, John Wycliffe wrote, *'The Bible is for the Government of the People, by the People, and for the People'* (Refer to Familiar Quotations by John Bartlett, 1951 edition). Bartlett cites Theodore Parker using this phrase in a sermon in Boston's Music Hall on 4 July 1858, noting Lincoln's law partner, William H Herndon visited Boston and returned with some of Parker's sermons and addresses. Subsequently, Herndon has said that Lincoln marked the portion of the Music Hall address with pencil—*'Democracy is direct self-government over all the people, by all the people, for all the people.'*

The readers must note the presence of the word 'all' in the definition of the Greek word *'demos'* and in Lincoln's famous Gettysburg Address. Would it mean if 'all' people are not involved in choosing a government and/or the government does not serve 'all' people, the basic spirit and the requirement of the word 'democracy' is not served at all?

Is it possible, therefore, in a two-party system, such as in the US, or in a multi-party political system, such as in India, the interest of 'all' people cannot be practically met, as there will always be a considerable number of people who would not have voted for that government and/or will, therefore, feel to be on the wrong side of the ruling party?

In a classical ballot that results in 50.5 per cent to 49.5 per cent majority win for a particular political party, the victorious political party would come to power and form the government with the support of only half of the voters, with the remaining half feeling a sense of loss and misrepresentation in the government. Will such a scenario truly serve the spirit of the word 'democracy'?

It is not uncommon to see that the Opposition (a party or a cohort of opposition parties) sees its role in the Parliament mainly to oppose the opinions, decisions and actions of the ruling party and the Government, instead of working together constructively with the Government, as alternate government, and together work out solutions to address the issues facing the nation.

The extent of mindlessness of the Opposition can go to such an extent that if the Government says, 'Today the sky is blue', the Opposition, to oppose and discredit everything that the Government says, will react publicly with statements like, 'The sky is not blue, it is a myopic view of the Government to mislead the junta; the Government is actually colour-blind. The sky is bluish grey, with a few blue patches.'

To sum up, if the Parliament comprises people's representatives who see their main role only to oppose and malign one other, instead of working together for the overall benefit of people, the system of governance does not truly serve 'all' the people. To makes matters worse, any party that comes to power strives to remain in power as long as possible and at any cost. Power corrupts. People lose. The country loses. Only politicians gain.

If the people's representatives (MPs) are not sincere and loyal to their electorate and the country, democracy does not work for the benefit of 'all' people.

When peoples' representatives are not honest, evolved, conscientious and active citizens, and work for only their individual personal interest and not for the greater interest of the county, 'democracy' is degraded to be a farce and a sham. Such a pathetic situation should not be a surprise considering majority of voters don't make informed decisions at the time of casting their vote, predominantly due to their illiteracy and poor education; they fall for those melodramatic politicians who act the best (and shed crocodile tears), evoke the sentiments or shout the loudest in the election rallies. Plus, a token handout of free transport and some refreshment goes a long way in attracting a vote from those ignorant and heavily exploited masses. In many cases, the voters see their elected representatives only just before the next election. Is that 'democracy' in a true sense?

Liberal democracy

A liberal democracy refers to the governmental systems whose main objective is the development and well-being of every individual of the state. They are founded essentially on the following four beliefs in:

- *The individual:* on the basis of belief that the individual is both moral and rational;

- *Reason and progress:* on the basis of belief that growth and development is the natural default condition of mankind and politics is the art of compromise;

- *A society that is consensual:* on the basis of a human desire for order and co-operation, and not disorder and conflict; and

- *Shared power:* on the basis of a suspicion (of corruption, tyranny) of a concentrated power—by individuals, groups or governments—for example, by a dictator or an autocrat or monarchy.

The following four key elements define the liberal democracy—by limiting the power of the peoples' representatives – so that a government works within the framework of justice and freedom.

Legitimacy

This means a government must have the appropriate mandate and authority to rule, as demonstrated by a free electorate and conduct of periodical elections.

Justice

This means citizens should be provided with an environment where they are treated equally, with inherent human dignity and respect. It requires the demands made by vested interest groups seeking special privileges to be questioned and disallowed; instead the system should reward citizens based on their skills, talent and merit, and not based on their privileged status or rank.

Author's comment: The reservation policy in India does not serve justice to all her citizens. People from the mainstream are generally disadvantaged and feel discriminated against.

Freedom

Freedom provides the citizens with:

- Self-determination to make their independent decisions, learn from them and accept responsibility for them;

- The capacity to choose between alternatives;

- The autonomy to do what the law does not forbid; and where prohibitions do exist, they should be for the common good; and

- Respect for political and civil liberties. For example, government intervention in political, economic and moral matters affecting the citizenry is limited or regulated; and the scope for religious, political and intellectual freedom of citizens is not limited.

Power

A liberal democracy requires a written constitution to define and limit power, and the necessary checks and balances, such as the separation of powers between the Parliament, the Cabinet and the judiciary. It also requires conventions of behaviour and a legal system to complement the political system so that the civil liberties are defended against the encroachment of governments, institutions and powerful forces in society.

Definitions of democracy

There is no one absolute definition of the term 'democracy'. Historically, the term 'democracy' and its common interpretation has invariably become specific to the time, place and circumstances.

The following list of definitions as provided by some experts in this area provides an idea about its flexibility and complexity in an indirect sense.

Jim Kilcullen: For a city to be called a democracy, the affairs of the city had to be subject to an Assembly, to which all 'male' citizens belonged, and in which decisions would be made by a simple majority vote.

Andrew Heywood: Democracy means 'rule by the people'. Democracy implies both popular participation and government in the public interest, and can take a wide variety of forms' (Ref. Palgrave Macmillan, *Political Ideologies: An Introduction, Third edition*, 2003, p. 330).

Dr John Hirst: 'A democracy is a society in which the citizens are sovereign and control the government' Ref. Papers on Parliament Number 42, *The Distinctiveness of Australian Democracy*, p.10/13[2]

Joseph Schumpeter: 'The democratic method is that institutional arrangement for arriving at political decisions in which individuals acquire the power to decide by means of a competitive struggle for the people's vote ... the classical theory of democracy attributed to the electorate an altogether unrealistic degree of initiative which practically amounted to ignoring leadership... the purpose of democratic method [is] not to select representatives who carry out the will of the people, but to choose individuals who [will] govern on their behalf.'

---

[2] Ref. http://www.cric.ac.uk/cric/events/schumpeter/papers/27.pdf

Definitional issues in the term 'democracy'

- What defines 'the people'? What qualifies one to be a voter?

- Is it possible for 'the people' to rule in largely differentiated societies for example as in India?

- How do we define systems in which leaders are not elected directly by the people but nevertheless are supported by the majority of population?

Characteristics of a typical democracy

- The elected officials have constitutional control over government decisions and policies.

- The people's representatives are elected via elections that are frequent and fair, without any coercion or rigging. (*Author's comment*: This did not happen in the Kashmir 1987 elections.)

- Most adults have the right to vote in the election.

- Most adults have the right to run for office in the government.

- Citizens have a right to express themselves on political matters broadly defined without the risk of facing any punishment or retribution.

- Citizens have a right to seek alternative sources of information which are protected by law.

- Citizens have the right to form independent organisations, including associations, interest groups and political parties.

- The elected people's representatives are able to exercise their powers without fear of being overridden.

- The polity is self-governing, and able to act independently of constraints imposed by others.

- People have the freedom of speech and expression, and are able to speak and publish dissenting views.

Types of democracies

Direct democracy

In this form of democracy, citizens are continuously involved in the exercise of power and the final decision is by the rule of majority. The citizens are invited to participate in all political decisions. For example, in ancient Athens, only adult males who had completed their military training were considered as the citizens with eligibility to vote. As such, women, slaves and plebs were not considered as citizens and, therefore, were not eligible to cast vote.

Representative democracy

The people's representatives are elected by the people and entrusted to carry out the business of governance. For example, Australia and India are representative democracies.

Constitutional democracy

In a constitutional democracy, a constitution outlines who will represent the people and how. For example, Australia and India are constitutional democracies.

Monitory democracy

In this form of democracy, government will be constantly monitored in its exercise of power by a vast array of public and private agencies, commissions and regulatory mechanisms. (Ref. *See Life and Death of Democracy by John Keane, published by Simon and Schuster UK in 2009*).

The Indian Democracy

Democracy Index

The Democracy Index was introduced by Economist Intelligence Unit (EIU), in 2006, to measure the state of democracy in 167 countries.

As per Wikipedia,[1] the Democracy Index is 'based on 60 indicators grouped in five different categories measuring pluralism, civil liberties and political culture. In addition to a numeric score and a ranking, the index categorises countries as one of four regime types: full democracies, flawed democracies, hybrid regimes and authoritarian regimes.'

India has a 'flawed' democracy, according to EIU. In 2016,

---

[1] https://en.wikipedia.org/wiki/Democracy_Index

India was placed at 32nd place in the world, with its Democracy Index of 7.81 (out of 10). However, in 2017, India fell ten places and was ranked at 42nd place, with its Democracy Index of 7.23.

In 2006, as per EIU,[2] India's Democratic Index was 7.68. Since then, it has fluctuated between a low of 7.23 (in 2017) and a high of 7.92 (in 2014).

According to Wikipedia, as of 2017, of the 167 countries:

- Only 19 countries qualified to be called '**full democracies**'. These countries are located mainly in Northern America, Western Europe, Australia and New Zealand, and contain about 4.4% of the world population. They scored between 8 and 10.

  Norway (9.87) topped the group, followed by Iceland (9.58), Sweden (9.39), New Zealand (9.26), Denmark (9.22), Ireland (9.15), Canada (9.15), Australia (9.09), Finland (9.03) and Switzerland (9.03) at the tenth place. The UK (8.53) stood at 14th place.

- Fifty-seven (57) countries were categorised as '**flawed democracies**'. These countries are located mainly in Latin America, the Caribbean and south Asia (India), and contain about 44.3% of the world population. They scored between 6 and 8.

  South Korea (8.00) topped the list (at 20 rank overall), followed by the US (7.98), Italy (7.98) and Japan (7.88). France (7.80), Israel (7.79), Greece (7.29), South Africa (7.24), India (7.23) and Singapore (6.32) stood at 29th, 31st, 38th, 41st, 42nd rank overall and

---

[2] https://infographics.economist.com/2018/DemocracyIndex/

70th place, respectively.

- Thirty-nine (39) countries qualified to be called **'hybrid regimes'**. These countries are located mainly in Asia, Australasia, Central and Eastern Europe and Sub-Saharan Africa, and contain about 17.7% of the world population. They scored between 4 and 6. Fiji (5.85), Bangladesh (5.43), Nepal (5.18), Kenya (5.11) and Pakistan (4.26) fall in this category at 81st, 92nd, 94th, 95th and 11th rank, respectively.

- Fifty-two countries (52) were categorised as **'authoritarian regimes'**. These countries are located mainly in the Middle East and North Africa, and contain about 32.3% of the world population.

The above assessment indicates only about half the world's population lives in democratic countries, an overwhelming majority of whom being 'flawed'.

Wikipedia provides the following definitions:

- Full democracies—where civil liberties and basic political freedoms are not only respected, but also reinforced by a political culture conducive to the thriving of democratic principles. These nations have a valid system of governmental checks and balances, independent judiciary whose decisions are enforced, governments that function adequately, and media that is diverse and independent. These nations have only limited problems in democratic functioning.

- Flawed democracies—where elections are fair and free and basic civil liberties are honoured but may have issues (eg media freedom infringement). Nonetheless, these nations have significant faults in other democratic aspects, including underdeveloped political culture, low levels of participation in politics, and issues in the functioning of governance.

- Hybrid regimes—where consequential irregularities exist in elections regularly preventing them from being fair and free. These nations commonly have governments that apply pressure on political opponents, non-independent judiciaries, and have widespread corruption, harassment and pressure placed on the media, anaemic rule of law, and more pronounced faults than flawed democracies in the realms of underdeveloped political culture, low levels of participation in politics, and issues in the functioning of governance.

- Authoritarian regimes—where political pluralism has vanished or is extremely limited. These nations are often absolute dictatorships, may have some conventional institutions of democracy but with meagre significance, infringements and abuses of civil liberties are commonplace, elections (if they take place) are not fair and free, the media is often state-owned or controlled by groups associated with the ruling regime, the judiciary is not independent, and the presence of omnipresent censorship and suppression of governmental criticism.

The Indian democracy—what others say?

According to Democracy Index, India has a 'flawed' democracy, which, by definition, means it may possibly have 'significant faults in other democratic aspects, including underdeveloped political culture, low levels of participation in politics, and issues in the functioning of governance.'

The author is not the first one to raise questions about the effectiveness, adequacy and the suitability of the current model of democracy for the country. There have been a number of noted personalities who have raised this question in the past, some of them are noted below:

- *Democracy put to test*, KC Singh, *The Tribune*, 15 March 2018[3]

This article by a former Secretary, Ministry of External Affairs, Government of India, provides a fresh and oven-hot snapshot of the current state of Indian democracy and a broader world view of the term 'democracy' in 2018.

The article is very much in line with the theme of this book. The following excerpts from the article, which have been reproduced unchanged to prevent any distortion in its message, are self-explanatory:

> While Prime Minister Narendra Modi accompanied visiting French President Emmanuel Macron on the Ganges at Varanasi, at times hand-in-hand, for an iconic view of the Ghats, India hovered over multiple domestic inflexion points. While agreements were signed with France for strategic engagement ... farmers marched, many barefooted and hungry, towards the centre of India's financial capital Mumbai. Rural India, where still a majority of Indian voters reside, was signalling that India could not become a great power by lopsided growth and mere promises of *achhe din*.

---

[3] http://www.tribuneindia.com/mobi/news/comment/democracy-put-to-test/557779.html

The Modi government has, at best, just a year left or less, if early Lok Sabha elections are held ... But the Modi slogan of a corruption-free India is no longer paraded.

The article makes the following important speculations and observations about the future course of the Indian general elections and the prospects of the ruling BJP party:

- Based on the recent by-polls in Rajasthan, Madhya Pradesh and Uttar Pradesh, the re-election of Mr Modi's government may not be taken as a certainty.

- A Belfer Center, Harvard Kennedy School report and two recent books — Steven Levitsky & Daniel Ziblatt's book *How Democracies Die* and Yascha Mounk's book, *People vs Democracy*—raise the possibility of potential risks of cyber-attacks and information operations on the outcome of forth coming elections. The lessons derived from those books could be deemed applicable to India's democracy also under the Modi government.

- In their book *How Democracies Die* the authors argue that in this century, democracies are potentially under threat through the election of populist autocrats, similar to Mussolini and Hitler, who also took the electoral route; although in this century, the methodology may be a little subtler, such as state institutions may be debased, judiciary weakened, Election Commission controlled by compliant appointees, the investigative agencies handed over to reliable and ruthless protégés for targeting businessmen and opposition figures, Parliament emasculated by negating its checks and balances. In addition, intelligence agencies may be co-opted or devalued, and media may be bought or bludgeoned into submission.

- In the book, *People vs Democracy*, the author explores flagging interest in democracy amongst youth and the millennials, with a downward trend of late. The book notes that 71 per cent people born in the 1930s in Europe and the US value living in a democracy, but only 29 per cent people born in the 1980s do so, with a quarter of the millennials believing democracy is not the right way to run a nation.

- The Indian polls show a tendency to favour authoritarian rulers. This tendency feeds Modi's personality as a leader, which is unmatched by his peers.

- The social media algorithms control the users with prejudices and curtail debate. The leaders use the social media—Twitter and Facebook—to propagate their thoughts, whilst browbeating their opponents directly. As an example, a former Indian Army Chief, who is a minister in the Modi government, coined the phrase '*presstitutes*'.

- The Belfer report reflects a debate, which the Aam Aadmi Party initiated—the integrity of EVMs being possibly compromised and the electoral process getting highjacked by the ruling party.

The report concludes that 'voting machines can be compromised via physical tampering (including using removable media) or through external connectivity (eg WiFi)'. It recommends that the *optical scanners* (OS) are safer than the *direct recording electronic* (DRE) machines, as used in India, including the *voter-verified paper audit trail* (VVPATs). The report recommended that this matter needs to be debated in India, due to the potential use of power by a powerful Prime Minister. The integrity of the electoral process needs to be safeguarded and done publicly.

The article warns: 'The next year is critical for Indian democracy, as indeed the idea of India as enshrined in the Constitution. In 1975-77, when the Emergency was declared, the world was still mired in Cold War and democratic rule had not flowered globally. Now even the US and its Western allies are casting doubts on the efficacy of its functioning. President Xi Jinping having seized almost total power from the party and the military posits the Chinese model of economic success via authoritarian structures. Can India keep the flame of democracy and liberalism alive in Asia as a counterpoint? That is the drama that is about to unfold in the coming year.'

The above article gains immense significance in wake of the fact that a 70-year-old man was beheaded by a mob in northern India on 16 March 2018 after he named a *chowk* (street crossing) near his home after Prime Minster Modi. This sad incident illustrates the level of intolerance in some parts of the country.

- *The Crisis of Indian Democracy*, Pulapre Balakrishnan, *The Hindu*, 27 July 2016[4]

The following excerpts from the article provide interesting dimensions about the Indian democracy, in particular from the point of view of oppression of the poor and backward class:

---

[4] http://www.thehindu.com/opinion/lead/The-crisis-of-Indian-democracy/article14509784.ece

While India's economy has received periodic attention… the workings of its democracy have received next to none. This reflects complacency…the neglect is evident in every angle from which the country has been approached…its condition is related to the failings of its democracy, which in one dimension has remained more or less unchanged since 1947. The majority of the population has been left with weak capabilities. Whatever may have been the vision of India's founding fathers, Indian democracy has not lived up to their expectations. As a matter of fact, it has done far worse.

So what can we do now? For those outside the corridors of power, the task is to shape the discourse on Indian democracy. Its goal must now be redirected towards human development while ensuring the security of all vulnerable groups. In fact, a genuine commitment to socialism should have helped here.

The task, envisaged by Nehru, of creating the institutions necessary to support individual freedom, did not materialise. India today hosts the world's largest number of the poorly educated and prone to poor health, a development disaster in spite of being the world's third-largest economy in purchasing power terms. One need only occasionally travel third class on the Indian Railways in most parts of the country, which Gandhi did, to comprehend the scale of the deprivation and estimate how close public policy today comes to addressing it.

For a democracy to be complete, however, something more than just focus on the individual, however deserving they may be, is necessary as members of a democracy must engage with one another lest we remain equal but separated. Public policy should engineer spaces where Indians meet on the basis of a participatory parity…Repeated interaction in public spaces would make us realise our common humanity and enable us to see any residual identity for what it really is…There has been far too little effort in Indian public policy to create spaces where citizens may interact freely and peacefully.

In its inability to contain these forces, India's democracy can be seen to be flailing. Bertrand Russell had remarked that we can never guarantee our own security if we cannot assure that of others…

- *Do we Deserve a Democracy?*, Biranchi Narayn Acharya, Orius, 10 March 2014[5]

The following excerpts from the article sum up the situation well and are worth noting:

During 2009 election, one of my friends, a political party worker, contacted the village head. The head immediately asked what would be party's bargain for each vote. That means the villagers authorised the head to negotiate the cost of each vote. Clear indication was the highest auctioneers would get at least 80 per cent vote of the village voter list. My friend tried to talk about the manifesto, but the (village) head clearly said that no one was interested to read so many promises. That was business time and he should straight away come to the point!

But this is order of the day. We call politicians corrupt, but we bargain with the contestants for our votes. Some do sell their votes for cash, some for kind and others in the name of community, religion, caste and other biases. Fact is many

---

[5] https://qrius.com/deserve-democracy

of us are corrupt in voting or electing our representative yet we never tire in blaming politicians as corrupt.

To be in a democracy, we need to deserve to be in a democracy. You can't expect everything to be alright and systematic without your participation. A monarchy can run systematically if the king is right. But a democracy can't run righteously if its masters are irresponsible, opportunists and unaccountable. A master with a dual character always became a liability to his kingdom! Have we ever thought that? No, because we are here just to enjoy our rights and not to fulfil our duties.

India, despite being the largest democracy & ancient civilisation, we are one of the corrupt, anarchic and irresponsible nations. Do we ever hold ourselves accountable for this embarrassment? If not, then we must not deserve to be in a democracy. If yes, then let's start our citizen responsibility, duty and obligation as early as possible!

- *Indian democracy is shallow, a failure, Hindustan Times, 28 September 2013*[6]

The following are the excerpts of the advice and views of India's powerful neighbour, China, on India's democracy:

'*Democracy in India is shallow and has failed to provide stability and overall growth for its citizens,*' Chinese state media said. In a scathing editorial, the *People's Daily*-owned *Global Times* said democratic institutions have failed to provide equality to its citizens. '*Democracy only exists in India in the framework but is empty inside,*' it added. The editorial added, '*By always defending itself as a democratic nation, India's general*

---

[6]   https://www.hindustantimes.com/world/indian-democracy-is-shallow-a-failure/story-gDfmY9QkuYnTqD13Z1mMAK.html

election and rule of law can only constitute a well-recognised outer form instead of an inner force, because those democratic institutions have failed to bring about overall stability, equality and well-being to its citizens.'

There is criticism when it said that votes in India often become an important baton to instruct power players rather than an agreement to guarantee fast and effective progress. *'India needs to objectively estimate its democracy,'* the editorial advised. *'Without the ability to lift the nation from poverty, it appears that 'democracy' itself is no help to transform India to a great power,'* it said.

Quoting the book authored by Indian strategic analyst, Bharat Karnad, *India's Rise: Why It's Not a Great Power (Yet),* the editorial said there were a number of deficits in India hampering development including *overly bureaucratic system, the ineptitude of local governments and policy infirmities, social and political fragmentation, corruption, and unbelievable poverty.*

It is understandable why China would like to criticise India on very available opportunity and justify to the world that its system of governance has worked better than India's democracy. For that matter, China has the figures to support it. Nevertheless, there is indeed a grain of truth in China's assessment about India. With reference to military power, economic growth, industrialisation and manufacturing, population control, some control on air pollution, world politics, sports (eg Olympic medals) and the overall standard of living, China heavily scores points over India. Their end product is definitely better.

One may argue about China's human rights and human happiness. The answer would be that, despite a democratic structure supporting human rights, India does not figure even in the world's top 100 happiest countries in the world.

As per an article, *India ranks a low 122 amongst world's happiest countries: Pakistan, Nepal fare better.* Published on the online version of The Indian Express[7], dated 21 March 2017, India ranked a lowly 122 on a list of the world's happiest countries, dropping four slots from last year. China (79), Pakistan (80), Nepal (99), Bangladesh (110), Iraq (117) and Sri Lanka (120) fared better than India on the ranking.

The World Happiness Report 2017, which ranks 155 countries by their happiness levels, maps happiness on the parameters of GDP per capita, social support, healthy life expectancy, freedom to make life choices, generosity and perceptions of corruption. The top ten counties in order were: Denmark, Iceland, Switzerland, Finland, Netherlands, Canada, New Zealand, Australia and Sweden. The US ranked 14th.

If happiness is considered as the ultimate goal of life, China scores many points over India, which is in addition to its proven superiority over India in the areas of military, economic and industrial development, educational infrastructure, and environmental awareness and sustainability.

The only area in which China scores lesser points than India is its freedom of press. One may argue that if the country is strong and people are happy what does the 'freedom of press' mean? Is it justified that for the 'freedom of press', i.e. for the sake of a very small percentage of the population, the country's health and sustainability should be comprised? But that is exactly what would happen if China, like India, had a so-called

---

7   http://indianexpress.com/article/india/india-ranks-a-low-122-among-worlds-happiest-
     countries-pakistan-nepal-fare-better-4578297/

'democratic' system of governance, with decisions being taken based on a majority vote, and different political parties and politicians, with their personal agenda, pulling the country in different directions.

- *Democracy in India: A success or Failure*, TVP Editorial by Sumati Arora, dated 11 June 2009[8]

The following are some excerpts from this interesting article, which add new dimensions to the debate on India's democracy.

'Have we ever given heed to the kind of democracy we have in India and under what conditions it had been established? …It is impossible to define Indian democracy as liberal, participatory or deliberative, because it is a blend all of these at the same time …It is not enough to only examine the formal presence of democracy but checking how effective are the institutions and procedures. According to Sameul Huntington, Indian democracy as an institution was facing few crises at the eve of independence. They were: crisis of national integration, crisis of identity, crisis of participation, crisis of penetration and crisis of legitimacy. Thus we see the number of challenges, which the newly independent and decolonised India was facing while adopting the system of democracy. The major problems before India were linguistic problems, caste system (which further took a new form of economic class system), poverty and illiteracy. To add to them malnutrition and poor health conditions, poor housing, poor work capability, lack of occupational

---

8   http://theviewspaper.net/democracy-in-india-a-success-or-failure/

adaptability and an inadequate level of savings reflected the clear picture of India.

Many scholars compare the status of development and democracy since independence. Does democracy lead to development or development leads to democracy? This dilemma still remains. India had a firm nationalist base with the strong leadership of Pt Jawaharlal Nehru as the first Prime Minister. But during that time, the members of legislative assembly were elitist. The democracy was functioning smoothly but in their favour because the masses were illiterate. Congress at that time was working for indigenous bourgeoisie. Thus, Congress became a party of social status quo...'

The above article is loaded with a nationalistic hope and optimism and obvious reluctance to see anything beyond 'democracy'. One reason could be it was written about nine years ago, in 2009, when not many people in India would have woken up to the fast diving liveability levels of the country.

Although Sumati Arora has covered a number of social issues, the obvious deteriorating conditions across the country did not seem to be on the radar of the author in 2009. Many people, well-educated and not-so-well-educated, seem to confuse bettering of lifestyle of the upper half of the population with bettering of the conditions in the country. It seems clean air, clean water, fast and smooth traffic, women's security, authentic food and medicines and compulsory free education to all children in the country are not very important to them. It is baffling why most educated people judge India's progress since 1947 by the growing affluence and (lavish) lifestyle of a minority population belonging to the upper rung of the socio-economic ladder.

The Indian elections—a case of Three Ts

The majority vote system makes a mockery of the basic objectives of democracy. The concept of democracy requires that an elected government represents most people, if not all people. But, in practice, the election process invariably results in a partial representation of the people, in many cases less than 50 per cent of voters, leaving the remaining voters unrepresented and dissatisfied. As a classical example, the May 2018 elections in Karnataka have amply demonstrated that the election process in democratic India is grossly inadequate in satisfying the basic objectives of democracy. The whole system looks to be a sham, rather a farce.

It appears the Indian election process is mainly about the three Ts—*Tactics, Tricks* and *Trading,* which the political parties adopt, and that too not clandestinely, to win the elections and form the government. After winning seats or the government, politicians cannot contain their pride and excitement; they tweet boisterously.

In India, politics and governance appear to be mainly about enjoying and exhibiting power, as raw as it can get. Governments and political parties are run as businesses. After winning a term, the politicians first endeavour to recover fast the 'investment' made by them and/or their parties during the election campaign and the subsequent horse-trading. Once that is done, they strive to recover more 'returns on their investment', some of which is kept aside as their personal gains and some is reserved as investment for running and winning the next election campaign. The remaining money, generally a minor fraction of the budget, is then used strategically for the benefit of people, with slogans of pride, achievement and fulfilment of the election promises—in particular, those people who are understood to have voted for the ruling party.

The whole election process is just about winning the elections and staying in power in order to keep accumulating more wealth and influence. It is not surprising that India has such high poverty and illiteracy rates, although some people will blame India's massive population for her woes. Yes, but why have the successive governments allowed the country's population to grow fourfold in the last seven decades since independence?

In the May 2018 state elections in Karnataka, out of a total of 222 seats declared, BJP won 104 seats, Congress won 78, JD(S) won 37 and others 3 seats. A party or a coalition needs to secure 112 seats to form the government. On their own, as such, none of the parties had qualified to form the government.

The Times of India (TOI)[9], dated 16 May 2018, published a news report, titled, *Why Congress gained vote share but lost seats*? Some interesting statistics are as follows:

- BJP emerged as the single largest party, winning 104 seats, i.e. 46.8 per cent of total seats but won only 36.2 per cent of the total vote share.

- With 78 seats (i.e. 35.5 per cent of total seats), Congress won 26 seats less than BJP, but won 1.2 per cent more votes (38 per cent) than BJP.

- JD(S) won 37 seats, i.e. 18.6 per cent of the total seats, which comprise 18.3 per cent of the vote share.

- On average, BJP took far less number of votes to win

---

[9] https://timesofindia.indiatimes.com/india/why-congress-gained-vote-share-but-lost-seats/articleshow/64182815.cms

each seat as compared to both Congress and JD(S). BJP took 1.27 lakh votes to win each seat, as compared to 1.77 lakh votes by Congress and 1.80 lakh votes by JD(S).

On the basis of the above statistics, it appears BJPs smart strategic polices and plans, and the three Ts, earned them disproportionately higher number of seats in comparison to their total vote share.

The following excerpts from the above TOI news report are interesting:

- The decline of the Congress tally from 122 seats in 2013 to just 78 this time round may suggest a significant anti-incumbency factor was at work in Karnataka, but a look at the vote shares of the various parties belies this assumption. The fact is that the Congress actually polled a higher vote share of 38 per cent in these elections than it did in 2013 when it got 36.6 per cent.

- Despite winning 26 seats less than BJP, the Congress ended up with almost two percentage points more in terms of vote share...Also working for it (BJP) was the fact that its votes were less scattered than the Congress. Thus, it was able to convert votes into seats much more effectively.

- The JD(S) won just 18.3 per cent of votes, almost two percentage points lower than its share of 20.2 per cent in 2013, but it too had a more effective conversion of votes to seats than the Congress.

- Congress outscored the BJP in vote share in the rural seats and in the rurban seats, but was outgunned in the urban ones. In fact, the biggest gap between the two parties was in the 20 rurban seats where the Congress got 38.7 per cent against the BJP's 32.3 per cent. Yet both finished with seven of these seats.

- There was an interesting inversion in the reserved seats. In the seats reserved for SC candidates, the Congress got a higher vote share than the BJP, but won fewer seats (12 against 16). In the ST reserved seats, on the other hand, the BJP got a higher vote share but won only 6 seats compared to the Congress' 8.

- In the 120 Lingayat-dominated seats, the Congress did increase its vote share compared to 2013, from 35.9 per cent to 38.1 per cent.

Given that no party had won the absolute majority, under the Constitution of India, the decision rested with the State Governor. He could take any decision he liked and, interestingly, his decision could not be challenged even by the Supreme Court of India. Is that really democracy? How is that different from being authoritarian?

Interestingly, but not unexpectedly, the Governor took more than 24 hours to announce his move after the results were declared, which kept everyone guessing. All television channels were abuzz with debates, discussions and speculation. The delay allowed Karnataka and New Delhi see warlike political activities, including closed-door lobbying and horse-trading. Many news reports alleged that huge sums of money were being offered by a party to lure the winning members of other parties and independent candidates to cross over.

To keep it simple, the Governor had only three options

which should not have logically taken more than a couple of hours to be announced and exercised:

- He could have asked BJP, the largest single party to prove they have the support of at least 112 members, in which case BJP would have to pinch at least eight members from other parties. The horse-trading process needed time, so the delay in Governor's announcement;

- He could have asked the coalition of Congress and JD(S) to prove they had the required numbers, through a collation of signatures or the actual presence of the members on the floor. Note that these two parties, after having fought bitterly against each other in the election campaign had decided to join hands to keep BJP out of power, but only after the results were declared; or

- He could have asked for re-election, given that no one party had secured the required 112 seats.

But the Governor took his own time in announcing something after a delay of more than 24 hours, which the Congress and JD(S) parties contested, not unreasonably so. Any person of common sense and reason would raise questions on his credibility and honesty given the recent practices in India wherein the minor parties made the government—for example, in Goa and Assam, BJP formed the government despite winning fewer seats than their opponents. One can't blame Congress and JD(S) for fuming and vocally being up in arms.

Governors are not elected directly by people through a voting process; they are appointed by the President of India on the recommendations of the Prime Minister and their position is tenured for five years, which can be extended at the convenience of the Central government and the President. In relation to their appointment, although it is not a constitutional requirement for the President to consult the Chief Minister of the State, a general convention of consulting the Chief Minister has evolved with time. They can be transferred from one State to another, or even appointed as Governors of several states at one time. In a nutshell, they are meant to work as the agents of the President and, thus, indirectly for the Central government. As such, they can be dismissed as per the convenience of the Central government if they do not serve its interest.

In an ideal world, Governors are expected to serve the following intentions:

- As they usually come from other states, they are meant to represent India's unity given India's vastness and diversity.

- They are expected to keep a close eye on the working of the state government and ensure it meets the Constitution of the country. To serve this purpose, they basically serve as the agents of the Centre.

- As they are not supposed to have any stake in the State politics, they are expected to act as impartial advisors to the Chief Ministers.

- They are expected to address the actual and potential conflicts between the State and Centre. If the State is ruled by a political party other than the ruling party at the Centre, some such conflicts can potentially precipitate constitutional crises.

On the basis of the above, it would not be unreasonable

to not rule out that Governors can exhibit, overtly or covertly, their own sets of loyalties.

Regardless of who would form the government, the following facts clearly defeated the objectives of democracy:

- The ruling party would come to power based on mandate given by less than 50 per cent voters.

- If BJP was invited to form the government, they would not represent 63.8 per cent voters who did not vote for them.

- If Congress was invited to form the government, they would not represent 62 per cent voters who did not vote for them.

- If JD(s) was invited to form the government, they would not represent 81.7 per cent voters who did not vote for them.

The above facts clearly put serious question marks on the veracity of the democratic election process in India. For practical reasons, therefore, if the elected governments are unable to represent all people, at least more than 50 per cent people in an election, democracy in India could be deemed to be a myth. It appears to be a defective system overall, where elections are fought on technical grounds, with three Ts, and where money makes the mare go, rather than fairness and common sense.

Excerpts of NDTV news, dated 17 May 2018—*Karnataka Elections Live: 14 Days Encouraging Sin of Poaching, Says Congress in Supreme Court*—are as follows, which sums it up:[10]

---

[10] https://www.ndtv.com/india-news/karnataka-election-result-live-updates-bjp-jds-to-meet-governor-today-1852720

'In a big setback for the Congress, the Supreme Court has refused to stay the swearing-in ceremony of BJP leader BS Yeddyurappa, in an unprecedented overnight hearing. Mr Yeddyurappa had been invited by Karnataka governor Vajubhai Vala, last evening, to form government in Karnataka and was given 15 days to prove majority on the floor of the house. The Congress wanted the Governor's decision to be cancelled, calling it an "encounter of the Constitution". The BJP contends that it should be allowed to form the government as it is the single largest party. The Congress disputes the claim, citing the precedence set by the BJP in Goa and Manipur last year. In both states, the Congress emerged as the single-largest party but the BJP cobbled up alliances and was invited to form the government.'

Criminal records of Indian politicians

For this rather very sensitive topic, reference is made to an interesting article, dated 4 Feb 2017, published in *The Economist*, titled, *A penchant for criminality is an electoral asset in India, the world's biggest democracy.*[11]

The article gives reference to '*When Crime Pays: Money and Muscle in Indian Politics*', a 2017 book published by Yale University Press and authored by Milan Vaishnav of the Carnegie Endowment for International Peace, which claims to track the political success of India's criminals—'accused murderers, blackmailers, thieves and kidnappers' as a first thorough study of the co-existence of crime and politics in democratic processes in India, establishing a symbiotic relationship between the two.

---

[11] https://www.economist.com/news/books-and-arts/21716019-penchant-criminality-electoral-asset-india-worlds-biggest

The following are some of the important excerpts of the article that throw light on the reasons and a growing trend on why many crooks run for office in India:

- Indian politicians who have been charged with or convicted of serious misdeeds are three times as likely to win parliamentary elections as those who have not…

- Thirty-four per cent (34%) of the members of parliament (MPs) in the Lok Sabha (lower house) have criminal charges filed against them; and the figure is rising…over a fifth of MPs are in the dock for serious crimes, often facing reams of charges for anything from theft to intimidation and worse—because the Indian judicial system has a backlog of 31 million cases, even serious crimes can take a decade or more to try, so few politicians have been convicted.

- After independence in 1947, thugs used to bribe politicians to stay out of trouble and to secure lucrative state concessions such as mining rights. It helped that candidates from the dominant Congress party were sure to win a seat and then stay there. From the 1980s, as Congress started to fade as a political force, bribing its local representative became less of a sure thing for local crooks…the dons promoted themselves into holding office, thus providing their own political cover.

- The supply of willing criminals-cum-politicians was met with eager demand from voters, as proven over the past three general elections, during which a candidate with a rap sheet of serious charges has had an 18 per cent chance of winning his or her race, compared with

6 per cent for a "clean" rival.

Mr Vaishnav has dispelled the conventional wisdom that crooks win because they can get voters to focus on caste or some other sectarian allegiance, thus overlooking their criminality. If anything, the more serious the charge, the bigger the electoral boost, as politicians well know.

- As so often happens in India, poverty plays a part. India is almost unique in having adopted universal suffrage while it was still very poor. The upshot has been that underdeveloped institutions fail to deliver what citizens vote for. Getting the state to perform its most basic functions—building a school, disbursing a subsidy, repaving a road—is a job that can require banging a few heads together. Sometimes literally.

- Who better to represent needy constituents in these tricky situations than someone who "knows how to get things done"? If the system doesn't work for you, a thuggish MP can be a powerful ally.

- Political parties, along with woefully inadequate campaign-finance rules, have helped the rise of the thug-candidate. Campaigns are hugely expensive. Voters need to be wooed with goodies—anything from hooch to jewels, bikes, bricks and straight-up cash will do. Criminals fill party coffers rather than drain them, and so are tolerated.

- In 2008, government whips desperate to avoid parliamentary defeat, sprung six MPs out of prison for a few days to get them to cast their votes, never mind the 100-odd cases of kidnapping, arson, murder and so on that the MPs faced between them. Some of the gangster-statesmen are straight out of Bollywood films. A fan of a local politician at one point explains that his man "is not a murderer. He merely manages murder."

- Mr Vaishnav does spell out the perils of India's elevation of lawbreakers to lawmakers. Constituencies represented by crooks suffer economically. A bigger cost is in the legitimacy of the public sphere as a whole when even MPs can flout the rule of law so brazenly. The Prime Minister, Narendra Modi, has pledged to clean up the system, for example, by recently scrapping large-denomination bank notes, which he thinks contribute to corruption. One presumes that the 13 alleged lawbreaking MPs he appointed to his first cabinet (eight of them facing serious criminal charges) all supported the move.

Criminal Records of MPs and MLAs against women

Reference is made to the online version of *Hindustan Times*, dated 31 August 2017. The article makes reference to studies by Association for Democratic Reforms (ADR), a non-government organisation working for electoral reforms, and National Election Watch.[12]

ADR and National Election Watch are reported to have analysed 4,852 out of 4,896 election affidavits of current MPs and MLAs, which included 774 out of 776 affidavits of MPs

---

[12] https://www.hindustantimes.com/india-news/bjp-has-highest-no-of-mps-and-mlas-with-cases-of-crime-against-women-study/story-UKFaWnMeVYCXCED03AZdGP.html

and 4,078 out of 4,120 MLAs from all the states of India. Of the analysed affidavits, thirty-three per cent (33%) of 1,581 MPs and MLAs had declared criminal cases, which included 51 declared cases related to crimes against women.

In addition, 334 candidates analysed, who had declared cases related to crime against women, were given tickets by recognised political parties.

The following are the excerpts of the article:

- 'There are 51 MPs and MLAs who have declared cases of crime against women such as charges related to assault or criminal force to woman with intent to outrage her modesty, kidnapping, abducting or inducing woman to compel her marriage, rape, husband or relative of husband of a woman subjecting her to cruelty, buying minor for purposes of prostitution and word, gesture or act intended to insult the modesty of a woman', the ADR study said.

- The BJP has the highest number of MPs and MLAs (14), followed by the Shiv Sena (7) and the All India Trinamool Congress (6) who have declared cases related to crime against women.

- Forty (40) candidates were given tickets by parties for Lok Sabha or Rajya Sabha elections. Various recognised parties have given tickets to 294 candidates with cases related to crime against women for state assembly elections.

- The analysed 122 independent candidates, with declared cases related to crime against women, had contested for the Lok Sabha or the Rajya Sabha and state assembly elections in the last five years.

- In the last five years, 19 independent candidates, with declared cases related to crime against women, contested in the LS and RS elections. Similarly, 103 independent candidates with declared cases related to crime against women contested in the state assembly polls.

- Among major parties, over the last five years, 48 candidates with declared cases related to crime against women were given tickets by the BJP. The second highest number of candidates (36), who had declared cases related to crime against women, were given tickets by the BSP, followed by 27 candidates from the INC, which had contested for LS/RS and state assemblies elections.

- Among the states, Maharashtra has the highest number of MPs and MLAs (12) who have declared cases of crime against women, followed by West Bengal (11) and Odisha (6).

- Also, among the states, Maharashtra has the highest number of candidates (65) in the last five years, followed by Bihar (62) and West Bengal (52) (including independents) who were given tickets by political parties even though they declared cases related to crime against women in their affidavits, the study added.

The above figures are baffling. Such criminal backgrounds of so-called lawmakers in a modern democratic system is unbelievable and unthinkable, especially if we talk about any western democracy. But India is different, as one finds out from the previous section of this chapter.

A question arises: 'How long will an average hardworking, honest, and educated Indian wait before raising his/her voice, which will be loud enough that the whole world will hear—a voice that will change India for the better?'

Why Do Many Indian MPs Have Criminal Records?

To give a peep into this query, reference has been made to an article, dated 25 September 2013, written by Andrew North – BBC's South Asia correspondent.[13]

The article suggests that illiterate voters are intimidated by candidates with criminal records into casting their votes for them and, therefore, it works well for the political parties to field such candidates. The article concludes with calling India an 'immature' democracy, despite being called a 'vibrant' democracy.

The following are the excerpts from the article:

- 'We need to build a consensus on how to prevent individuals with a criminal record from contesting elections.' When Sonia Gandhi uttered this (in 2010), her main opponent, the leader of the BJP agreed. Yet, since then, things have gone in the opposite direction, with more alleged lawbreakers among India's lawmakers than ever, a third of the current parliament according to a watchdog called the Association for Democratic Reforms (ADR).

- Politicians with a criminal record are more likely to be elected than those with a clean slate because, says the

[13] http://www.bbc.com/news/world-asia-india-24269113

ADR, they have more illicit funds with which to buy votes.

- India's cabinet sought to ensure there was even less chance of criminal politicians facing their own laws. It issued an order overturning a Supreme Court ruling demanding the disqualification of any politician convicted for crimes punishable with more than two years in jail. This was 'to ensure that governance is not adversely impacted,' the government had argued…

- Arguably, of course, the government is right. Losing tainted local or national politicians—among them many accused murderers, rapists and fraudsters—could upset delicate political alliances and make it even harder to get laws passed. So often derided for doing nothing, this time round the cabinet acted with unusual speed.

- Many politicians in India have criminal records because Indian political parties are more likely to select and field candidates with criminal records. Political parties especially, if facing a higher degree of electoral uncertainty, prefer such candidates. This is one of the many remarkable conclusions of Aidt et al.'s brilliant study, titled *Incumbents and Criminals in Indian National Legislature*. Political parties are more likely to choose candidates with criminal background in response to greater electoral competition and in constituencies with a higher illiteracy rate.

- The intuitive interpretation is that "alleged" criminal candidates have a higher capacity to intimidate voters compared to non-criminals. The presence of these candidates depresses electoral turnouts. It is used more in areas with low literacy rates as intimidatory tactics are more likely to work on illiterate voters. Political parties are also more likely to field them when facing a strong incumbent who cannot be defeated by fair electoral competition. This incumbent might be an "alleged" criminal himself in which case the optimal strategy is to field one. This creates a strong feedback loop in which non-criminal candidates are slowly being crowded out.

• These findings document that the well-known disadvantage of the Indian legislative incumbent is a product of whether he faces a known criminal among his opponents. That two-thirds of India's electoral districts saw at least one acknowledged party sponsored criminal on the ballot in 2009, representing a massive diffusion of candidate criminality over 2004, suggests that self-reported criminals are driving out non-criminals at the national level of the Indian polity.

• The broader forward looking implication of this phenomenon is very interesting as it seriously calls into question standard political science theory that electoral competition improves accountability. The trend here is quite the opposite. Now why are Indians tolerating this? The electorate is collectively dumb. Even after being a vibrant democracy for over seven decades, India still is an immature democracy. This is just one of the many metrics to prove it.

Criminal Records

International Business Times, dated 19 May 2014, in an article titled, *186 Indian Members of Parliament Have Criminal Cases Including Murder and Rape*, has provided some interesting statistics about the criminal records (in 2014) about Indian parliamentarians, which are in line with the numbers as presented in the earlier articles in the chapter:[14]

The following are the excerpts of the article:

- Going by the statistics, the general election of 2014 has seen the highest number of politicians with criminal records being elected to the Indian parliament. As per records, every third newly elected MP in the Indian parliament has a criminal record.

- An analysis of 541 of the 543 winning candidates by Association for Democratic Reforms (ADR) shows that 186 (about 34 per cent) of the newly elected MPs have confessed in their election affidavits that they have criminal cases against them. In the 2009 Lok Sabha, the figure was 158 (about 30 per cent) of the elected members of Parliament.

- Among the newly elected leaders to the Indian Parliament, 112 have declared that they have serious criminal cases, including the ones related to murder, attempt to murder, communal disharmony, kidnapping and crimes against women, against them.

- The report reveals that nine Indian leaders in the Parliament have murder cases, while another 17 have

---

[14] http://www.ibtimes.co.in/186-indian-members-parliament-have-criminal-cases-including-murder-rape-600584

attempt to murder against them. Similarly, there are two MPs who have cases related to crimes against women.

- The report notes that among the elected leaders in the Parliament, there are 16 with cases related to communal disharmony registered against them. There are 10 MPs who been charged for robbery and dacoity, and seven have cases related to kidnapping.

- Sixty-three elected MPs from the winning party— Bharatiya Janata Party (BJP), had serious criminal charges against them. The report notes that three out of 44 winners from Indian National Congress, three out of 37 winners from AIADMK, eight out of 18 winners from Shiv Sena and four out of 34 winners fielded by AITC have declared serious criminal cases against themselves in their affidavits.

- Interestingly, the report also notes that the chances of winning were higher for candidates with criminal cases, compared to the candidates with a clean record.

- There has been some other criticism outside but not much. Indians have become very used to these kinds of shenanigans.

- Almost forgotten already are calls in the Verma Commission report into the December 2016 Delhi gang rape case for all politicians accused of sexual crimes to be barred from office. Instead, six politicians charged with rape remain in office.

- The world's largest democracy is not alone in allowing so many questionable people to run it. Fellow BRICS member, Brazil, has similar numbers of alleged criminals running the country. The difference though is that, in Brazil, brazen political abuses have provoked major protest. Indian MP Baijayant Panda says: 'This is a phase all democracies have gone through—look at the US.' Voters will start to demand change, he predicts: 'This is the last era of brazenness.'

Character building

As a nation of 1.35 billion people, India needs massive character (re) building, right from the grassroots, across all sections of the society—the rich and the poor, the literate and the illiterate.

Indians living in the cities must fast review their current (hybridised) lifestyle and try to revert to a more traditional, simpler, value-based lifestyle, intertwined with spirituality. Horses for courses! What may have worked in the West may not necessarily work in India. Indians must not copy the West blindly. There must be some reason why many wealthy, educated and successful westerners turn towards the eastern philosophy, spirituality and a simpler lifestyle.

Currently, Indians seem to be generally focussing on the material prosperity, and not human development. As a consequence, they are reaping the effects of materialism—a fast growing population, lopsided/uneven affluence, patchy industrialisation, monstrous consumerism, dwindling agricultural land space, polluted air and water, lesser sleeping hours, and noise—all of which seemingly keep eroding the human happiness, well-being and the peace of mind. How many people really know what 'development' means? The country is seemingly paying a heavy price for its industrial growth and the growing affluence of some sections of the community. Masses, who live in the rural areas, continue to remain poor.

The ever-growing human struggle to survive and a sickening competition between the people at all levels of the lifecycle have seemingly taken a massive toll on the civic sense and the environmental awareness of general masses and their ownership of the country. It seems most people do not own their country. Pity is that people are not trained to accept other people from across numerous man-made division in the country—religious, caste, region, class, profession etc. as their own family members. As such, true nationalism is missing.

It is so unfortunate that, in the modern India, if a person talks about Hinduism or Lord Ram, the person is branded as a BJP or RSS supporter. And if one does not follow BJP, one is branded as a Congress supporter or a Communist. It seems it is very hard to remain non-aligned and neutral, and keep one's mind/eyes open and intellect clean...

At the author's book launch at Chennai, on 17 November 2017, the eminent panel members unequivocally agreed that India urgently needs a national character (re) building exercise at all levels and in all communities. The question is how to do it, considering India is a multi-racial, multi-ethnic and multi-faith country. Religion, caste and ethnicity play a major part in people's general outlook and behaviour. The rest of the world sees the people living in India and those coming out of the country as 'Indians', but the people living in India don't see themselves first as Indians; they see themselves first as Hindus, Muslims, Sikhs...or Bengali, Bihari, Punjabi...or Dalits, and even along the regional divide—North or South Indians. The essential sense of belonging is seen to be missing in most people living in the country. Therefore, how and from where to start the seemingly uphill, rather impossible task of national 'character building'? The million dollar question is if this task is worth doing at all? Don't the wise and the intelligent in India keep low, and go about their daily lives without causing any fuss or attracting attention to themselves? Are they not waiting for the chaos to sort itself out naturally?

Will writing books on the subject really help, considering most people are happy messaging on the social media and watching those television debates with interest? Books are not generally considered attractive or important, which also reflects a character of its own kind! How ironical is that some communities, who claim to be literary and intelligent, don't generally buy and read books; they keep busy messaging on the social media and show a clear preference for dining out at expensive eating places, showing off their expensive clothing and jewellery, and hosting/attending lavish social and wedding parties. Literary, really! How to build a national character? A task for God!

Prayers and prostration

How sad it is to accept the state of affairs in daily life in India, seeing those sickening issues as someone else's problem and hoping for a miracle to improve the liveability? India needs to wake up and not simply sleepwalk towards a catastrophic situation. People need to own the country and take responsibility for their actions and inactions, and help to turn things around.

Most politicians work for themselves. People must stop the common culture of prostrating before their *netas* (politicians/leaders), *abinetas* (actors) and the so-called celebrities; instead the citizens must guide them. No human can be considered to be superior to the other. Under that beautified and made-up skin and the (expensive/designer) clothes that we wear, we all look and smell the same.

Very bad things happen when people just give up and don't fight at their own levels to address the issues that they face on a daily basis. Praying to God or prostrating before a politician or an actor will never help. People must discover their individual potential and be proactive to help to change things for the better.

People power

Watching television and those numerous television debates will not help to improve the liveability in the country. No one gains from these shows except those who run them. Indians cannot leave it all to one man who leads them. They must start owning the country; help themselves and the man who leads them.

In democracy, various essential tasks needed for the nation—national integration, raising awareness about the population control; restoration of environmental health; promotion and improvement of education; elimination of various social issues, such as gender inequality, girl education and women empowerment etc. cannot be left to any particular individual or any politician. These tasks are for all Indians, especially the educated ones. They must start various campaigns. Every citizen needs to step up and raise community awareness.

People cannot afford to bury their heads in the sand like ostriches and believe everything is hunky-dory—it is not; the country is just sleep-walking to an existential problem. The Kodak moment!

Most politicians will never help to control the alarmingly

growing population, which is the root cause of the most, if not all, menacing issues in India. They have a sinister vested interest in the vote-bank politics under the pretext of demographics etc. Their aim is let the population keep growing so that the poor and the illiterate continue to remain in the country, only to be exploited by them for their own benefits. Educated people must help the country, take the initiative and educate other people around them. For example, discuss and tell everyone why it is urgently needed to control the population rate. Many Asian countries such as Iran and Bangladesh have been running successful population control/sterilisation programmes. Social campaigns are important to ensure girl education and gender equality, as well as for the education of the older people.

Leadership & solution

The Indian people and their leaders may have just about five years in the worst case scenario and about ten years in the best case scenario, if not more, to evade a potentially pathetic liveability situation in the future. The Indian leaders must without any further delay, on a war footing, get both Houses of the parliament, the country's President and the Supreme Court, as well as the experts on population and civil defence, together with the people who man the country's law and order, under one umbrella, with one Mission—*Save India*.

It is most important that everyone in the government and the parliamentary machinery is taken on board before the solution—*One Child Policy*—is implemented across all demographics (as the law of the land), at least for 10 to 15 years before it is reviewed for its effectiveness. As that happens, all required educational and civil infrastructure must be extended to all rural areas so that people get educated uniformly across the country (and not only in cities) and find employment in their own hometowns, which will also help to stop any further migration of people from villages to cities, thereby allowing cities to breathe!

Most importantly, India must weed out corruption at all levels. Corruption is an insidious disease that has gripped the entire nation across all levels and in all dimensions of everyday life in India. It is in the DNA of Indians, as they say. Corruption is a way of life for many Indians; they see nothing wrong with it. Most people don't even know the difference between a corrupted life and a non-corrupted life; for them corruption is a new norm.

Most of these reforms require a firm hand from the top. A well-meaning, visionary and benevolent dictator, supported by an equally benevolent and dedicated team, with passion to turn around this huge nation and set it back on the track to health and happiness is the need of the day.

Population & Liveability Issues

India's growing population

India occupies about 2.41 per cent of the world's land area but disproportionately contains more than 18 per cent of the world's population.

India has a National Population Commission (NPC), which is chaired by the Prime Minister of the country and its vice-chairman is Deputy Chairman of Planning Commission. Chief Ministers of all states, ministers of the related central ministries, secretaries of the concerned departments, eminent physicians, demographers and the representatives of the civil society are members of the commission.

Wikipedia[1] indicates it has the following mandate:

- To review, monitor and give direction for implementation of the National Population Policy with the view to achieve the goals set in the Population Policy;

- Promote synergy between health, educational environmental and developmental programmes so as to hasten population stabilisation;

- Promote inter-sectoral coordination in planning and implementation of the programmes through different sectors and agencies in centre and the states; and

- Develop a vigorous people's programme to support this national effort.

The above mandate does not provide any direct reference to any need for the country's population control, although the word 'stabilisation' has been mentioned. Does that mean the people at the helm are waiting for population to stabilise 'automatically'—by disease or as per God's will—and not do anything that a responsible government ought to do proactively to prevent it from crossing a certain threshold number which the experts deem as a sustainable limit?

A discussion on National Population Policy, as noted in the above mandate, is provided in the next section of this chapter, along with the author's comments.

As per Wikipedia[2], India's population is projected to be about 1.53 billion in 2030; that is an increase of about

---

[1] https://en.wikipedia.org/wiki/National_Commission_on_Population
[2] https://en.wikipedia.org/wiki/Projections_of_population_growth

200 million in the next 12 years. In doing so, India would have overtaken China as the world's most populated nation. By comparison, the population of China in 2030 is projected to be about 1.41 million; that is an increase of only 40 million in the next 12 years. This means India will add five times the population increase of China.

By 2050, the population of India is projected to be 1.57 billion as against China's population of 1.46 billion. This means, India will maintain a lead of 110 million between 2030 and 2050. In 2050, India will also have the honour of featuring three of its cities in the top five most populated cities of the world. Mumbai will top the list at 42.4 million, with Delhi at the 3rd spot with 35.2 million and Kolkata at the 5th spot with at 33.0 million. By contrast, the Melbourne (Australia) population is tipped to be about 8 million in 2050 and Australians are already making a lot of noise about its negative effects on the city's liveability.

An article by Scroll. in[3], dated 29 May 2017, has stated that India may have a population of around 1.7 billion by 2050. The article expresses serious concern about how the country will feed her population in that scenario.

Hindustan Times, dated 22 June 2017, has projected India to overtake China as the world's most populated country in the next seven years, i.e. by 2024, which is backed by a UN study.

As per the 2001 census, 72.2% of the Indian population lived in about 638,000 villages and the remaining 27.8% lived in more than 5,100 towns and over 380 urban agglomerations. In 2016, the rural population in India had dropped down to

---

[3] https://scroll.in/article/838970/food-for-thought-india-will-have-1-7-billion-people-by-2050-how-will-it-feed-them-all

about 66.86%, according to reliable sources.

(Readers are referred to the author's book, *Issues White-anting India*, for insight into author's serious concerns about the rate at which India's population has been allowed to grow.)

Towards the end of 2017, the author lived four eventful and memorable weeks in India, crisscrossing the country, covering six cities, in a warm and humid climate in the central, west and the south of India, and a colder but relatively smoggier environment in the north. One common denominator in all cities was the sickening traffic congestion. He also attended a number of wasteful and lavish weddings in India.

During his tour, he was interviewed by the media as well as many book distributors and retailers in every city he visited. He also had many engaging, emotional and educational interactions with many taxi drivers, porters, workers, shopkeepers and the common man in all cities, all of whom taught him many lessons about life in India.

National Population Policy

By definition, the population policy of a country is anticipated to get its population to an optimal level that it deems right for the country's sustainability. It can be aimed at either reducing the rate of population growth or increasing it.

Reference has been made to a PRS blog by Rohit, dated 4 August 2010, which provides interesting insights into the subject matter:[4]

- This post is pursuant to the discussion on population stabilisation being held in Parliament currently.

---

[4] http://www.prsindia.org/theprsblog/?tag=national-population-policy

- India is the second most populous country in the world, sustaining 16.7 per cent of the world's population on 2.4 per cent of the world's surface area. The population of the country has increased from 238 million in 1901 to 1,029 million in 2001. Even now, India continues to add about 26 million people per year. This is because more than 50 per cent of the population is in the reproductive age group.

- India launched a family planning programme in 1952. Though the birth rate started decreasing, it was accompanied by a sharp decrease in death rate, leading to an overall increase in population.

- In 1976, the first National Population Policy was formulated and tabled in Parliament. However, the statement was neither discussed nor adopted.

- The National Health Policy was then designed in 1983. It stressed the need for 'securing the small family norm, through voluntary efforts and moving towards the goal of population stabilisation'. While adopting the Health Policy, Parliament emphasised the need for a separate National Population Policy. This was followed by the National Population Policy in 2000. The immediate objective of the policy was to address the unmet needs for contraception, health care infrastructure and personnel, and to provide integrated service delivery for basic reproductive and child health care. The medium-term objective was to bring TFR (Total Fertility Rate – the average number of children a woman bears over her lifetime) to replacement levels by

2010. In the long term, it targeted a stable population by 2045, "at a level consistent with the requirements of sustainable economic growth, social development, and environmental protection".

• India's TFR was around 6.1 in 1961. This meant that an average woman bore over 6 children during her lifetime. Over the years, there has been a noticeable decrease in this figure. The latest National Family Health Survey (NFHS III, 2005-06) puts it at 2.7. TFR is almost one child higher in rural areas (3.0) than in urban areas (2.1).TFR also varies widely across states ... states like UP, Bihar, MP, Rajasthan, Orissa, Uttaranchal, Jharkhand and Chhattisgarh, where over 40% of the population lives, TFR is still high.

The blog identifies the following factors that affect population growth in India:

• **Low socio-economic development**: This is considered as the overarching factor...Uttar Pradesh has a literacy rate of 56 per cent...records an average of four children per couple ...

• **Infant Mortality Rate (IMR)**: In 1961, the Infant Mortality Rate (IMR) ie deaths of infants per 1000 live births, was 115. The current all India average is much lower at 57...Empirical correlations suggest that high IMR leads to greater desire for children.

• **Early marriage**: Nationwide almost 43 per cent of married women aged 20-24 were married before the age of 18. This figure is as high as 68 per cent in Bihar. Not only does early marriage increase the likelihood of more children, it also puts the woman's health at risk.

- **Level of education**: Fertility usually declines with increase in education levels of women.

- **Use of contraceptives**: According to NFHS III (2005-06), only 56 per cent of currently married women use some method of family planning in India. A majority of them (37 per cent) have adopted permanent methods like sterilisation.

- **Other socio-economic factors:** The desire for larger families particularly preference for a male child also leads to higher birth rates. It is estimated that preference for a male child and high infant mortality together account for 20 per cent of the total births in the country.

The blog identifies the following initiatives undertaken by the government:

- The National Population Policy 2000 gave a focused approach to the problem of population stabilisation. Following the policy, the government also enacted the Constitution (84th Amendment) Act, 2002. This Amendment extended the freeze on the state-wise allocation of seats in the Lok Sabha and the Rajya Sabha to 2026. It was expected that this would serve 'as a motivational measure', in order to enable state governments to fearlessly and effectively pursue the agenda for population stabilisation contained in the National Population Policy 2000.

- The National Commission on Population was formed in the year 2000.

- The *Jansankhya Sthirata Kosh* (National Population Stabilization Fund) was set up in 2005 to undertake activities aimed at achieving population stabilisation.

- Programmes like the National Rural Health Mission, *Janani Suraksha Yojana*, ICDS (Integrated Child Development Services) etc. have also been launched ... also expected to contribute to population stabilisation.

- Free contraceptives ... monetary incentives are given to couples undertaking permanent family planning methods like vasectomy and tubectomy.

- Nutritional and educational problems are being targeted through programs like the mid-day meal scheme and the recently enacted Right to Education.

The blog provides a very useful insight into the core factors leading to the population growth in India, as well as how the Indian government has been historically trying to address the issue. The identified factors leading to the population growth appear to be valid.

One would assume that if the identified issues are directly tackled head on, through a multipronged, time bound, direct action, the population issue could be addressed and the alarming population rate brought under control. But, obviously that has not happened. The government's initiatives, as noted in the blog, seem to be reasonable. However, given the continued growth in the country's population, choking of the Indian cities and high levels of pollution, nothing that the successive governments have been doing can be deemed to be truly effective. The government policies and actions, if any, have obviously fallen short of their intended targets, not much different to those numerous under-strength antibiotics that are being sold in the country that are making many dangerous bugs drug-resistant.

It shows that the past governments either did not have the vision about the extent of damage that a fast rising population would do to the Indian cities and the country's environment, or the will, to prevent it from crossing a certain pre-defined limit (eg 100 crores—1.0 billion) through effective and timely measures.

Policies alone are not sufficient; follow-up actions too are important and, for that, honesty, dedication and pure intent of the people at the helm, as well as the administrators sitting in air-conditioned offices and the workers on the ground, are vital. Timely achievements of targets are crucial for the planners and the enforcers in any country.

Obviously, as all the people have not played their respective roles to its intended target effect, the country now urgently needs a 'direct action' to control its population without wasting any further time. Every day matters, but going by the Indian television channels and newspapers, political parties and politicians mainly engage in proving their counterparts wrong with power-struggles taking the centre-stage, leaving the country neglected. Just because most politicians and some prominent (cocky and influential) businessmen are becoming richer, it does not mean the country is becoming a better place to live and thrive.

The blog says: In 1976, the first National Population Policy was formulated and tabled in Parliament. However, the statement was neither discussed nor adopted.

In 1976, Indira Gandhi was the Prime Minister of India

and the country was under a State of Emergency (1975–1977). Those days, many people and most students used to say, 'India is Indira, Indira is India.' After India's decisive victory over Pakistan in the liberation war of Bangladesh in 1971, she was hailed as Goddess Durga by Atal Bihari Vajpayee, the opposition leader at that time. The author distinctly remembers, as a young school student in the seventies, widespread campaigns, slogans on buses, walls, billboards, skits in schools, cinema halls, skits on the radio and the television—about urgent need to control the population. This was the time when Indira Gandhi was the Prime Minister. The slogans were obviously intended to generate awareness amongst the public, through democratic mechanism and education, against potential issues due to high population.

Indira Gandhi lost the general elections of 1977, possibly because the timing of the elections was miscalculated. One of the principal reasons of her defeat could have been that, during the Emergency when civil liberties were suspended, Indira's son, Sanjay Gandhi, was on a campaign to forcibly sterilise poor men. The campaign features in Salman Rushdie's novel *Midnight's Children*. Reportedly, 6.2 million Indian men were sterilised in just a year.

In order to win the elections of 1980, Mrs Gandhi approached the then Shahi Imam of Jama Masjid, Syed Abdullah Bukhari, before the elections and entered into an agreement with him on the basis of a 10-point programme to secure the support of the Muslim votes. In the elections held in January, Congress returned to power with a landslide majority.

It is obvious that after Indira Gandhi lost the general elections in 1977, and her subsequent pact with Mr Bukhari in 1980, the first National Population Policy of 1976 was buried in files under dust till they were rediscovered 24 years later, in 2000. The damage caused by those lost 24 years is very clear on the streets and roads of all cities and villages of India. What a tragedy! In India, politicians are still scared to talk about population control.

- In 1952, India's population was 388.5 million, which is based on a projected population from the 1951 Census of India, which was 361.09 million. In 1951, only about 18 per cent of Indians were literate and the life expectancy was 32 years. Hindus comprised 83 per cent of population and Muslims 9.8 per cent.[5]

- In 1976, India's population was 635.8 million, i.e. it added 247.3 million (63.6 per cent increase) in just 24 years. In the same year, China's population was around 930.7 million. In 1976, about 40 per cent of Indians were literate and the life expectancy was about 52 years. Hindus comprised 82 per cent of population and Muslims 11.5 per cent.

- In 2000, India's population was 1.063 billion, i.e. it added about 427 million (67.1 per cent increase) in another 24 years. In the same year, China's population was around 1.263 billion. In 2000, about 64 per cent of Indians were literate and the life expectancy was about 63 years. Hindus comprised 80 per cent of population and Muslims 13.4 per cent.

The above figures indicate that after India launched its family planning programme in 1952, its population grew about

---

[5] https://en.wikipedia.org/wiki/1951_Census_of_India

2.7 times in the next 48 years. Also, after the first National Population Policy was formulated and tabled in 1976, Indian population grew by 67 per cent before the current National Population Policy was launched in 2000. Despite that, India has added about 340 million in the last 18 years. In a nutshell, nothing that India has done to manage and control its population since 1952 has really worked.

A country needs a vision from the top—a constant vision and guidance about the direction the country should be made to take irrespective of which political party is ruling the country or who is the country's Prime Minister. The broader picture of the country must not be dependent on the party politics; it must be drafted and painted by the visionary leaders of the country for all times to come.

The blueprint of the country should have been made decades ago by its leaders so that the country could meet the demands of the future and not land in its current state. Unfortunately, the major political parties mainly indulged in cronyism, nepotism, and vote-bank politics to stay in power. The country was neglected. Application of band aids will not now cure the roots of the infection which has grown to alarming levels.

No one in the country dares to speak about the root causes of the country's issues—dwindling liveability, lack of security for children and women, corruption, sectarianism, and environmental degradation. What is the purpose of bringing more people into the country when the existing population is struggling to live and the environment is not healthy enough to accommodate them? Is it not sinful, immoral or unethical to let those unborn children arrive into this world, only to let them struggle and suffer through their lives. Why can't the country first fix its mess and create a healthy and sustainable living environment for the future? Is that not the duty of the country's leaders? Is staying in power so important?

Power corrupts people and politicians alike in all forms of government be it a so-called democracy like India or a dictatorship elsewhere on the planet.

And who are politicians? They are just the sample representatives of the people living in the country; they have not come from outside the country.

Readers must note that, as of March 2018, Australia does not have a national policy on population. Due to perceivable and imaginable negative effects of a growing population, mainly through immigration, on the liveability of several big Australian cities, many Australians have been raising the population issue which goes to prove the high level of awareness of the people and their care for the country's health. Sooner or later, the politicians will have to listen to the people and formulate polices.

'Like people, like politicians,' one can conclude.

Effect of population on liveability

Too many people struggling for survival are pushing and elbowing away everyone else to move ahead in a seemingly perpetual rat race in India for survival. This behaviour is clearly seen on the roads. Honking, which means show of nil respect for the fellow commuters, and which is considered extremely offensive in the west, is acceptable in India. People frequently honk and bully other commuters. A perpetual rat race ... but to where?

Indian cities are well and truly choking and heading towards a complete gridlock in not too distant future, due to ever worsening traffic congestions in all Indian cities.

Roads and streets can be likened to the blood vessels of a country. India's roads and traffic congestions reflect the health of the country. Similarly, the behaviour of the road users reflects the country's values.

The following elements of the basic life supporting system must be improved on a war footing:

- Quality of air for breathing
- Quality and availability of water for drinking
- Authenticity and quality of food—vegetables, fruit, dairy etc.
- Authenticity of medicines
- Security of life in general, in particular, for women
- Ease of movement on the roads

Indian city dwellers are fast moving (in the next 5 to 10 years) into a lifestyle wherein they will be working 10 to 12 hours a day and commuting 8 to 10 hours a day for work, leaving just 2 to 4 hours for the night sleep and family time. What a life? The following vignette illustrates the level of frustration and harassment one can potentially face in the nation's capital, New Delhi. On 27 November 2017, it took the author about three hours from NCERT's Delhi campus (Aurobindo Marg) to reach New Delhi Railway Station. With just under half a minute remaining, the author and his wife boarded the train. It was like a thriller, rushing against time. First, they encountered a paralysing traffic jam near Safdarjung flyover for more than 45 min, due to some VIP's presence in the area. Later, another paralysing traffic jam in Connaught Circus, caused by a protesting procession of a religious community and the inefficiency of the traffic wardens, forced their cab driver to take several internal clogged streets in that overcrowded part of Delhi. Later, to add to the drama, with barely 12 minutes to go, the driver was forced to park his car by the roadside at a distance of about 500 m from the station. With their luggage in their hands, they stopped the traffic on both sides of a crowded road to cross it and then ran to the station with just five minutes to go. The author and his wife, each carrying two bags, ran frantically through a long queue and then the x-ray machine and finally up the escalator, huffing and puffing, and miraculously boarded the train in the nick of time, with hearts pounding and profusely perspiring. It is not hard to guess that many people, especially the old, sick, children and women, would have missed their trains. Does anybody care?

A young army officer also boarded the train a few seconds after them. He sounded very angry and frustrated while speaking over his phone. He had left his home at Dwarka four hours prior to the scheduled departure of the train. He wished the Indian army had the opportunity to govern the country for just five years!

When a young and well-educated, English speaking army officer undergoes such harassment and, thereafter, vents such thoughts, the country's administrators are put on notice. The army is trained and committed to protect the country's borders against external threats and enemies. In discharging their duty towards the nation, soldiers remain ever ready to sacrifice their own lives. But they are also human. Therefore, one must not keep assuming that soldiers will commit themselves to fight only against the external enemy. If they see enemies of the state living and enjoying within the country, that may not forever remain passive witnesses, like *Bhishma* from the *Mahabharata* did; hopefully, they may act decisively.

Indian politicians and so called VIPs seem to have lost touch with the reality of life faced by the ordinary citizens. The only way to make them see the reality is if they are made to commute, on a daily basis, like other ordinary Indian citizens— through heavy traffic and clogged streets and roads—without the assistance of traffic wardens, who keep their roads open and cripple other commuters in the process. They must not be provided with any flying services, in particular the government's taxpayer-funded helicopters to commute short distances on their unscheduled trips, similar to erstwhile royalty.

Liveability issues

One does not need to have a PhD degree to see the current sorry state of liveability in the country or predict its future catastrophic state. It is so obvious.

One just needs common sense but, unfortunately, common sense is not so common. Indian school education is mainly rote-based, so 'common sense' is not encouraged to be developed. Most people form their opinions based on what is fed to them by the social media, the television and the politicians. Unfortunately, in many cases, the literate and educated people fail to see the obvious; they rely on the information that is fed to them by the social media and television.

During the author's book launch tour across India, between September 2017 and December 2017, he spoke with many taxi drivers, porters, street vendors, coolies and shopkeepers in every city he visited. Their feelings and thoughts were quite distressing. Each and every individual with whom he spoke talked about a continued struggle, constant depletion of happiness and a sharp increase in anxiety and mental depression, general helplessness and frustration. One taxi driver in Delhi said that Indian cities would definitely choke in the next five years. He desperately wished for some form of Divine intervention, such as massive earthquakes, devastating floods, outbreak of diseases and even a nuclear war to break out, so that the population could reduce. He did not show any trust in the country's politicians and the leadership.

Another taxi driver wanted strict regulations on the production and sale of new vehicles. He also wanted the regulatory authorities to closely look into the bank lending processes and questioned why banks chased and lured people into borrowing money easily to buy new vehicles.

A 29-year-old taxi driver said he scored himself as 10/10 on the happiness scale in 2010, but only about 5/10 in 2017. He said he slogged 17 to 18 hours every day to support his family. Growing traffic woes have been making his life difficult and unhappier with each passing day.

Effect of population on mental health

In a situation where demand keeps on increasing but supply just can't keep up with the increasing demand, anxiety to survive drives an unhealthy competition between the people.

Mental anxiety starts building up in children and parents from a very early age at all following stages:

- **Childbirth**—access to a 'good' gynaecologist and a hospital for delivery, cost involved, waiting time and travel distance at the time of regular consultations before birth and at the time of the final delivery. The increasing population keeps increasing the travel time because of increasing traffic on the roads, which can become critical at the time of traffic jams and gridlocks, and the waiting time at the doctor's clinic, which keeps increasing with increase in the number of people. One would expect that the foetus is already exposed to stress anxiety through the anxiety suffered by the parents, in particular by the mother.

- **Pre-school life**—the child needs to be immunised and taken to the doctor from time to time. In addition, working parents need to organise a domestic help to look after the baby if the mother is working. Availability and trustworthiness of such domestic helps is itself a big challenge. For working parents, this is a source of significant stress.

- **Nursery and primary school admissions**—Despite a mushrooming growth of nurseries and primary schools in almost every street, parents remain worried about securing the admission in time (sometimes even before the child's birth) and the safety aspects of the school. In addition, capitation fee (donation to school fund) needs to be organised. The increasing demand to supply ratio makes securing the admission in itself a big achievement.

- **Competition at school**—every parent wants to see his/her children to be the best all-rounder in school—at studies, sports, extra-curricular activities. By the law of probability, it is not possible for every child to be the best in everything. But most parents don't want to understand that reality; they just want their children to develop the habit of excelling in everything and be at the top of the class, each and every time. So, they transfer their anxieties to their children by constantly pushing them. The children, in turn, feel pressured to perform and not disappoint the parents. Thus, parental expectations start building up mental anxiety in children from an early age.

High school, college and university admissions— the aforementioned cycle of anxiety repeats at every stage—high school admission followed by college and university admissions. As for the child, the burden of carrying parental expectations and keep performing, to justify their 'significant monetary and physical investment' in the child's education, exacerbates the child's mental anxiety with time. With growing student numbers each year, the competition to stay at the head of the race keeps getting stiffer. The household mantra becomes: 'work, work, work…harder, harder, harder… be the best, be the best, be the best…' Most students and their parents want to secure admission in streams that can offer the best scope (in terms of job opportunities and salary) regardless of whether the student is fit for that stream in terms of calibre and temperament; it is all about job and salary. At each of these stages, many students cannot cope with the mental stress associated with a growing competition and many suffer from the anxiety and depression disorder. Unfortunately, many also commit suicide.

- **Securing a job, retaining that job and promotion at work**—at each of these stages, mental anxiety kicks in. With increase in the number of job applicants, reservations at the work places, a person is constantly subjected to worries, anxiety to survive and move ahead. Many people borrow significant amounts of money from banks or loans from their organisations, to buy motor vehicles, apartments and household gadgets—to stay alive in social competition, as a show of prosperity in a rat race—which brings in considerable anxiety in terms of job security. With high rates of unemployment, for employers it becomes relatively easier to exploit the needy employees, given a high supply of potential recruits waiting to pounce on any job vacancy. The workplace exploitation can result in long work hours, reduced salaries, less family time, frustration and unhappiness, and poor physical and mental health.

The above are only some of the common scenarios that provide a snapshot of a constant build-up of mental stress, leading to various serious diseases, such as diabetes and cardio-vascular diseases (eg hypertension). It is not surprising that India is not listed even in the world's top 100 hundred happiest countries, lagging far behind its immediate neighbours—China, Pakistan and Bangladesh.

Effect of population on adulteration and corruption

The author believes that, instead of providing statistics and a commentary, it would much easier to write a short story to illustrate how population growth encourages people to dilute and adulterate common commodities of everyday life— food, medicines and general consumables. The story goes like this:

The year was 1970. A student hostel had the capacity to accommodate maximum of ten boarders. The hostel also had a mess facility which provided a glass of milk to every student as part of the daily breakfast. A milkman, who lived nearby and had a small dairy (two cows), would deliver two litres of pure and undiluted cow's milk every morning to the Mess Manager. The chef would boil the milk and provide each student with a glass of milk. That year, the milkman, Mess Manager and kitchen cook were all honest. Therefore, all students got pure and undiluted milk. This continued for the next decade.

Ten years later, in 1980, the hostel capacity suddenly doubled to twenty because of an increasing demand. The milkman had in the meantime also increased the number of his cows to three to service more customers. The Mess Manager decided to double the quantity of milk supply and accordingly requested the milkman to deliver four litres of milk. Due to demands from his other customers, the milkman could neither afford to spare four litres of pure and undiluted milk for the hostel, nor purchase a new cow to keep up with a growing demand for milk. For fear of losing his old customer, he decided to dilute the milk. This was the first time he had become corrupt. He mixed half a litre of water with pure milk and started supplying four litres of diluted milk to the hostel. A growing demand for milk and his inability to procure additional resources to meet that demand had corrupted him. The Mess Manager did not at first notice what happened. Some old students noticed the difference and complained to the Mess Manager, who took up the matter with the milkman. But the milkman assured him that there was no difference in the milk. The Mess Manager believed him and the milkman got away with cheating.

After discovering a trick of the trade, the milkman gradually increased the quantity of water to one litre in the next six months to produce four litres of (diluted) milk. The hostel students slowly got used to the 'diluted' milk, which became a new quality standard for the milk. As most other milkmen had started a similar practice, an average customer slowly forgot the taste of original, pure and undiluted milk. This continued for the next five years. During all this while, the Manager and Kitchen Master remained honest.

In the year 1985, the mess capacity was increased by five more students. Now the Mess Manager had to procure milk for twenty-five students, which meant he had to increase the milk supply to five litres to maintain 200 ml of milk for each student. The milkman could not, however, deliver more than 4.5 litres of (diluted) milk. To make things easier, and make some money in the process, the Mess Manager clandestinely started adding half a litre of water to the 4.5 litres of milk supplied by the milkman and pass on five litres of (diluted) milk to the Kitchen Master. On paper, he showed payment for five litres of milk to the milkman, but pocketed the cost of half a litre of milk on a daily basis. The students could not see much difference and the Mess Manager got away. Thus, the Mess Manager also became corrupt. Once day, when the Kitchen Master spotted him diluting the milk, the Mess Manager explained why he had done so and offered to share his new income, which the Kitchen Master readily accepted, as he did not want to lose his job. This was the first act of successful bribery in the chain of events at the hostel.

With time, the Kitchen Master settled down with his 'cheating' act and accepted it as a normal practice. He rationalised his act with the thought that the whole world cheated and made money so why not him; after all, he also had a young family to support. This practice continued for the next 15 years.

It was the year 2000. Due to population growth and ever growing demands for hostel accommodation, the mess capacity was increased to forty students. This increased the demand for milk to eight litres. Although the milkman, now a much wealthier person, had increased the number of cows in his dairy to ten, he could not meet the suddenly increased demand of the hostel. So, after further dilution, he started supplying eight litres to the hostel every morning. The Mess Manager and Kitchen Master immediately understood what the milkman had been doing. As they had themselves been indulging in a similar act, they negotiated with him. It was decided the milkman would supply 4.5 litres of milk at the earlier (diluted) consistency and the additional 3.5 litres at a new (more diluted) consistency. On paper, the milkman would receive full payment for eight litres but in practice, he would be paid the cost of only six litres. Thus, the Mess Manager and Kitchen Master shared the savings from two litres of milk between them.

The students complained against the diluted milk. Both the Mess Manager and Kitchen Master cleverly dodged the complaints and the students were silenced.

Amongst the students was one Sheroo, who came from a rich and influential background with political connections. His father was a businessman. The family's newly found wealth was on complete display on Sheroo's body—designer clothes, a thick gold chain, a broad gold bracelet on his right wrist, gold rings with precious stones on several fingers of his right hand (seemingly on some astrologer's advice). He rode an expensive motorbike and carried a fat wallet. His gait and demeanour reflected his confident mind and lack of respect for other people. The Mess Manager would stand up when Sheroo would walk up to him.

Sheroo used to be constantly shadowed, rather escorted by five other students—Martin, Jaswinder, Suhail, Kartik and Raghav. One could call them his henchmen or sidekicks. All five belonged to working middle class families and came from different parts of the country. Incidentally, their fathers were government servants. Kartik came from a high caste Brahmin family, but his father was a middle-tier employee in a government organisation. Raghav was from a Scheduled Caste background and his father was a second generation doctor in the family. The other three students came from 'law and order' background. All of them rode motorbikes, but their motorbikes were not as expensive as Sheroo's. From their behaviour and attire, it was obvious they were constantly trying to keep up with Sheroo but Sheroo was definitely the boss. He had the influence which his sidekicks would avail from time to time, and he had the money to spend on them in return for their loyalty.

When Sheroo moved into the hostel, he made sure he received all facilities that befitted his rich background. He had several private introductory conversations with the Hostel Warden, security personnel, Mess Manager, Kitchen Master, all cooks and workers around the place.

It is understandable that Sheroo would find the food in the mess rather *feeka* (bland). So, he started making regular payments to the Kitchen Master. He would not eat at the designated lunch or dinner times. In fact, he did not have to follow any mess rule. His *dal* would be rich with *desi ghee* and *rotis* would be served to him in the form of *paranthas*. In a predominantly vegetarian mess, with meat being served only on Sundays, Sheroo was served meat and chicken dishes on a daily basis. His sidekicks also shared his delicacies. In return for good food and other services, such as consumption of alcohol in the mess and arrangement of access for his girlfriends to his hostel room under cover of darkness, Sheroo also helped the Kitchen Master, who had five children, with school admission for three of his children at a good private school. He also assisted the Mess Manager with a police case involving his teenage son who was caught indulging in an illegal activity. As Sheroo knew how to get any job done, everyone tried to befriend him. He enjoyed the attention and the services from others.

One day, Sheroo caught the Kitchen Master red-handed diluting the milk. The Kitchen Master's eyes begged him to keep quiet. Sheroo smiled back. After all, the Kitchen Master had been serving him well with good food and 'other facilities'. But when the sidekicks learnt about it, they decided to make money. They struck a deal with the Kitchen Master. It was decided that he would serve the 'diluted' milk to unsuspecting students who paid normal mess fee. But those students who would pay 100 rupees every week to the Kitchen Master would be served with 'better quality' milk and, in return, he would share his profits with them.

Finally, it came to year 2010. The mess capacity was further increased. The nexus between the milkman, the Mess Manager and the Kitchen Master saw milk being adulterated. Instead of traditional dilution with water, the milk was adulterated with paint, caustic soda or detergents, both at the dairy itself or in the kitchen, with no set rules. It all depended upon the 'demand and supply' and the depth of pockets of consumers. Those students who were willing to pay more than the regular mess fee had access to genuine milk, albeit diluted. Other unsuspecting students would consume anything but milk. Everybody made money, except the unsuspecting students who paid for genuine milk but instead were provided with spurious and adulterated milk.

This is what a disproportionately increasing 'demand to supply' ratio, due to rapidly increasing population, does to a community and its ethics and morality. This story, or a similar story, would be applicable to most other consumables and medicines in India.

Humans rights & population control

Can children be considered as 'humans'? If yes, do they have 'human rights' and, therefore, 'free will'? If yes, are they free to do anything they want? Do their parents and teachers allow them to exercise their 'free will'—play anytime they want; eat and drink anything they want, and watch TV for most of the time? Are children free to choose whether or not they want to study, go to school, wake up so early in the morning and carry that big ten kg school bag on their back, sit for the examination etc.? The answer to most of these questions would be: 'No, in the interest of their well-being, education, personal development, career, health, livelihood, parents and teachers cannot and do not allow children to exercise their 'free will' as to how they spend their time.' In essence, therefore, it is the system—parents, society, school, government, law & order etc. that dictates what children must do and, more importantly, must not do.

As children grow into young adults, and then into adults, their behaviour and lifestyle continues to be dictated by the 'system'. There is no 'free will'! Because, in a civilised society, an individual's overall well-being (much beyond an individual's instincts and tendencies) and the society's greater interest dictate what an individual can and cannot do.

In the light of the above, as an extrapolation on a much larger scale, if a country is suffocating and urgently warrants a strict control on her population growth, why should the pseudo-intellectuals construe 'population' control as infringement of 'human rights'? Is an individual's (human) right to produce an unlimited number of children higher than the basic survival and sustainability of the country itself? Doesn't improvement in the liveability of a country, and her environmental sustainability and, therefore, her very survival, be considered as a common cause for one and all?'

Don't children have the basic right to grow and live in an environmentally healthy and habitable country, with access to abundant clean air and clean drinking water, security, authentic food and medicines, ease of movement on the roads etc.?

Australia & liveability issues

The author lives in Australia. Many readers may ask why this guy is so paranoid about liveability issues in India, if at all there are any liveability issues in India. How about Australia? Don't they have any issues?

This section answers all such questions.

Australia is home to about 25 million people, coming from nearly 160 ethnic backgrounds—so that makes the country a very multi-cultural, multi-faith and multi-ethnic country. In terms of population, the entire population of Australia could fit in one of the largest cities of India. The comparison between the two countries becomes alarmingly uncomfortable and a little unreasonable considering India's land area is nearly one-third the size of Australia, but contains nearly 54 times as many people as Australia does. Arithmetically, one could assess that the liveability issues in India should be nearly 160 times that of Australia. By that measure, one could then assess Australia as having negligible issues as compared to India (mathematically less than one per cent). But all liveability issues can't be assessed using linear relationships; many issues become compounded, some exponentially, as population exceeds certain sustainable levels.

Undoubtedly, Australia has its own set of issues, many of them due to the growing population of its cities. Despite that, four of the seven largest cities of Australia figure in the world's top ten liveable cities, with Melbourne being at the top of the table for several years now.

The major difference between the two countries is that many voices have constantly been rising over the years in Australia about potential threats to liveability in the Australian cities, so people seem to be alert and aware about the threats. Once there is awareness in the people, solutions will follow to address the threats perceived. But in case of India, the author is simply baffled. It is hard to imagine common Indian people raising voices, considering the poverty and struggles of daily life they have to face just to put food on the table at the end of the day. Tragedy is the country's so-called leaders and politicians are napping, without any vision or concerns about the health of the country. People do talk about a need for infrastructure development, but not many politicians talk about improving the liveability in the country; simply because most of them have no awareness. And that is a dangerous situation. It puts a big question mark on the country's leadership itself. In India, there is a lot of talk, lot of promises, but the ground reality is different. The author's sensitivity towards liveability can be gauged by the fact that he is even concerned about potential threats to the Australian cities, which could be described as virtually heaven on earth.

Voices in Australia have risen since the nineties.

A scholarly article by Sharon Beder, titled, *Population and Environment in Australia—Urban Problems*, on the University of Wollongong website, based on Sharon's book, *The Nature of Sustainable Development*, 2nd ed. Scribe, Newham, 1996, pp 161-3, is worthreading.[6]

The following are important excerpts from Sharon's article:

- A major contributor to air pollution in Australian cities is the motor vehicle, the number of which increases with rising populations. Motor vehicles are responsible for 80 to 90 per cent of carbon monoxide and lead emissions, and 50 to 80 per cent of hydrocarbon and nitrous oxide emissions. Although technological changes and regulations have kept some emissions in check, ozone and nitrogen dioxide have increased to

---

[6] https://www.uow.edu.au/~sharonb/STS300/limits/studies/urbanprobs.html

unacceptable levels in the large cities. Photochemical smog sometimes goes above national health guidelines in areas of Sydney, such as the south-west, and around Melbourne. It is because of concerns about air quality that the NSW Government has decided to limit housing development in the south-west of Sydney. However, since the pollutants flow there from elsewhere in the city, this may be a rather limited solution.

• Water pollution resulting from flows of domestic sewage and urban run-off is also related to population levels (although it is also a function of treatment and urban design). Sydney's river system is already under severe stress because of urban development. Nutrient, bacteria and virus levels are high because of inflows of sewage and agricultural run-off. Yet the NSW Government is proposing to develop additional housing for thousands of families within the catchment of this river system, adding to its load.

• Water supply is said to be another potential constraint on population growth in many parts of Australia. For example, the population issues committee estimates that new sources of water will have to be found early next century if increases in population and use of water per person in the Sydney area continue to grow as they have been. Nevertheless, while water is in relatively short supply in Australia, its use depends not only on population levels but also on agricultural and industrial consumption and how efficiently the water is collected, distributed and used.

- Disposing of the solid waste from large populations causes environmental pressure in cities. Domestic solid waste generated by households accounts for one-third to one-half of all solid waste generated in large cities. This amount depends on the numbers of people and the amount of rubbish they each generate. The population issues committee estimates that almost half of the growth in solid waste is due to population growth, and just over half is due to increased resource use per person.

- Each year, Sydney and Melbourne residents generate hundreds of thousands of tonnes of paper, cardboard, glass, plastic and other wastes. Solid waste is generally buried in the ground, which has a number of adverse environmental consequences. Resources are wasted, land is used up, smells and visual nuisances are created, and groundwater may be polluted. The waste often has to be transported long distances to be buried. If it is incinerated, the resources are still wasted and toxic air emissions are generated.

- Population increase also puts pressure on existing housing, raising prices and forcing some people out of the city because they cannot afford to live there. Some people respond to rising prices by moving to the outer fringes of the city, promoting urban sprawl. Generally, these fringe areas are poorly served by public transport and other community facilities, so urban sprawl involves additional motor vehicle travel to work and to community facilities. It can also mean that prime agricultural land is turned over to residential developments.

• The NPC's population issues committee concludes that, although there is still far more to learn about the links between population levels and environmental impacts, "there is some significant evidence of negative influence of urban population growth on urban ecological integrity". Some people move out of the cities because they find them congested and unpleasant. Often, they move to the coastal regions where they find a beautiful natural environment. However, as more people move to these areas, species preservation can be threatened and the natural environment damaged.

The article establishes a direct relationship between population growth and environmental pollution (air and water), garbage disposal and urban development.

Sharon's book, originally published in 1993, reflects the level of heightened awareness in the Australian academics about a quarter of century ago. And the message was not only relevant to Sydney in 1996, but has one hundred per cent validity for all cities on the planet in 2018, including all Indian cities.

Melbourne has been judged the world's most liveable city for several years now in a row, but Australians are already well aware about the liveability issues that the beautiful city could potentially be facing unless timely actions are undertaken now to prevent those issues from occurring in the future. That speaks of people's vision and imagination and, of course, their love for their city and the country as a whole. Obviously, Australians are not complacent. They believe in implementing timely measures to prevent undesirable future outcomes rather than using a reactionary attitude when things go wrong. That is why Australia is one of the world's happiest, most liveable, sportiest, richest, first-world countries, despite being small in terms of its population. Australia has been punching well above its weight.

An article, *The 20 things that threaten Melbourne's liveability*, written by Aisha Dow in an Australian newspaper, *The Age*, dated 4 June 2015, provides an insight into the depth to which Australians go for the upkeep and maintenance of high living conditions in their country.[7]

The following excerpts from the article identify the factors:

- Influenza pandemic: A deadly virus outbreak in Melbourne could see the city shut down … an influenza pandemic might cause the "greatest problems" in the inner-city, where large numbers of people live and work.

- Lower rates of community participation: The time demands of modern life…with increasing numbers of new arrivals to the city, has resulted in a drop in the percentage of Melburnians who belong to a sporting club or volunteer.

- Unemployment: Melbourne's unemployment rate increased from 4.9 per cent in December 2010 to 6.5 per cent in December 2014...

- Family violence: Family violence is the leading cause of death and disability in Victorian women under 45…

---

7   https://www.theage.com.au/national/victoria/the-20-things-that-threaten-melbournes-liveability-20150604-ghh4cj.html

- Cyber-attack: This is an "emerging risk" for Melbourne, especially for the business sector...

- Increasing social inequality: There are concerns about a growing divide between those living in middle and inner suburbs and those on the city's fringes, who often have to endure long car commutes to work every day. There are calls for more resources to be put into car-pooling networks.

- Chronic illness: The rates of heart disease, cancer, osteoporosis, stroke, diabetes and depression are all predicted to rise.

- Age-related diseases and disability: More Victorians will face sickness and disability as the population ages. (The number of Australians reaching their 100th birthday grew by 490 people in the year until June 2014).

- Climate change: As temperatures rise,...it is expected Melbourne will have to survive with less drinking water...more weather-related disasters....

- Alcohol and drug abuse: Across Victoria, heavy drinking among young adults is rising significantly....

- Increasing pressure on healthcare: Extreme climate events such as heatwaves will exacerbate the strain on medical services....

- Transport infrastructure emergency: During past heatwaves, tram tracks have buckled and power outages and fires played havoc with train timetables, crippling the transport network.

- Heatwaves: The Mallee district is considered at greater

risk from extreme heat, as are residents and workers in the city's skyscrapers.

- Electricity supply disruption: Melbourne relies heavily on electricity infrastructure located outside the city. If air-conditioning systems were paralysed by a widespread power outage, almost 300,000 people could be forced to evacuate their offices in the CBD.

- Radicalisation and terrorism: Victorians are not only flying overseas to join terrorism groups, now there are allegations of home grown terrorism plots being hatched in Melbourne's suburbs.

- Hazardous materials incident: More likely to be an immediate risk in heavily industrialised municipalities...

- Marine pollution: A danger mostly for beachside areas and industries reliant on a healthy ocean environment.

- Bushfire: Not just a problem in country areas, but for people on the suburban fringe of Melbourne with back fences looking out over grass paddocks.

- Flood: A risk for those living near the beach or along Melbourne's major rivers or creeks. A study has found more than a $1 billion damage could be inflicted on waterside communities in the next 90 years and that parts of Rosebud foreshore could be completely submerged by 2100.

- Loss of green space and drinking water catchments: Melbourne's growing urban sprawl is putting pressure on the supply of fresh air and clean water. A recent study found Melbourne's suburbs already have some of the lowest urban tree canopy ratios in Australia.

The position of chief resilience officer is a $236,544-per-year role, funded by the Rockefeller Foundation, with the end goal of producing a Resilience Strategy for Melbourne.

From the above article, amongst several other factors, '*lower rates of community participation*', '*increasing social inequality*', and '*loss of green space and drinking water catchments*' have universal detrimental effect on the liveability of any city of the planet.

Another article, *Will population growth ruin a city's liveability?*, dated 20 Feb 2017, throws light on issues that some people identify as affecting Melbourne's liveability unless its population is brought under control. As per the article, *The Age's* politics editor, Josh Gordon, believes Melbourne is growing at an unsustainable rate. Josh is reported to have listed the following five reasons why Melbourne no longer deserves the title of the *world's most liveable city*:[8]

- Unsustainable growth of traffic congestions
- Rapid rise in crime rate
- Drop in housing affordability
- State schools struggling to cope with demand
- Deterioration of Victoria's environment

Some important excerpts from the article are reproduced as follows:

- Melbourne is also just another big city that is rapidly

---

8 https://blogs.crikey.com.au/theurbanist/2017/02/20/will-population-growth-ruin-melbournes-liveability

getting bigger, more expensive, more troubled. Underpinning many of these problems are unsustainable rates of population growth. Unless we wake up to this, our problems will only continue to grow.

- While the Economist Intelligence Unit's (EIU) ranking has many relevant metrics, their combined purpose isn't to measure liveability for permanent residents... it describes liveability for expatriate business executives on temporary assignments...

- The nub of Mr Gordon's complaint though is unsustainable population growth. The term "unsustainable" is potent, but it's misused in this context. Melbourne can easily keep growing; there are around 100 cities in the world with a larger population than Melbourne and about 40 with double its population...

- The implicit assumption that rapid growth means a significant loss of liveability overlooks the reality that cities adapt to the forces driving growth eg residents change the location of their job and/or dwelling, or they change how they travel... For example, Mr Gordon complains it currently takes more than an hour to drive from outer suburban Epping to the city centre in peak hour; and he estimates by 2037, it will take an extra 45 minutes! But residents will adapt by taking the train to the city centre rather than driving...

Standards of liveability in Australia

The current expectations about standards of liveability in Australia can be judged from an interesting article titled, *This is what our cities need to do to be truly liveable for all,* dated 12 October 2017, published in *The Conversation,* authored by Julianna Rozek (Research Officer) and Billie Giles-Corti (Directors) from Healthy Liveable Cities Group, Centre for Urban Research, RMIT University.

The RMIT research team, in a recently released report, *Creating Liveable Cities in Australia,* defined and produced the first baseline measure of liveability in Australia's capital cities. They broke down liveability into the following seven 'domains', identifying them as critical factors for creating liveable, sustainable and healthy communities:

- Walkability
- Public Transport
- Public Open Space
- Housing Affordability
- Employment
- The Food Environment
- The Alcohol Environment

Each domain was linked by evidence to health and well-being outcomes, and also measurable at the individual house, suburb and city level.

Some important excerpts from the article:

Walkability

'Liveable cities, streets and neighbourhoods are designed to encourage walking instead of driving. Homes, jobs, shops, schools and other everyday destinations are within easy walking distance of each other. The street network is convenient for pedestrians, with high-quality footpaths ...

Walkability is an important factor in liveability because it promotes active forms of transport. Increasingly physically inactive and sedentary lifestyles are a global health problem, and contribute to around 3.2 million preventable deaths a year ... walkable neighbourhoods achieve their full potential only when residents have easy access to employment, particularly by public transport.'

Public Transport

'Liveable cities promote public transport use instead of driving... Good access to public transport supports community health in two ways: by encouraging walking and by reducing dependence on driving... Each hour spent driving can increase a person's risk of obesity by around 6 per cent. Road-traffic accidents are the eighth-leading cause of death and disability globally...

Cars are also a major source of urban air pollution and noise, which are harmful to mental and physical health. Our team found that people were more likely to walk for transport if they had a public transport stop within 400 metres of their home. The service frequency was also important ...'

Public Open space

'In liveable communities, most people live within walking distance of a green, publicly accessible open space such as a park, playground or reserve.

Green space has many physical and mental health benefits for people, and social and environmental benefits for communities. Parks provide opportunities for physical activity, such as jogging, ball sports and dog walking.

Increasingly, research is finding clear links between living in neighbourhoods with lots of parks and higher physical activity.

Urban green spaces are also important for plants and

animals displaced by urban development and provide other environmental benefits. The cooling effect of trees and green spaces can play an important part in maintaining the liveability of Australian cities…'

What do prominent people say about liveability issues in Australia?

Over years, Dick Smith, a well-known and iconic Australian philanthropist and adventurer, has been championing for a control in the growth rate of Australian population and immigration into the country to more sustainable levels so that the country continues to provide the best living conditions to its existing population. He maintains the country's infrastructure is not adequate to accommodate more people.

Many people are also seen now on the national television (ABC) discussing potential liveability issues in the country's biggest two cities—Sydney and Melbourne—due to forecasts about their population growth. Of late, the country's former Prime Minister, Tony Abbott, too has been raising his voice for population control and squeeze on the immigration for similar reasons.

The online version of *The Guardian*, dated 19 February 2018, in an article titled, *Tony Abbott repeats claim immigration cut will improve quality of life*, reported:

Tony Abbott has seized on (Home Affairs Minister) Peter Dutton's claim that Australia needs to cut its migration intake and signalled he will renew his push to do so by linking migrant numbers to quality of living issues. The former Prime Minister (Tony Abbott) said he would make the case for cutting migration.

Abbott told 2GB Radio, 'Just at the moment we've got

stagnant wages, unaffordable housing, clogged infrastructure and there is no doubt the rate of immigration impacts on all of these things.'

Earlier, on 15 February 2018, *The Guardian* published an article, *Peter Dutton calls for migration cut: 'We have to reduce the numbers'*. Some excerpts of the article are as follows:

Dutton said it was a 'perfectly legitimate argument' that Australia's cities were 'overcrowded' including 'gridlocked traffic in the mornings' and use of services like hospitals. 'We have to try and encourage people out into regions. We have to reduce the numbers where we believe it's in our national interest,' he said.

The Home Affairs Minister said the migration program should always 'be operated in a way that it acts in our best interests' such as refusing to allow migrants who were 'going to be a burden' in favour of people who 'make a good contribution.'

Education & Secularism

Education—what and how?

Many people claim that education will address all issues faced by India. Well, that is true. But how many people know about the current state of the Indian education system and how many years will be required to educate all people in India. Importantly, how many people know what the term 'education' really means and what are its basic objectives? Understandably, the objectives will change with time and could be country-specific based on the issues faced by the country. But one objective that must never be overlooked and allowed to be changed, regardless of the time and place, and that is, education must make good, happy and responsible citizens and harmonious communities. The term 'good' herein refers to its common definition of inherent goodness in humans.

All living beings are born with some 'natural' intelligence. Thereafter, education received from the external sources initially from home or later from school—results in their 'cultivated' intelligence. In time, both forms of intelligence combine to shape a person's wisdom and outlook. As one would expect, natural intelligence grows with one's interaction with Mother Nature because humans are a part of nature and not outside of it. When one constantly studies and interacts with nature, through self-learning, one understands the natural laws. As a result, one's natural intelligence increases which, in turn, increases the scope and capacity for cultivated intelligence, and hence the wisdom. In simple terms, the cup that holds and assimilates the knowledge and information provided by the world deepens as one studies nature, not from the books, but being out there under the sky—in sun, rain and snow—and on the earth—in meadows and on hills and mountains—and in water bodies—brooks, streams, rivers, seas and oceans—and everything that comprises nature. For holistic development, it is essential that young minds are exposed to observe and study the flora and fauna out there in nature, and not from books alone, and interact with various elements of nature, play with soil, rocks, water and snow.

In India, the common perception of education seems to be information gathering. Practically, it is the person's general knowledge based on which a person is gauged. An educated person's benchmark is considered as knowing the names of prominent personalities—leaders, actors, sportspersons, countries and their capital cities; remember dates of historical events; and past and current political issues.

One sees the radiant and proud faces of young parents

when their child reproduces, like a parrot, the names of various bones of the human skeletal system, capital cities of Indian states and other countries, the country's Prime Minister and the President—past and present, etc.

People generally refer to books or other known people when asked about possible solutions to common issues. When asked what would be their solution, they look confused because the educational system, home and community culture, and the media do not allow them to develop their independent and critical thinking. They have not been trained to ask questions. First, at home, their parents expect them to listen and not ask questions; later, at school, teachers are no different.

The exact direction the Indian school education system is intended to take the students is not very clear. One common observation is that the existing system practically promotes cramming or rote learning and information gathering. How many parents send their children to school, or how many students go to school for the sake of learning or for the love of knowledge?

What are the combined effects of the current education system coupled with a fast paced materialistic lifestyle, in a generally competitive and survival mode, and an ever growing addiction to the media and the social media on the young minds?

- It bombards them with information, arguably most of which is useless in the context of human development and which leaves them with lesser opportunity to think critically and independently.

- It makes them adopt rote learning and reproduce like a parrot, without first developing an independent thought and the conceptual understanding of the subject matter.

- It makes them extremely competitive and, as a result, they have the potential to become mean, arrogant and selfish, devoid of respect for others. Any one in competition is seen as a threat and an opponent, who needs to be conquered. People talk of virtues of 'healthy competition' but that expression itself is oxymoronic. Students learn shortcuts to achieve their targets by hook or by crook. They believe it is all about them and everything is for them to grab and run with it. It becomes a case of *me, me, me*!

- It makes them anxious and mentally depressive, given that all students cannot top their classes and secure the coveted prized top positions. They don't realise that their failures are more probable given the constantly dwindling 'supply to demand' ratio as a result of a fast growing population in an already populous country.

- It makes them much more materialistic and remote from nature, devoid of nature's nourishment. Nature's role is essential for the growth of one's natural intellect, and the wisdom, both of which are necessary for living in coherence and harmony with nature and fellow living beings.

Young students are expected to do what they are told to do, nothing less or more. As an example, a teacher at a private Jammu school, about two decades ago, was heard telling a student that his father was a mad person (*'tumhara baap pagal hai'*) just because the student had correctly solved a mathematical problem, as instructed by his father at home, and not how the teacher had taught at school. In another instance, a computer science teacher at a prestigious private school, again in Jammu, failed a student just because the student had written a much updated computer programme as instructed by her aunt who was a computer programming professional. Generally, teachers assume they are the last word on the subject matter and expect their students to follow their instructions to the hilt.

It seems the policy makers and educationists have forgetter to ask themselves: 'What is the purpose of receiving formal education? Is it for earning one's livelihood or for human development, human well-being and happiness?' A logical answer would be, 'All of these'. It seems the education system in India, as well as in most of the rest of the world has significantly deviated from the original objectives, as outlined by the founding fathers of the modern western education—Socrates, Plato and Aristotle, the great philosophers and teachers. In India, it seems the mechanism of learning and teaching has moved tangentially in the past seven decades and the education system has been driven mainly by social divisions—religious, regional, ethnic and caste—history and politics, and lately by materialism and consumerism. In its current state, it looks more like a patchwork, at the cross roads between the western and eastern education system. The current education system does not foster holistic development of young students, nor does it encourage their independent critical thinking and self-learning. Young minds lose the simplicity of thought and natural creativity at a very young age. Receiving education becomes a chore, and drudgery in most cases, and a necessity for survival. As a direct consequence, environmental ethics and responsibility don't make their home in minds of young people. Sickening competition with peers steadily erodes civic sense, social ethics and compassion. Life is seen as a constant battle to survive and be ahead of others. The lopsided education generates lopsided humans. Unhappiness grows. Before it is too late, one must revisit the founding principles of education, as laid out by the aforementioned masters of philosophy, as well as the thoughts of great philosophers and poets from the Romantic era, such as Rousseau and Wordsworth, and the modern day educationists, with a core objective—what is the education meant for and how to get educated?

Socrates (circa 470 BC–399 BC)

Socrates, the son of a Greek sculptor, was a teacher and philosopher, and known to be an enigmatic man. He was possibly influenced by early Greek philosophers, such as Heraclitus and Parmenides, who may also have been his teachers. In his earlier days, he had also been a soldier and he received recognition for his valour in the Peloponnesian War.

Socrates' philosophy and teaching methods have significantly influenced the world of learning and education. As such, he is recognised as the father of Western philosophy. As he did not write any books, his 'quotes' are sourced from the writings of his students—Plato and Xenophon. A couple of his quotes are reproduced below:

'Education is the kindling of a flame, not the filling of a vessel.'
'The unexamined life is not worth living.'

It may be deduced that, based on Plato's writings, Socrates believed society would not see real justice or order without education. As such, education was required by all those in power and all other people regardless of gender. He believed women had intellectual potential equal to men despite being physically weaker.

In Socratic teaching, focus is maintained on giving students questions, not answers. Socratic questioning is a highly disciplined process in which students are posed questions, which they are required to answer. The teacher then challenges them to prove or support their answers. The process helps students to develop critical thinking abilities. The conversational teaching process encourages the use of hypothetical questions and the inclusion of additional facts to fine tune statements or clarify beliefs. As a consequence, students achieve deeper understanding of their beliefs, exceptions to their thoughts, and the limits of their ability to defend their views. Socrates' philosophy and conversational teaching methods are widely accepted these days in law schools, humanities and other higher schools of learning and teaching.

Socrates' philosophy included the development of both body and the mind (soul) to create moral and just people. He maintained that education of a person happens when the following three things happen:

- The person must recognise what he/she does not know, as wisdom begins in admitting one's own ignorance;

- The person must realise that self-knowledge is required, as self-knowledge is the ultimate virtue; and

- People can arrive at truth through questioning.

Socrates said, '*I know that I am intelligent, because I know that I know nothing.*' In Plato's *Apology*, after visiting a well-regarded wise man, Socrates said, '*Although I do not suppose that either of us knows anything really beautiful and good, I am better off than he is, for he knows nothing and thinks that he knows; I neither know nor think that I know.*'

On the importance of acquiring self-knowledge, Socrates said, '*The only good is knowledge and the only evil is ignorance.*' He believed self-examination and gaining self-knowledge to develop one's own understanding was important to be good and just. As such, he valued knowledge much more than wealth and status, which he reconfirmed in his last hours:

'*While I have life and strength I shall never cease from the practice and teaching of philosophy, exhorting any one whom I meet and saying to him after my manner: You, my friend—a citizen of the great and mighty Athens—are you not ashamed of heaping up the greatest amount of money and honour, and reputation, and caring so little about wisdom and truth and the greatest improvement of the soul, which you never regard at all?*'

Socrates' greatest contribution to education is perhaps his theory of questioning. He believed, to recognise contradictions and distil the truth, an issue must be broken into smaller questions. In Xenophon's *The Economist*, Socrates discussed this method with another thinker:

'*Really, Ischomachus, I am disposed to ask: Does teaching consist in putting questions? Indeed, the secret of your system has just this instant dawned upon me. I seem to see the principle in which you put your questions. You lead me through the field of my own knowledge, and then by pointing out analogies to what I know, persuade me that I really know some things which hitherto, as I believed, I had no knowledge of.*'

Socrates' education can be disseminated in the following theories:

- Theory of Value: The most important of all knowledge is 'how best to live'. Most people live in ignorance regarding matters of ethics and morals. The goal of education is to learn what you know but, more importantly, what you do not know.

- Theory of Knowledge: Knowledge exists in two different forms—*ordinary* and *definitional*. Ordinary knowledge does not bring any expertise or wisdom. Definitional knowledge, i.e. knowledge of definitions and concepts, is important for philosophical discussions. People who know what is good or true will live well and truthfully. Ignorance of goodness and truth prevents a man from being wise and honest.

- Theory of Human Nature: The being in humans is inner-self, which is divine and immortal. Human beings can distinguish virtue (i.e. knowledge) from ignorance, which is the root cause of moral evil. The human being is designed to know the good and will, therefore, follow the good and not the evil.

- Theory of Learning: Learning means seeking of truth in all matters, which happens only when one questions, interprets the wisdom and knowledge of others, and recognises one's own ignorance.

- Theory of Transmission: No one person or any one school of thought is authoritative or has the wisdom to teach. Socrates repeatedly disavowed his personal knowledge and methods, possibly using it as a technique to engage others. His dialectical teaching method used critical inquiry to challenge the credibility of established doctrines.

- Theory of Society: Individuals are not self-sufficient, and no one working alone can acquire all the necessities of life. Education can take place anytime and anywhere—magnificent buildings, large open areas, market places and public squares. The best life means acquisition of virtue (i.e. knowledge). A good Athenian was expected to strive to do good things for the city, strictly obey law, honour parents and ancestors, and scrupulously pay homage to the gods of the city by strictly obeying the conventions governing prayer and sacrifice.

- Theory of Opportunity: Ignorant people who mistake themselves as knowledgeable should be educated, challenged, questioned and debated to promote their intellectual and moral improvement.

- Theory of Consensus: Self-knowledge is important. Goodness and truth, and ethical and moral instincts are embedded divinely in the soul but can be brought to consciousness only when awakened or learned. Man is destined to seek virtue, such as courage and self-control, and master one's desires, ambitions and emotions that cloud the quest for truth. Ignorance stands in the way of consensus. When one learns what one does not know, disagreements change. Recognition of the value of virtue can improve the quality of one's life. The value of virtue will take precedence over personal power and the gratification of desire and pleasures. The life-long pursuit of self-improvement, the desire for wisdom is attainable only when one can see one's own faults, weaknesses and negative tendencies.

During his lifetime, Socrates frequently created controversies by challenging the ideas and status of the elite class. As a consequence, he was charged with immoral behaviour and accused of corrupting the youth. According to his student Plato's *Apology*, despite knowing the consequences, he did not attempt to escape with his friends. Instead, he strongly defended his views at court but was sentenced to death. He carried out his death sentence by willingly drinking a cup of hemlock.

The Socratic Method is most relevant to India where materialism and aggressive competition have gradually overtaken the traditional simpler and spiritual thought and lifestyle. As a consequence, people value wealth much more than knowledge. Sadly, all acts, including education, are aimed mainly to acquire wealth, status and power, all of which become addictions with time. It is not surprising that corruption is ripe in India because, as Socrates maintained, people tend to do wrong things due to ignorance. The most unfortunate part is that average consciousness has dwindled to such a level that people don't see anything wrong with corruption; it has sadly become a way of life—to survive, succeed and thrive. The combined effects of various belief systems and their religious scriptures, the media and the social media don't allow questioning the status quo and attainment of self-knowledge, which Socrates believed was the ultimate virtue. Furthermore, the autocratic education system and parental education work against the development of independent critical thinking in students. To make the situation worse, most teachers in India pretend to know more than they actually do, all of which goes against the Socratic Method. It is time for the people at the helm to think!

Plato (circa 428 BC–348 BC)

Plato, a Greek philosopher and teacher, was one of the two outstanding students of Socrates, the other being Xenophon.

Later in his life, Aristotle was his student. In circa 385 BC, he founded his Academy (near Athens), believed to be the first university. As Socrates did not leave any writing behind, Plato's book, *The Republic*, provides information about Socrates and the Socratic Method of teaching.

Plato's works are divided into three periods:

The *early* works: These comprise the 'dialogues' and provide much of what we know of Socrates and the Socratic Method, as discussed previously in this book.

The *middle* period: These are characterised by dialogues in which Socrates, a character in his book *The Republic* is the main speaker. It is generally accepted these dialogues are actually Plato's own words. One can note the development of his thought around knowledge and the Forms, the Soul (psyche –psychology), and political theory.

The *late* period: In this period, the dialogues are largely concerned with revisiting the metaphysical and logical assumptions of his middle period.

Plato's thoughts about education and the ideal society are best portrayed in *The Republic*. He set out the shape and curriculum of an education system, and plans for an educational organisation in *The Laws*. In the ideal state, matters are overseen by the guardian class, who are educated.

The relevance of Plato's beliefs about education to educators can be summarised as follows:

- Educators must have a deep care for the well-being and future of the students they work with. Educating being a moral activity, it is the duty of educators to search for truth and virtue and guide their students.

- A teacher must know one's subject but, as a philosopher, the teacher must also know the limits of one's knowledge. The power of dialogue leads to joint exploration of a subject matter by the teacher and the students. Knowledge will not come from teaching but from questioning—the Socratic Method.

- Various life stages demand differing educational requirements. Plato's work reflects the classical Greek concern for body and mind (soul). The works emphasise the importance of exercise and discipline, of storytelling and games. In Plato's model of 'lifelong education', children start school at six where they learn reading, writing and counting, and also music and sports. Thereafter, those students who are to be the guardians, undergo military and physical training at 18; start higher studies at 21; begin to study philosophy at 30 and serve in the army or civil service; and are finally ready to rule at 50. The model reflects a 'learning society', where members continue to grow with time and training.

- Plato regarded education as a mechanism to achieve individual justice as well as social justice. He believed individual justice can be obtained when each individual develops to the fullest. Justice meant excellence which, for the Greeks and Plato is virtue and, as per Socrates, virtue is knowledge. Thus, knowledge is required to be just and comprise (a) knowledge of one's own job; (b) self-knowledge, and (c) knowledge of the Idea of the Good. Social justice can be attained when all social classes in a society—rulers, workers and warriors—

live harmoniously with one another. Plato believed that people can coexist in harmony when society gives them equal educational opportunity from an early age to compete fairly with one other. Without equal educational opportunity, an unjust society is created because the political system is run by unqualified people and the system is ridden with timocracy, oligarchy, flawed democracy, or even tyranny.

The Republic defends justice and offers an equally powerful defence of philosophical education. Socrates posits two differing visions of education—of the warrior guardians and the philosopher-kings—via a subtle account of education through his pedagogical approach with interlocutors, Glaucon and Adeimantus. An explicit account of education is made available after Glaucon questions Socrates' suggestion that an austere, moderate and plain lifestyle is necessary for producing a just city, whereas Glaucon desires it be rather luxurious. But, as soon as Socrates allows fineries, the city quickly becomes rife with issues, eg more land needed to house a flourishing and growing population, and a specialised military needed to undertake conquests and guard the city from its neighbours. Furthermore, due to a potential danger of tyranny accompanying a military rule, necessary efforts are required to curb the guardians' tendency to take over the city and lord over the citizens.

Socrates suggests that the guardians must be controlled through an education designed to make them think and act like noble puppies, which are fierce with enemies and gentle with citizens. For shaping their thought and behaviour, and to prevent them from lording over citizens, Socrates suggests guardians to receive musical education for the mind (soul) and gymnastics for the body. Their education is primarily moral in nature, one that requires blind acceptance of beliefs and accepted behaviours. As such, they are not meant to have a particular moral nature before their education. Their education should not help them to develop the ability to think critically or independently. For receiving guardian's education, Socrates requires the students to be *philosophic, spirited, swift,* and *strong* by nature. Unlike the philosopher-kings, the guardians must accept only that with which they are familiar with and attack whatever looks unfamiliar or foreign. Socrates' musical education includes speeches, music and tales. Tales must be strictly censored because young children are malleable. Socrates claims, '*A young thing can't judge what is hidden sense and what is not; but what he takes into his opinions at that age has a tendency to become hard to eradicate and unchangeable*'. Unable to distinguish between good and bad, children will use bad examples to justify their own bad behaviour. Through carefully crafted tales, mothers and nurses will shape their children's souls. Children are expected to accept whatever they are told with little free-thought.

Tales should instil virtue, foster courage and justice; glorify and encourage temperance in drinking, eating, sex, love of money and possessions; display obedience to superiors and show bravery in the face of danger. Gods must never be shown as unjust, as children may think it acceptable and honourable to do injustice. Children must be told that citizens have never been angry with one another. By hearing such tales, they will learn the importance of unity. Children must be told that the gods are not the cause of all things and cannot be said to punish (unless it is for the punished person's benefit), change shape/form, or lie. Children must look solely to human guardians and the law for guidance. They should grow up fearing slavery more than death.

Socrates suggests gymnastics for preventing illness. He maintains a healthy soul and a healthy intellect produces a healthy body. By eating and drinking moderately and undertaking simple physical exercises, the body will be fit. Although music is the most important component in the Socrates' guardians' education, equilibrium between music and gymnastics is important. A solely gymnastic education can potentially cause savagery and a purely musical education potentially causes softness, therefore, the two must be balanced. Education in music and gymnastics should be compulsory for the youth.

Socrates says the city should be ruled by philosopher-kings and admits the nature required in philosopher-kings is rare. He says quick and fiery natured people, who are suited more to music, will usually not show courage in war. On the other hand, trustworthy and brave people who excel in war are generally intellectually slow. Therefore, potential philosopher-kings must be given a form of education that will identify, test, and refine their philosophical nature, as education serves to identify those who are capable of philosophising.

To make his student Glaucon grasp the concept of good, Socrates uses the *cave analogy* to illustrate that the good can be known through education. The analogy also explains why philosophical education is often resisted.

Socrates describes a cave in which prisoners, restrained right from birth, face a wall. Behind them, puppet-masters carry figurines that cast shadows on the wall which is in front of the prisoners. Because they do not know the actual reality, the prisoners assume the shadows to be their extent of reality. Now if a prisoner was unchained and allowed to leave the cave, at first, he would be irritated and disoriented by an unfamiliar foreign and bright surrounding outside. If he was told that his experience in the cave was not entirely real, he would possibly react in disbelief. If he tried to look at the sun directly after leaving the cave, he would possibly be blinded and, out of irritation, may want to rush to his familiar darker cave environment. Socrates says if someone were to drag him *'away from there by force along the rough, steep, upward way, and didn't let him go before he had dragged him out into the light of the sun'*, the prisoner would resist, possibly fight and be resentful, although he would not be entirely able to see his new surroundings immediately. However, his eyes would adjust slowly. He would observe many actual things, shadows, reflections in water, the night's sky and, finally, the sun, which represents image of the good and the reality. Once he focuses on the reality, he will be happier than ever before and possibly will never want to return to his former darker cave environment. If he did try to return to the cave and help the other prisoners, they would possibly disbelieve him and call him delusional because their reality is still limited to the shadows in the cave.

As a learning from the above, one could say that the good is beyond the perceived reality and hard to see. But once the good is seen and understood, it becomes clear that it *'is the cause of all that is right and fair in everything,'* and must be understood by prudent rulers. An education that teaches men to use their existing capacity for knowledge is what Socrates intends for the philosopher-kings. He says, 'Education is not what the professions of certain men assert it to be. They presumably assert that they put into the soul knowledge that isn't in it, as though they were putting sight into blind eyes ... but the present argument, on the other hand ... indicates that this power is in the soul of each and that the instrument with which each learns—just as an eye is not able to turn toward the light from the dark without the whole body turned around....The ability to know is always within man, never faltering, but useful only depending on whether it is focused on the truth.'

Socrates says that good guardians must not be prisoners nor should they be philosophers who selfishly stay outside of the cave. They must escape the cave, get educated in the good through philosophy, and then return to the cave to enlighten others and rule.

Socrates claims a study of mathematics—calculations and forms (geometry, cubes etc.)—is not only useful for practical matters, but its abstractness enables students to exercise their intellect and ask questions about the reality. He says, '*It leads the soul powerfully upward and compels it to discuss numbers themselves*'.

The study of complex and elusive concepts pushes a student to study what is permanent and perfect. Socrates insists that recipients of an education in mathematics and dialectics must have a suitable nature. The students must love to work hard and must be steady, courageous, noble, tough and quick learners.

He insists that education in philosophy begins in childhood and is something to be loved. Children should be allowed to come to the truth on their own rather than by force. Never tell them what to think in order to help them realise their own thinking and natural potential. He says, '*Don't use force in training the children in the studies, but rather play. In that way you can better discern what each is naturally directed towards.'*

Socrates also says that education should be more like play than work; however, play must have serious intentions and must not be without responsibility. Children must not be allowed to play with dialectics unless they are able to do so responsibly because they may become corrupted and lawless.

Plato completely disagrees with the current educational system in India which lays more emphasis on the economic development of the country rather than the human and social development.

Children in India are not allowed to develop their own independent thinking and ask questions to arrive at the truth. There are non-uniform opportunities for the school-age children in India to learn, as Socrates and Plato would like them to learn, and poor/limited access to good functional schools, despite the RTE.

In India, the reservation policy benefits generations of some social categories but at the cost of relatively brighter candidates coming from the general category. Additionally, the method of teaching and school curriculum do not encourage self-learning and a holistic development of young students due to absence of targeted social, moral, ethical and environmental education.

In India, flourishing of private institutions—schools, and universities—reflects education being seen more as a business rather than a noble cause. Businesses are concerned mainly with profit whereas true education, according to Socrates and Plato, is concerned with the common good based upon the rational principle of individual and social justice.

Aristotle (circa 384 BC–322 BC)

Aristotle, widely adjudged as the best educated man who has ever lived, was a Greek philosopher, psychologist, logician, moralist, political thinker, biologist, and literary critic. His father, Nicomachus was a court physician for King Amyntas of Macedonia. Following the tradition of hereditary at that time, Aristotle was taught in the area of medicines and then trained for the position of court physician. At 17, he joined Plato's school, and stayed there for 20 years.

After Plato's death, in 348 BC, Aristotle taught philosophy. He went to Atarneus in Asia Minor where he met with Hermias, the ruler. After a few years, when Hermias was murdered, King Philip II of Macedonia called upon him to return to Stagira, where he became the tutor of then 13-year old Alexander, who later came to be known as Alexander the Great. Alexander greatly profited from Aristotle's influence and the knowledge he received from him. Once Alexander acceded to the throne in Macedonia, Aristotle returned to Athens in circa 335 or 334 BC where he opened a school of philosophy. Later, stepping into the footsteps of his teacher, Plato, he formed a school in a gymnasium, called the Lyceum, which included a school, a research institution, a library, and a museum where he taught philosophy.

For 13 years (335 BC–322 BC), Aristotle taught at the Lyceum and came up with 'dialogues', which were the writings that he frequently wrote. He had a habit of walking about while he would be in the process of teaching.

Various great philosophers defined Aristotle differently.

- Eusebius called him '*nature's private secretary, dipping his pen in intellect.*'

- Dante called him '*the master of those that know.*'

- Alexander Bain called him '*a devotee to facts and a master of the highest abstractions.*'

- Hegel called him '*a man beside whom no age has an equal.*'

It is believed that the legendary trinity—Socrates, Plato and Aristotle—represents a real unity and that Aristotle's work fulfils the Socratic impulse.

Aristotle's writings related to 'logic' developed as an art of discourse and was used as a tool for finding out the structure of the world. It is believed that, before him, there was no rigorous system for determining the truth of a proposition. He addressed this issue by developing a system in which rules were formulated to examine the internal consistency of any argument.

Aristotle advocated a well-rounded education where students studied science, mathematics, and philosophy; were exposed to play and physical training, music and debate. He believed that education should also include ethics and political philosophy. He wanted education to be undertaken through reason and students to have an active role in their education. He stated that: '*Anything that we have to learn to do we learn by the actual doing of it ...We become just by doing just acts, temperate by doing temperate ones, brave by doing brave ones.*'

Aristotle's first writings, modelled on Plato's examples, comprise treatises on a wide range of subjects which are investigative reports possibly presented by Aristotle as lectures and notes taken by his students. The treatises were recovered in the Middle Ages and studied widely across the globe by many prominent thinkers. Each of the treatises includes:

- Aim of the subject matter;
- Consideration of ideas of other thinkers;
- Examination of various principles proposed to

determine the one that can best explain the subject matter;

- Search for the facts that illustrate the proposed principle; and

- Explanation of the subject matter by illustrating how the proposed principle explains the facts observed.

The treatises, deemed to have been essential to the work of the Lyceum, are classified into the following three types:

- Theoretical sciences, such as metaphysics, mathematics and physics, aimed to know for the purpose of knowing;

- Productive sciences, such as poetics and rhetoric, aimed to know for the purpose of developing things of beauty and use; and

- Practical sciences, such as ethics and politics, aimed to know for the purpose of conduct and working.

Aristotle suggested the Theoretical sciences can only be understood by principles that are certain and as they are; and their study is necessary. However, the Productive sciences and the Practical sciences can be understood by principles that are less than certain; and their study is contingent.

Aristotle believed:

- Distinct sciences exist and the nature of each is to be determined by principles found in the midst of the subject matter that is characteristically its own.

- Many subject matters exist, with corresponding principles that explain their individual facts. Most importantly, he said, what is learned in any subject matter may be useful in studying other subject matters, without any hierarchy of principles.

Aristotle's educational thinking was focused on pursuing the *highest good for human beings in the life of a community.* He believed the good life is essentially a social life, which is a life of good conduct in a community. He maintained ethics is a part of politics and equally, politics is a part of ethics and, accordingly, argued that the end of individuals and states is the same; therefore, an investigation into the nature of society is necessary for investigating into the nature of ethics.

'*The Good of man must be the end of the science of Politics.*'
… Aristotle

Aristotle maintained that one may have a rough idea about the 'highest good'—one that is required by 'reason'—one will never find out what actually it is until one learns to live with the highest principles of 'reason'. The 'highest good' is never completely known because its pursuit leads one to an unending series of actions. The contingent nature of social existence requires one to discover what is good for us in what we do; as such, one cannot truly learn what it is apart from one's 'conduct'. Although 'reason' is an essential part of 'conduct', it is not adequate for actualising the 'highest good'. Only by one's 'conduct', one can discover one's possibilities; and only by further 'conduct', one can strive to actualise those possibilities.

In community life, the activity of 'doing' can only result in further 'doing'. Similarly, education, being one of the activities of doing, must be a continuing process that has no end except further education. Education, being a Practical science, is a way of conduct and actions.

Aristotle's *The Politics* cites three aims of education: the possible, the appropriate, and the happy mean. In the pursuit of the good life, the aim of education is to know the nature of the 'best state' and the 'highest virtues' which humans are capable of achieving. Such knowledge enables humans to know what is possible in education. Educational activity determines the mechanism for pursuing that which is possible, thus, being a kind of 'making' as well as a kind of 'doing'. In doing, one tries to make things happen. Education is an attempt to find the kind of unity of 'doing' and 'making', enabling individual people to grow socially and ethically.

As per Aristotle, two kinds of virtues—moral and intellectual—define the human conduct. Moral virtues are learned by habit and intellectual virtues through education. Although humans are not considered temperate or courageous by nature, they have the potential to become temperate and courageous by acquiring appropriate habits and by conducting themselves appropriately, they can learn to realise their moral virtues. For example, children learn the moral virtues even before they know what they are doing or why they are doing it. Aristotle emphasises inculcating habits to train children, as they cannot control their conduct through intellectual principles. Children must first learn the moral virtues and then, once their intelligence has matured, they will learn to use their intellectual virtues and exercise reason while conducting themselves.

Before his time, private education had prevailed in most states in the Greek world, which Aristotle rejected. He insisted that state (i.e. government) should be responsible for educating its citizens. In his book, *The Politics,* he identified four bases for public education:

- The constitutional requirements;
- The origins of virtue;

- The common end to be sought by all citizens; and

- The inseparability of the individual and the community.

There are numerous ways that the Aristotelian theories, philosophies, ethics, writings, and styles of teaching have significantly influenced the western education system and most likely will continue to influence in the future. He strongly believed in the importance of an education which studies the real world, draws conclusions, and gains knowledge through analysis. Another aspect in which Aristotle has influenced education today is his views on realism. Throughout its history, realism has had a common theme, called the *principle or thesis of independence*, which holds that reality, knowledge, and value exist independent of the human mind.

Jean-Jacques Rousseau (1712–1778)

In the mid-18th century, childhood was beginning to be viewed positively and associated with positive meanings and attributes, such as freedom, innocence, spontaneity, emotion, creativity and malleability, which fitted well with those entrusted with raising and educating children. This change in perception and belief influenced several famous 18th and 19th century writers, some wishing they could preserve childhood indefinitely. This shift was in complete contradiction to the earlier Puritan belief that maintained humans are born out of sin, as a consequence of mankind's 'fall'.

One such philosopher was Jean-Jacques Rousseau, a political philosopher and educationalist, who not only rejects the doctrine of Original Sin, but maintains that children are innately innocent and become corrupt only through experience of the world. Rousseau was a French Genevan philosopher, writer, and composer. His political philosophy influenced the Enlightenment across Europe, as well as aspects of the French Revolution. During the period of the French Revolution, he was the most popular of the philosophers. In 1794, he was declared as a French national hero, sixteen years after his death.

Rousseau's novel, *Emile* (1762), is an invented account of an experiment in raising a boy named Emile, using Rousseau's method. Emile is allowed to develop naturally in nature by following his own instincts, which are shown as naturally healthy. Rousseau showed this method of raising children preserves the special attributes of childhood resulting in well-adjusted adults who will also turn out to be good citizens. Rousseau recommends education should take place in natural environment. As reflected in *Emile*, he suggests countryside as a more natural and healthy environment for learning than the city environment, but under the guardianship of a tutor who guides the student through various learning experiences. The tutor should, however, ensure that no harm is caused to the student through those learning experiences. He believes children learn to differentiate between the 'right' from the 'wrong' by way of experiencing the consequences of their actions rather than through physical punishment. In essence, he maintains vice and error, which are alien to a child's original nature, are introduced by external agencies. Therefore, the tutor must try to counteract those agencies by using tactics and methods that are coherent with nature. This method, called *'the method of natural consequences'*, is somewhat similar to the Indian ancient system of *Gurukul*.

Rousseau greatly influenced the overall development of modern political and educational thought. His Discourse on Inequality and The Social Contract are considered as cornerstones in modern political and social thought. His novel, *Emile*, has been considered as the most significant book on education after Plato's *The Republic*. His other works have had a profound impact on political theory and practice, romanticism and the development of the novel.

Rousseau's philosophy of education does not consider any particular technique of teaching, or imparting knowledge and concepts. It is mainly concerned with developing the student's character and moral sense, so that he learns self-mastery and remains virtuous even in the unnatural and imperfect society in which he will have to live.

Rousseau's ideas have greatly influenced child education. He was an early advocate of developmentally appropriate education. His description of the stages of child development reflects his conception of the evolution of culture. He divides childhood into the three following stages:

- In the first stage, up to the age of about 12, children are guided by their emotions and impulses;

- In the second stage, from the age of 12 to about 16, reason starts to develop; and

- In the third stage, from the age of about 16 onwards, the child develops into an adult.

Rousseau had an unusual childhood; he had no formal education. His mother died a few days after his birth and he was brought up initially by his father, Issac, and later by an aunt and an uncle.

As per Wikipedia[1], Rousseau had no recollection of

---

[1] https://en.wikipedia.org/wiki/Jean-Jacques_Rousseau

learning to read. But the following admission by him provides an interesting example about how his father encouraged his love of reading when he was about five or six years old: 'Every night, after supper, we read some part of a small collection of romances (adventure stories), which had been my mother's. My father's design was only to improve me in reading, and he thought these entertaining works were calculated to give me a fondness for it; but we soon found ourselves so interested in the adventures they contained, that we alternately read whole nights together and could not bear to give over until at the conclusion of a volume. Sometimes, in the morning, on hearing the swallows at our window, my father, quite ashamed of this weakness, would cry, "Come, come, let us go to bed; I am more a child than thou art."' (Ref. Confessions)

Oddly, in his childhood, he was not allowed to play with children his own age. Despite that, he had happy memories of his childhood. His father taught him to read and helped him to appreciate the countryside. He increasingly turned to the latter for solace.

Rousseau recommends young adults should also learn a manual skill, such as carpentry, smithy etc. which requires creativity and thought. This could keep him out of trouble in the event of a change of fortune, as a fall-back means of making a living.

Rousseau's ideas soon found way into children's literature, such as in his disciple Thomas Day's popular *Sandford and Merton* (1783-89).

Rousseau emphasised that students should learn the habit of reasoning. He said, '*The noblest work in education is to make a reasoning man, and we expect to train a young child by making him reason! This is beginning at the end; this is making an instrument of a result. If children understood how to reason they would not need to be educated.'*

William Wordsworth (1770–1850)

William Wordsworth was an English Romantic era poet, renowned around the world as one the greatest poets of all times. He and Samuel Taylor Coleridge initiated the Romantic Age in English literature, via their joint publication, *Lyrical Ballads* (1798). He was Britain's poet laureate from 1843 till his death in 1850.

The 18th century saw a new era, characterised by advocacy for reason and intellect, and Romanticism emphasised on the feelings and matters of the heart. Following Rousseau's remarkable ground-breaking work, childhood came to be perceived in a good light and as a force for good. Thereafter, thanks to such great Romantic poets as William Wordsworth and William Blake, the purity and idealised version of childhood found its way in children's literature in the 19th century, and continued into the 20th century.

Wordsworth's greatest work is generally considered to be *The Prelude*, a semi-autobiographical poem of his early years, which was posthumously titled and published. In his lifetime, the poem was generally known as '*the poem to Coleridge*', which he had revised and expanded a number of times.

Pantheism and mysticism were interwoven in the Romantic era's Nature poetry. In the Romantic era poets, mysticism was seemingly born out their communion with Nature, and possibly founded upon an instinctive or experienced conviction of oneness (unity) of likeness in all things. The founding philosophy is that a spiritual force lives and breathes through all the works of Nature. The emotional intensity of the thinker can alone reveal the presence of the spirit beneath the material and outward appearances of this phenomenal world. So, it is just a matter of scratching under the surface—by observations and interaction with Nature and contemplation.

One of Wordsworth's greatest poems, *Tintern Abbey* (1798), which is one of the nineteen poems in *Lyrical Ballads*, is based on his childhood memories of communion with natural beauty, a subject essentially close to his heart. The poem, characterised by its striking simplicity, is written as a monologue, imaginatively spoken by the poet to himself.

Tintern Abbey signifies the first emotional change in the Romantic era poetry in the sense that it defined the power of nature to develop and sustain the imagination and creative faculty of humans. The scene is in the narrow gorge of the river, Wye, located between Tintern and Monmouth. Wordsworth had visited it in the summer of 1793. After five years, in July 1798, he visited it again with his sister. The poem opens with the poet's declaration that five years had passed since he had last visited the location. He describes the objects that he sees again with a new perception and how they provided 'tranquil restoration' to his mind, whilst also describing his memories when he was away in crowded towns and cities. Gleefully, he thinks that his newfound experience with Nature will provide him with many happy memories for his future years. He feels greatly rejuvenated.

Wordsworth's poetry essentially illustrates his philosophical beliefs:

- The inherence of the universal spirit (God's soul) in Nature;
- Intercommunion between God's soul in Nature and

God's spirit in Man; and

- The chastening effect of the communion in tranquillising and elevating the human spirit and aligning it with the infinite.

On education, Wordsworth's thoughts could be summarised as follows:

- Nature and human life are one. The laws that bind Nature are the same as the laws that bind humans. Anything that enables humans to realise the meaning of things and Nature is worth studying.

- Simple things have underlying freshness.

- One must return to Nature— return to the spirit.

- Man must return to childhood. The starting point or the benchmark for the man is the wholeness of the child's nature. The child is with Nature, he is one with himself.

- Through self-discovery, one must discover that the simplest things in life that all men have in common— birth and death, rest and labour, parents and children, home and country—are the most important factors underlying human happiness. Anything that enables us to realise their meaning, such as wholesome surroundings and the best of books, is of essential human value. On the contrary, anything that estranges us from them, such as artificial things in the modern industry and civilisation, is the enemy of true human peace and happiness.

- One must be in touch with one's inmost being; it

extends and deepens one's hold upon life, tranquils the soul, strengthens the will and penetrates the character. The inmost being moulds our body features in the reflection of the underlying harmony of Nature.

- Any education which fails to lay stress on the development of the soul is hopelessly inadequate and unworthy of learning.

- All schemes of education are futile if not directed to the prolongation of the prenatal innocence or the childhood.

  On early education of children, Wordsworth said that through early contact with Nature and human life in its simpler forms, children should have the amplest opportunity of forming for themselves the association out of which the sentiments on which one discourses are born.

Education, similar to all other vital areas, must be self-education. Nothing can replace self-appropriation, the inwardising by the soul of its first-hand experiences and impressions. For this process to occur, leisure and time for assimilation are required. Therefore, one must be allowed to be free from distraction and officious interferences, fuss and worry.

He believed that separating the child at the most impressionable age from its proper environment—i.e. Nature—was nothing short of a sin against Nature. He strongly objected to early severance of children from the (natural) objects and (natural) events that formed the natural stimulus of its growing powers. All those things that are really valuable in early school education i.e. the development of attention, imagination and memory—are far better obtained by leaving the child alone.

Wordsworth denounced the mistake of overrunning the child's infancy with moralising books. Instead, he recommended that formal education must begin *'by putting the child in the way of acquiring, without measure or limit, such knowledge as will lead him out of himself; such knowledge as is interesting for its own sake; things known because they are interesting, not interesting because they are known; in a word, by leaving him at liberty to luxuriate in such feelings and images as will feed his mind in silent pleasure. This nourishment is contained in fairy tales, romances, the best biographies and histories, and such parts of natural history relating to powers and appearance of the earth and elements, and the habits and structure of animals as belong to it not as an art or science, but as a magazine of form and feeling.'*

Wordsworth emphasised that early education should be concerned with the production of a state of mind from the start to the end. He maintained if early education is right, all else will be right. However, if early education is wrong, no technical acquirement can compensate for the loss. As such, he is mainly concerned with first principals and could be seen as being a little indifferent to details of later education

On later education and learning science, he says, *'Admiration and love, to which all knowledge truly must tend, are felt by men of real genius in proportion as their discoveries in natural philosophy are enlarged.'*

Following Wordsworth's philosophy on early education, in the present world, it seems the aim of the teacher should be to procure in the child a condition of mind as well as a condition of feeling and will in respect to the objects that are brought before it. The child must then initiate an inward process of assimilation, which requires time and an atmosphere of large leisureliness.

John Dewey (1859 – 1952)

John Dewey, an American philosopher, psychologist, Georgist, and educational reformer, is considered to be one of the primary figures associated with the philosophy of pragmatism. He was born in Burlington, Vermont, US, to a family of modest means. As one of the fathers of functional psychology, he was influential in education and social reform, and a major voice of progressive education and liberalism. In addition to education, he also wrote about epistemology, metaphysics, aesthetics, art, logic, social theory, and ethics.

Dewey was a strong advocate of democracy. According to him, complete democracy required not just extending voting rights but also ensuring there is a fully formed public opinion, as a result of clear communication between citizens and politicians, with the latter being accountable for the policies they adopt.

'*The fundamental unity of the newer philosophy is found in the idea that there is an intimate and necessary relation between the processes of actual experience and education.*' (Dewey, 1938, p.6)

Dewey (1934) developed a procedure to support the construction of knowledge within a particular experience:

- Observation of surrounding conditions;

- Knowledge of what has happened in similar situations in the past; and

- Judgement which puts together what is observed to see what they signify.

'*Dewey treats human inquiry as continuous with the biological transaction between the organism and environment, hoping in this way to establish an objective basis for describing both what is problematic about problematic situations and what is determinate about their resolution*' (Schon 1992, p. 122).

Lev Vygotsky (1896 – 1934)

Lev Semyonovich Vygotsky was a Soviet psychologist. He proposed the theory of '*higher psychological functions*' in the field of developmental psychology, which sees human psychological development emerging through interpersonal interaction with the social environment.

In the early 1980s, much after his death in 1934, his notion of the '*zone of proximal development*' (ZPD) became a central component in the development of new paradigms in developmental and educational psychology.

ZPD is Vygotsky's term for the range of tasks that a child is in the process of learning to complete. Vygotsky viewed the ZPD as a way to better explain the relation between children's learning and cognitive development.

Prior to the ZPD, the relation between learning and development was believed to boil down to the following three major positions:

- Development always precedes learning (eg constructivism): children first need to meet a particular maturation level before learning can occur;

- Learning and development cannot be separated but instead occur simultaneously (eg behaviourism): essentially, learning is development; and

- Learning and development are separate but interactive

processes (eg gestaltism): one process always prepares the other process, and vice versa.

Vygotsky believed that learning should always precede development in the ZPD and, therefore, rejected all above theories. According to him, with the assistance of a teacher, a child can learn skills or aspects of a skill that go beyond the child's actual developmental or maturational level. The lower limit of ZPD represents the level of the skill learnt by the child working independently, which defines the child's actual developmental level. The upper limit of ZPD represents the level of potential skill that the child is able to achieve with the assistance of a teacher.

Jean Piaget (1896–1980)

Jean Piaget, a Swiss psychologist and epistemologist, is well known for his pioneering work in child development. His theory of 'cognitive development and epistemological view' are called 'genetic epistemology.' He placed great importance on the education of children. His theory of child development is studied in pre-service education programmes.

Ernst von Glasersfeld (1917–2010), a renowned philosopher and professor of psychology, called Jean Piaget '*the great pioneer of the constructivist theory of knowing.*' In 1934, as the Director of the International Bureau of Education, he declared, '*only education is capable of saving our societies from possible collapse, whether violent, or gradual.*'

Through his research, Piaget began to understand the investigative process as one in which individuals constantly interact with the environment. Piaget postulated that the process of knowledge creation was, in actuality, a series of recursive intuitions. Individuals move through a continual mental functioning process beginning with assimilation, transitioning to states of disequilibrium and accommodation, and ending with the integration of new knowledge.

'*Intelligence, viewed as a whole, takes the form of a structuring which impresses certain patterns on the interaction between the subject or subjects and near or distant surrounding objects.*' (Piaget, 1960, p. 167)

Piaget asserted that, by placing students in situations of cognitive dissonance and offering opportunities to equilibrate, students could build fully elaborated schemes of thought. Learning through inquiry can prompt scrutiny of the way knowledge becomes manifest and can open the possibilities for greater understanding. In this manner, knowledge loses the default assumption that is always absolute and eternal. Instead, claims to knowledge become tentative, susceptible to revision. Continual negotiation and reaffirmation are required for knowledge to be accepted as genuine

The Indian education system

With about one-fifth of its population comprising around 260 million children enrolled in more than 1.5 million schools (Years 1 to 12), across 36 states and union territories, with about 8 million teachers (in public and private schools), the Indian education system is one of the largest in the world and very complex (*School Education in India* 2014-15). As per the Right to Education 2009, schooling is supposed to be free and compulsory for 6 to 14 year olds in India.

India does not have an Education Minister. Since 29 August 1947, the education department in India has instead been administered by the Ministry of Human Resources

Development. The National Policy on education, originally formulated in 1968 (updated in 1986 and modified in 1992) recognised education as a precondition for development, setting out three critical issues—equity, accessibility and quality.

India's Scientific Policy Resolution (SPR) of 1958 resolves to *'foster, promote and sustain the cultivation of science and scientific research in all aspects'*. Science, technology and innovation have been identified as the drivers for India's faster, sustainable and inclusive growth (*Science, Technology and Innovation Policy, 2013*).

The earlier education policies failed to change the state of education in the country in the earlier years. Of late, the National Policy on Education 2016 recognised education as the most important tool for social, economic and cultural transformation, whilst emphasising on critical thinking, skill development, and innovation. The Policy identified four essential components—building values, awareness, knowledge and skills—to enable the skilled and competent citizens to contribute in the country's well-being, strengthen its democracy and foster social cohesion (*National Policy on Education* 2016).

On 19 July 2017, the Indian Prime Minster, Mr Modi, asserted that science, technology and innovation are the keys to progress and prosperity of India. He asked the officials to draw up clear goals to identify the brightest and best science talent amongst the school students and effective mechanisms to reduce the drudgery though interventions of science and technology by 2022, the 75th year of independence of India. On 14 October 2017, the Prime Minister also announced a package of Rupees 10,000 crore (about AUD $2.2 billion) to transform 20 universities in India into world class institutions.

Currently, Indian universities score very low in the world rankings.

The Indian National Education Policy has endorsed a sum of 6 per cent of GDP as the minimum expenditure on education (*National Policy on Education* 2016) and 0.88 per cent of its GDP towards R & D (*Research and Development Statistics* 2011-2012). However, the expenditures have never exceeded more than 4.3 per cent of GDP; currently being around 3.5 per cent (*National Policy on Education* 2016). Furthermore, the private sector's contribution in R & D is far less than Government of India's desire to invest 2 per cent of GDP on the R & D (*GDP in Science Research*, 27 November 2014).

Recent initiatives

India, traditionally an agrarian country, has thankfully recognised the need to embrace STEM (Science, Technology, Engineering and Mathematics) education for her development and to be able to compete in the world service sector. STEM is about the learning skills in science, technology, engineering and mathematics to assist in design processes through need based solution, development of technology and creativity.

India is committed to introduce the constructivist teaching approach and spend a major part of research budget on STEM programmes for school students. In the recent years, commendably, India has launched a number of skills development programmes to encourage, popularise and inculcate scientific temper amongst the students:

- Skill India (*National Policy on Skills Development and Entrepreneurship* 2015);

- National Children's Science Congress (NCSC);

- Innovation in Science Pursuit for Inspired Research (INSPIRE) Programme;

- The Initiative for Research and Innovation in Science (IRIS);

- Science Express (mobile science exhibition); and

- Science Exhibition.

The educational programmes aim to help to enhance the awareness about science and its prospective career options.

In addition to the above, India has also launched the Atal innovation Mission, which aims to *Cultivate one Million children in India as Neoteric Innovators*, by establishing Atal Tinkering Laboratories (ATL) in schools to foster curiosity, creativity and imagination in Year 6 to Year 10 students, whilst inculcating in them the design mindset, computational thinking, adaptive learning, and physical computing skills.

All above programmes are designed for students. But it seems India has overlooked a dire need to enhance the quality of instructors. For successful implementation of these programmes, as well as effectiveness of the main curriculum, the main focus must be first on the teacher development.

There are also a number of limitations in the programmes, which potentially disadvantage many students. For example, the selection of just top one per cent (bright) students in the INSPIRE programme (i.e. the students who score high in the Year 10 Board Examination) leaves behind numerous other students who may also have an equal, or perhaps higher aptitude for science but do not score high in the tests for some reason. Furthermore, the current system witnesses a repetition of many students and schools, mainly due to favouritism, in science competition programmes like NCSC and IRIS which also disadvantages numerous other students. To make things worse, there are no direct linkages of such programmes with tertiary institutions where they could be run with collaboration of tertiary institutions.

In addition to the above, Connected Learning Initiative (CLIx) is the first initiative undertaken by Tata Trusts in collaboration with Massachusetts Institute of Technology (MIT). It is a bold and innovative effort that aims to improve the professional and academic prospects of high school students from underserved communities in India. It supplements the high school curriculum in key areas, including digital literacy, Mathematics, the Science subjects of Biology, Chemistry and Physics. CLIx is currently being implemented in four states— Chhattisgarh, Mizoram, Rajasthan, Telangana, where it is available to approximately 1,11,000 high school students and some 4,500 teachers in over 1,100 government schools. CLIx was selected out of 143 entries from 79 countries worldwide for the 2017 edition of the UNESCO Prize for the Use of ICTs in Education.[2]

Importance of teacher training and quality teachers

India needs a trained and passionate team of qualified teachers and a well-resourced infrastructure to provide an innovative education system that will support students' inherited skills, interests and achievements.

High-performing countries (in education) concentrate on: (a) attracting brightest students as teachers; and (b) nurturing

---

[2] http://www.tiss.edu/view/11/connected-learning-initiatives-clix/

teacher leadership talent through adequate support and professional development programmes (Finland: Teacher and Principal Quality, 2017; Stewart, 2010).

Many international studies have analysed the commonalities of best performing school systems in the world and identified teachers as the single most important factor in improving students' performance within schools (Barber and Mourshed, 2007; Hattie, 2008):

- Barber and Mourshed (2007) highlighted their main point as being: *'The quality of an education system cannot exceed the quality of its teachers.'*

- Hattie (2008) announced: *'The only way to improve outcomes is to improve instruction.'*

Report of Australian Education Department suggests that the key to student engagement lies not so much in the nature of subject content, but rather with pedagogy (Tytler, Osborne, William, Tytler & Cripps Clark, 2008).

How education affects economy?

Education has been proven to be an essential driving tool for economic well-being worldwide in this ever-growing age of competition. Education directly impacts the economic growth of a nation.

The theoretical literature has identified three main mechanisms that impact the economy through education (Hanushek, Wobmann, Jamison & Jamison, 2008):

- Education increases the productivity and outcomes by integrating the human capital in the labour force (Mankiw, Romer & Weil, 1992).

- Education contributes in the growth of an economy by introducing new knowledge about new technologies, products and processes (Aghion, Howitt, Brant-Collett & Garcia-Penalosa, 1998; Lucas, 1988).

- Education facilitates the diffusion and transmission of knowledge to share or understand the available technical knowledge (Benhabib and Spiegel, 1994; Nelson and Phelps, 1996).

As an example, PricewaterhouseCoopers report has indicated that by changing just one per cent of Australia's workforce into STEM-related roles would add an amount of $57.4 billion to Australia's GDP (Australia, 2015: Perspectives on Education and Training: Australians with qualifications in science, technology, engineering and mathematics, 2010-11).

The earlier research also suggested significant positive relationship between quantitative measures of schooling and economic growth (Barro, 1991; Lavergne, Doppelhofer & Miller, 2004; Mankiw, et al., 1992).

Impact of education on economic growth of a country has also been mixed with many factors, such as differences in cognitive skills due to a combination of peers, families, health & nutrition (Hanushek, et al., 2008).

Recent literature confirms that critical thinking, problem solving, innovation, creativity, and profusion of new technologies become key to success of future economy and creation of jobs (Rothwell, 2013; Scientist, 2014).

A number of current global issues, such as climate change, health, biodiversity, ecological sustainability and economic prosperity, have been seen to have a relationship with declining STEM enrolment numbers, which has forced many policymakers around the world to take serious steps to create an interest and motivate children towards STEM education (Ali and Shubra, 2010; Elias, 2009; Sjoberg and Schriener, 2005).

India must also commit to train and inspire its youth to produce skilled workforce to make invaluable contributions to nation's STEM industries which will, in turn, help the country's economy to grow faster.

The current challenges

Indian history provides glorious examples of many Indian scholars such as Charaka and Susruta, Aryabhata, Bhaskaracharya, Chanakya, Patanjali, Vatsayayna and numerous others who have made strong contributions in many fields of science and technology. But that is past. The world has moved on and changed significantly. The challenges of the current world are different from the past and the future will present new challenges, so the country has to prepare its youth to meet those future challenges.

India's education system has evolved slowly over time through the country's ancient culture and moral practices, rooted in the Vedas, and subsequently influenced by the religions of its rulers. Therefore, the Indian education system has been facing many more challenges as compared to other nations mainly due to its cultural diversity and a huge population. For example, the Australian system has directly inherited a European modern system and evolved through a far more focused and competency-centred approach of education (Singh, 2014). With a far lesser population than India, and with an intensive and constructivist approach, Australia outperforms India at both school and university education levels.

The Indian education system is currently struggling with a

number of issues, such as poor educational infrastructure, tough competition within such a huge and growing population, dire shortage of well-trained teachers, limited resources, diversity in language and, of course, corruption at all levels.

It is reported that India is witnessing a shortage of more than half a million teachers in elementary schools and about 14 per cent government secondary schools do not have the prescribed minimum six teachers (*National Policy on Education* 2016). Reportedly, most of the vacancies are not filled because most teachers hesitate in relocating themselves due to absence of basic facilities in rural areas. Also, as some issues can be politically influenced, administration is not able to fully address the challenges of the teaching profession in many cases.

Science education in India has been facing the following three main challenges (Malti, 2017; Sarangapani, 2017):

- Availability of and access to basic infrastructure and scientific equipment required for classroom instructions while teaching science;

- Shortage of quality teachers in science education who remain updated with the current knowhow in their subject matters; and

- The country's science curriculum, which needs an urgent update.

Apart from a paucity of basic infrastructure and quality teachers, significant gaps between people in the administration and academic areas, and a casual attitude of the regulators have contributed to a diminished quality of parameters of the Indian education system (*National Policy on Education*, 2016).

One of the major reasons for a large number of dropouts

from science education at high school level includes inability of the school system to encourage critical thinking, inquiry-based learning and hands-on learning of the students.

Driven by the low confidence of educated parents in the school education, the business of coaching classes, parallel to schooling, indicates a lack of credibility of the Indian school system. In addition, unlike Australia, absence of formal linkages in India between vocational fields and academic areas, with no horizontal and vertical mobility of students to move between these two fields, makes another reason for students to leave the science field. The Indian government has now woken up to understand how the absence of vocational courses and pathways potentially affects the students' interest in science and their entry in highly competitive STEM streams. Accordingly, various education programmes, such as *Skill India*, have been launched.

Another reason for higher dropout rates in high schools is triggered by poor performance of students in mathematics and science subjects. This can be attributed to rigid (and fewer) options for numeracy. Unlike Australian system, Indian education system does not permit the student to choose the level, or move from a higher to lower level at which the student may feel comfortable with the Year 10 Board Examination. The Committee of National Education Policy 2016 recommends two levels in mathematics and science for students to exercise their choice in the Year 10 Board Examination: Part A at higher level and Part B at a lower level. This could potentially limit the eligibility of the students to pursue future courses incorporating higher mathematics and science (*National Policy on Education* 2016).

Facts indicate most of the primary school teachers do not have the confidence about their own knowledge of mathematics and science. One of the reasons for poor quality teachers could be their inappropriate education. The earlier one-year Bachelor degree in education (B Ed), with an option to obtain it through correspondence, possibly did not equip those teachers with either the subject knowledge or the teaching skills. The infrastructure and quality of most of educational institutions that provided such degrees is reported to be poor. This has resulted in the employment of numerous teachers with low academic and inadequate pre-service training in education, in the government schools in India during the last three to four decades.

Thankfully, for improving the teacher quality, RTE and NCTE now require Bachelor degree as the minimum entry level qualification for teachers in upper primary classes, with a compulsory 2-year B Ed course. However, the system continues to depend on in-service training of millions of not-so-proficient existing teachers for improving learning and teaching standards in government schools (*National Policy on Education* 2016).

In addition to the poor quality of the teachers, large scale corruption in teacher appointments and their transfers, and in approvals to affiliate and grant recognition to institutions, commercialisation of education and political interference, have damaged the overall quality of education and the functioning of the education regulators in India (*National Policy of Education* 2016).

Based on the report, there are a disproportionate number of young student teachers from the arts and social sciences backgrounds coming to be trained as teachers as compared to trainees from the mathematics and science backgrounds.

Although India has lately started talking and promoting STEM education, the school education in India, despite placing emphasis on the science and mathematics, does not engage engineering and technology as part of the regular curriculum of pedagogy (*National Policy on Education*, 2016).

The Australian government has introduced various national standards and established various organisations to improve the accountability of schools and the teachers. In addition to the formal education, vocational education and training (VET) is part of Australian school education. Australian education system focusses on strong linkages between the schooling and vocational and higher education systems, and provides movement between them. The Australian Science Curriculum is organised around three interrelated strands—science understanding, science inquiry skills and science as human endeavour; it aligns science with the Australian government's national priories *(Shape of the Australian Curriculum: Science, May 2009)*.

Going forward

India needs to focus immediately on its poor educational infrastructure, poor quality of teachers, shortage of well-trained teachers, non-professional management across higher education and vocational education, lack of collaboration between the industry and academia, and non-alignment of syllabi with the current industry trends.

India has been following a traditional approach to education. To meet its current demands and the demands of the future world, the country will need to promote a more sustainable environment for effective education and teaching by attracting its brightest minds to the teaching profession, as well as enhance the quality of its educational infrastructure and the curriculum. The country will need to promote constructivist teaching and implement a transparent education policy.

To move forward with the rest of the world India urgently needs to a raise a well-trained army of teachers, particularly in STEM education to guide the next generation of students towards a bright future.

A well-coordinated, focused and concentrated effort towards enriching the teacher quality is an important task for the country. The teacher education system needs to be revamped, redesigned and remodelled by making the process of trainee teacher selection, promotion, enumeration and transfer of teachers more stringent and transparent. In-service teachers must be made accountable for their performance.

To improve STEM education, India needs to undertake reforms in science curriculum, provide the necessary infrastructure, address the current paucity of quality teachers and introduce specialised education to be able to identify early talent in teaching. The overall quality of Indian education system could also be improved through an exchange of teaching tools, methodology, sharing of teacher training resources, and faculties between institutions within and outside the country. India must introduce and blend vocational training at different levels in schooling years with necessary pathways for mobility in both directions.

A nation which has its education system built on innovation has huge potential to become a leading and strong player amongst emerging knowledge economies in the world.

Indian Education—The World Bank Report 2018

The World Bank report 2018 includes references to India and other developing countries. It stresses the enormity of the task for developing countries in the domain of education of the students, especially living in rural and remote areas. The report draws on research and case studies to suggest how countries can improve the quality of learning. The report makes an important point that schooling is not learning and getting children into classrooms is insufficient. The report discuss the importance of teacher quality, system support, pedagogy, and appropriate metrics for making progress in the education sector.

The author finds the following excerpts from the report having direct relevance to India:

- 'Individuals already disadvantaged in society—whether because of poverty, location, ethnicity, gender or disability—learn the least. Thus, education systems can widen social gaps…poor service delivery that amplifies the effects of poverty and the deeper system level problems, both technical and political, that allow poor-quality schooling to persist. Most enrolment gaps in basic education are closing between high and low income countries.'

- 'Schooling is not the same as learning. In rural India, just under three-quarters of students in Grade 3 could not solve a two-digit subtraction, such as 46–17, and by Grade 6, half could still not do so…such data are for children and youth lucky enough to be in school.'

- 'In rural India, in 2016, only half of Grade 5 students could fluently read text at the level of the grade and curriculum, which included sentences in the local language, such as "It was the month of rains" and "There were black clouds in the sky". These severe shortfalls constitute a learning crisis.'

- 'In Andhra Pradesh, India, in 2010, low performing students in Grade 5 were no more likely to answer a Grade 1 question correctly than those in Grade 2. Even the average student in Grade 5 had a 50 per cent chance of answering a Grade 1 question correctly—compared with about 40 per cent in Grade 2.'

- 'In New Delhi, India, in 2015, the average Grade 6 student performed at a Grade 3 level in maths. Even by Grade 9, the average student had reached less than a Grade 5 level, and the gap between the better and worse performers grew over time.'

- 'When poor parents perceive education to be of low quality, they are less willing to sacrifice to keep their children in school—a rational response, given the constraints they face. Parents consistently cite student learning outcomes as a critical component.'

- 'Learning shortfalls during the school years eventually show up as weak skills in the workforce. The job skills debate reflects the learning crisis. Work skill shortages are often discussed in a way that is disconnected from the debate on learning, but the two parts are of the same problem...The problem isn't just a lack of trained workers; it is a lack of readily trainable workers. Accordingly, many workers end up in jobs that require minimal amounts of reading and math. Lack of skills reduces job quality, earnings, and labour mobility.'

- 'The skills needed in labour markets are multi-dimensional, so systems need to equip students with far more than just reading, writing, and math—but students can't leapfrog these foundation skills…the foundation cognitive skills are essential.'

- 'Given all the investments countries have made in education, shortfalls in learning are discouraging. One reason for them is that learning has not always received the attention it should have…Acting effectively requires first understanding how schools are failing learners and how systems are failing schools.'

Schools are failing learners

- 'First, children often arrive in school unprepared to learn—if they arrive at all. Malnutrition, illness, low parental investments, and the harsh environments associated with poverty undermine early childhood learning.'

- 'Second, teachers often lack the skills or motivation to be effective. Teachers are the most important factor affecting learning in schools. In developing countries, teacher quality can matter even more than in wealthier countries…the problems are even more severe in remote communities, amplifying the disadvantages already facing rural students.'

- 'Third, inputs often fail to reach classrooms or to affect learning when they do. Public discourse often equates problems of education quality with input gaps.

Devoting enough resources to education is crucial, and in countries resources have not kept pace with the rapid jumps in enrolment…inputs often fail to make it to the frontlines…'

- 'Fourth, poor management and governance often undermine schooling quality. School principals are not actively involved in helping teachers solve problems, do not provide instructional advice, and do not set goals that prioritises learning. School governance—particularly the decision-making autonomy of school, along with oversight provided by parents and communities—serves as the framework for seeking local solutions and being accountable.'

- 'Because these quality problems are concentrated among disadvantaged children, they amplify typically disadvantaged, marginalised communities—also resources are used less effectively there, exacerbating the problem. Public policy has the effect of widening social gaps rather than offering all children an opportunity to learn.'

Systems are failing schools

- 'Technical complexities and political forces constantly pull educational systems out of alignment with learning.'

- 'Even when countries want to prioritise learning, they often lack the metrics to do so.'

- 'To be truly aligned, parts of the education system also have to be coherent with one another.'

- 'Teachers need to be trained so that they can use more active learning methods, and they need to care enough to make the change occur because teaching the new curriculum may be much more demanding than the old rote learning methods. Even if teachers are on board with curriculum reform, students could weaken its effects if an unreformed examination system creates misaligned incentives.'

- 'If teachers are poorly educated, unmotivated, and loosely managed, giving them even more autonomy will likely make matters worse.'

- 'Successful systems combine both alignment and coherence. Alignment means that learning is the goal of the various components of the system. Coherence means that the components reinforce each other.'

- 'Bureaucrats may focus more on keeping politicians and teachers happy than on promoting student learning, or they may simply try to protect their own positions ... competing interests may loom larger than the learning-aligned interests.'

- 'Many systems are stuck in low-learning traps, characterised by low accountability and high inequality. These traps bind together key stakeholders through informal contracts that prioritise other goals such as civil service employment, corporate profits, or re-election, perpetuating the low-accountability equilibrium. It is often in the interest of each to maintain the status quo— society, and many of these actors would be better off if they could shift to higher quality equilibrium.'

- 'There are at least two reasons for optimism. First, as countries innovate to improve learning, they can draw on more systematic knowledge than ever available before about what can work at the micro-level—the level of learners, classrooms, and schools. A number of interventions, innovations, and approaches have resulted in substantial gains in learning—new pedagogical methods, ways to ensure that students and teachers are motivated, approaches to school management, technologies to enhance teaching learning. It is possible to improve learning outcomes. These interventions can provide substantial improvements in learning; almost one to two grade-equivalents for some students. Second, some countries have implemented reforms that have led to sustained system-wide improvements in learning.'

- 'The education system in Shanghai (China) and Vietnams today, and Korea decades ago, show that it is possible to perform far better than income levels would predict, thanks to a sustained focus on learning with equity. Brazil and Indonesia have made considerable progress despite the challenges of reforming large, decentralised systems.'

- 'Learning outcomes won't change unless education systems take learning seriously and use learning as a guide and metric.'

- 'When children have a growth mindset, meaning they understand their own great learning potential, they learn much more than when they believe they are constrained by a fixed intelligence. Societies have the same opportunity. One overarching priority should be to end the hidden exclusion of low learning.'

- 'Because reliable information on learning is so spotty in many educational systems, especially in primary and lower secondary schools, the way the system is failing disadvantaged children is a hidden exclusion. Systems should also track the critical factors that drive learning such as leaner preparation, teacher skills, quality of school management, and the level and equity of financing.'

Right to Education

On paper, India's literacy rate is reported to be around 75%. Interestingly, how is the term 'literacy' defined in India? Is it the ability to write one's name in an Indian language or ability to read and write at a certain meaningful level?

As per the census data of 2015, and with reference to the following links, only 4.5% of the population in India was university graduate or above.[3]

To ensure a vibrant democracy and prevent exploitation of the poor and the illiterate and, more importantly, to bring about equality amongst all her citizens, India needs to sincerely enforce the Right to Education Act (RTE Act) in letter and spirit to allow equal opportunities for all her children and generate equity across her society and across all gender groups.

---

[3] https://yourstory.com/2015/11/india-literacy-census/
https://www.ndtv.com/india-news/only-4-5-population-in-india-is-graduate-or-above-census-1240996

In 2002, India became a signatory to the Dakar Declaration. Following the Eighty-sixth Amendment to its Constitution, India made elementary education for children a fundamental right and included Article 21 A (Act 2002) in her Constitution, which states: "The State shall provide free and compulsory education to all children of the age of six to fourteen years in such manner as the State may, by law, determine." One would wish that the latter part of that statement should have been different for ensuring a more effective and quicker implementation.

The RTE Act was not enforced for the next eight years. It was not till April 2010, following sustained efforts of a wide range of civil society originations and, in particular, dedicated educationists and campaigners, such as late Dr Vinod Raina, things started becoming slightly visible.

Dr Vinod Raina, (who passed away at a young age in September 2013), left an academic position at Delhi University to forge the RTE ACT. As a prime mover, he recognised the potential in every child to become a creative person, and the need to bring out that creativeness. He recognised that creativity was not limited to only the mainstream school subjects, but could be brought out by a wholesome education system. Readers are encouraged to listen to Dr Raina via the following links:[4]

India needs firm implementation of the RTE with an aggressive educational campaign to:

- Make unequal societies equal to the limit possible.

- Stop exploitation of the poor and the illiterate by more

---

[4] https://www.youtube.com/watch?v=-CSDfS0qDIQ
https://www.youtube.com/watch?v=Tzk_AoNF85g

affluent and literate sections of the society.

- Breakdown the societal snobbery of the rich and influential.

- Break down the silos in which people live and operate.

- Let the lower socio-economic sections of the community come up the societal ladder via education, entrepreneurship and regular jobs, like in the west. Why can't the rich and more educated people work for themselves, like their counterparts in the west? Why do they need domestic 'slaves' to work for them?

- Restore gender equity which is a must in order to:
  - Stop female foeticide;
  - Restore dignity of all women;
  - Get rid of numerous societal ills and bad social practices/taboos/ stigmas due to the ignorance and exploitation of women; and
  - Stop mindless population growth.

All women must have equal opportunity and the skills to work professionally outside their home, like their male counterparts, instead of staying at home and serving as children-producing factories.

Given that about 70 per cent population lives in rural and backward areas, one can easily argue that more than 70 per cent children in India are marginalised based on where they are born and the family they are born to—educated/ uneducated or rich/poor? A person's background dictates that person's opportunities for undertaking high school and tertiary education.

However, due to the poor implementation of the RTE Act, all children are not in schools. As per National Coalition for Education (NCE), more than 34.5 million children were not enrolled in school in 2014.

Even for those students who were enrolled, the quality of education received was low.

Although the elementary school education is the State responsibility (as per the RTE Act), this responsibility is being shifted by the government to private organisations that run schools for profit. The current system, thus, promotes the growth of private schools. The elementary education and thereafter the opportunities in life are, therefore, monopolised by the children of the relatively richer communities.

In a nutshell, the current educational system in India, instead of eliminating inequalities, is further exacerbating the factors that lead to inequality. In a country like India, education must not be seen as business by private organisations. Of course they can contribute but the system needs to be more regulated by the government so that the overall objectives of the RTE are met without being a subject of financial affordability of the citizens.

Private education encourages formation of unequal societies with children coming from expensive private schools turning into social snobs as they grow. This dents the respect for inherent human dignity and the dignity of work itself. Humans and work are classified as 'superior' and 'inferior' based on the educational background and wealth of the individuals. Discrimination of humans based on their wealth and calling can be construed as blasphemous on both moral and spiritual grounds.

To ensure a homogenous and educated community which can respect and work with one another, aggressive enforcement of the RTE is a must. After all, all humans are born equal. Then, why should one enjoy more privileges than the other just because one is born in a more privileged community.

To bring equality across the country, the government must build more schools with adequate number of qualified permanent teachers especially in the rural and backward areas. Bright minded teachers should be attracted towards the government schooling system for working in the rural and backward areas with attractive remuneration and facilities. All teachers must be appraised regularly for their performance.

Sufficient budgetary allocation must be made for elementary education. As per the following link, India spends under 4% of her GDP for education. In comparison, Pakistan spends 5% of its GDP on education. Australia, the UK and the US spend between 5% and 6% of their GDP on education.[5]

The Kothari Commission Report (1966) suggested 6% of GDP to be spent on education but that recommendation has never been implemented.

The Indian education system begs for revamping of the whole system. Interestingly, India has an HRD minister, but not an Education Minster.

Internationally, the Indian secondary school students have performed poorly in their last international testing in science. In 2009, India was ranked at 72nd place out of 73 participating countries in Programme for International Student Assessment (PISA) organised by Organisation for Economic Co-operation

---

[5] http://wdi.worldbank.org/table/2.7

and Development (OECD) (Ref. OECD, 2012, PISA 2009 Technical Report, OECD Publishing). Thereafter, India has not participated in international tests. The assessment focused on reading, mathematics and scientific literacy of 15-year old students.

As for the university education international ranking, India does not score any better. According to the 14th annual edition of its World University Rankings (1,000 universities from 77 countries), India's performance has deteriorated. IISc Bengaluru dropped from the 201-250 band in the previous rankings to the 251-300 band; IIT-Delhi and IIT-Kanpur fell from the 401-500 band to the 501-600 band. IIT-Madras fell from the 401-500 band to the 601-800 band. The drop comes at a time when the IITs have sought more funding under the HRD ministry's Vishwajeet project aimed at helping them climb in global academic rankings.

For enforcement of the RTE, parents who don't send their children to school must face several punitive actions, enforced by a joint task force led by the education and the policing departments. One way could be that such parents potentially lose the custody of the child to the state, such as in Australia. Second way could be sterilisation of both parents to prevent them from having any more children. The following message must be sent boldly to all communities and enforced strictly:

'If you can't take care of your children and give them the RTE, you can't have them. You also forfeit the right to produce any more children.'

Sounds drastic? Well, yes? Unfortunately! Extraordinary situations warrant extraordinary solutions…and that is India, a country of 1.35 billion souls with an ever increasing population. It is a country that grows and consumes much beyond her means.

Indian secularism

An interesting article by Michel Danino, *The great secular confusion*, dated 19 March 2018, in *The Indian Express*, amply sums up the current state of Indian secularism. Michel is a guest professor at IIT Gandhinagar and a member of the Indian Council of Historical Research. The following excerpts from his article are reproduced herein as a credible account of the current state of secularism in India as viewed by a high-profile academician, one who also has educated knowledge about Indian history.

> 'India seemingly has armies of self-appointed guardians of secularism, such as those who recently petitioned the Supreme Court to turn Ayodhya's disputed site to a public purpose…But secularism in India is as enigmatic an animal as the proverbial elephant variously described by blind men: it has been all things to all people.
>
> The word 'secularism' did not appear in the 1950 Constitution of India; Nehru was initially cold to it: "Another word is thrown up a good deal, this secular state business. May I beg with all humility those gentlemen who use this word often, to consult some dictionary before they use it? It is brought in at every conceivable step and at every conceivable stage. I just do not understand it.'

The following observations, critical comments and quotes from Michel's article are noteworthy:

- Nehru's influential minister for Agriculture, PS Deshmukh is on record for questioning 'the specious, oft-repeated and nauseating principle of secularity of the state. I think that we are going too far in this business of secularity'.

- The principle of 'secularism' was introduced into the Constitution in 1976 through the 42nd Amendment, during the Emergency, transforming India from a *sovereign democratic republic* to a *sovereign socialist secular democratic republic.* However, the word 'secularism' was not defined, which is uncharacteristic of Constitutional amendments.

- On secularism, Oxford Dictionary says, 'The principle of separation of the state from religious institutions' and Webster adds, 'indifference to or rejection or exclusion of religion and religious considerations.'

- Questioning the need to introduce the word *secularism*, Michel asks, 'Was such a concept ever relevant to the Indian context, where compulsion in matters of religion and belief is repulsive to the ethos of the land? No Jain, Buddhist or Hindu king or emperor, to my knowledge, ever imposed a 'state religion'; nor was India the scene of 'religious wars,' whatever doctrinal frictions there may have been…Besides, the same Constitution which declares all Indians equal irrespective of their religion, caste or gender, proceeds, in Articles 28 and 29, to give religious and linguistic minorities the right to manage their places of worship and educational institutions.'

- Interestingly, as a counter to so-called *secularism*, the Civil Code is religion-specific in regard to social matters like marriages, divorces, inheritances, etc. which is anti-secular.

- Michel questions the validity of the term *secularism* and asks if the word 'actually means something else: for instance, equidistance from, or neutrality towards, all religions (which is not the case), tolerance (why not use this word, then?), or perhaps some combination of atheism, rationalism and agnosticism (why not those words?).'

- India's brand of *'secularism'* denies equal rights to a perceived *'majority'*.

- The word 'secularism' has no roots in the history of the land...does not exist in any Indian language (except for recent coinages).

- Rabindranath Tagore 1917 wrote in his essays on Nationalism: *'India has all along been trying experiments in evolving a social unity within which all the different peoples could be held together, while fully enjoying the freedom of maintaining their own differences.... This has produced something like a United States of a social federation, whose common name is Hinduism.'*

- Secularism has been a source of endless controversy and bitter feelings.

- Taslima Nasreen, an author, has been quoted as, *'Most secular people are pro-Muslims and anti-Hindu. They protest against the acts of Hindu fundamentalists and defend the heinous acts of Muslim fundamentalists.'*

- KM Munshi—advocate, statesman, educationist and litterateur—has been quoted as: 'The word "secularism" in India has no bearing on the attitude and conduct of

215

individuals nor of religious groups. However, it has been used as a slogan of varying significance. In its name, anti-religious forces, sponsored by secular humanism or Communism, condemn religious piety, particularly in the majority community. In its name, minorities are immune from such attention and have succeeded in getting their demands, however unreasonable, accepted. In its name, again, politicians in power adopt a strange attitude which, while it condones the susceptibilities, religious and social, of the minority communities, is too ready to brand similar susceptibilities in the majority community as communalistic and reactionary. How secularism sometimes becomes allergic to Hinduism will be apparent from certain episodes relating to the reconstruction of Somnath temple. These unfortunate postures have been creating a sense of frustration in the majority community.'

Michel concludes this article as: 'By another sleight of word, such a statement would be viewed as "communal" today. But whether this 'majority' really exists or is a construct deserves our attention. So does the important application of secularism to the world of education.'

The above article acquires a significantly high importance in the light of India's vast population, with an alarmingly high population growth rate; demographics, with numerous political, religious and social divisions; and vastly disruptive domestic and international politics, and interference from India's immediate neighbours. It also shows the direction the country may be heading into, which is not what the founding fathers must have envisaged. If the people of India are not bound together and made to genuinely identify themselves as Indian first (before identifying with their faith), this young nation, which came into being after the merger of more than 550 princely states about seven decades ago, may potentially tear apart and disintegrate due to a simmering deep mutual distrust and apprehensions that have been building between the two largest religious communities, especially following Kashmir (since 1986), Ayodhya (1992) and Godhra/Gujarat (2002) episodes.

The greatest danger arises if the majority religious community in India feels it is marginalised and discriminated against by the law and the system.

The article provides a hint about the reasons underlying a growing frustration amongst the so-called Hindu majority of the country and the rise of a new 'nationalistic' movement, which may potentially lead to a civil disorder in the country if that frustration is not addressed in a timely manner. It is not helpful for any country if its majority populations feels, for any reason whatsoever, that its political infrastructure and the Constitution discriminate against it under the cover of democracy.

A vast number of frustrated Indians belonging to the educated and professional class from the Hindu community believe that, in current India, it is fashionable to be called a secular, as exemplified by many pseudo-secular and pseudo-intellectual public figures, which practically means indulging in public criticism and bashing of the Hindu philosophy and Hindu rituals. These people add that it is only the tolerance of Hinduism that allows these pseudo-intellectuals to indulge in such irresponsible and careless gossip and get away unscathed; no other religion, other than Hinduism, will leave them unpunished if they criticise the practices of that religion.

Many young people, educated and professional, belonging to the Hindu faith, living in India and Perth and possibly elsewhere on the planet, live with a sad feeling that Hindus are fast losing India as their motherland, considering the way the things are shaping in India. Alarmingly, they apprehend they may have nowhere to go after a few years when India potentially slips towards Islam if the population of the Muslims in India keeps growing at the current rate. Recently, one such person, Chaman (name changed), asked the author many questions.

'If India cannot be called a Hindu land, where is our land then? Why is the word 'Hindu' considered to be a bad word by so-called intellectuals and pseudo-intellectuals in India? Why can't India be renamed as *Hindustan* to reclaim its roots; after all, it has been the traditional land of the Hindus; many other religions came from outside? Why can't we reclaim our land? Why can't Hinduism be the state religion of India? Why India has to be secular? Aren't the Hindus characteristically secular and the people of other religions intolerant against all other religions?'

It is true that, historically, the Hindu India accommodated all other religions because Hinduism does not claim to be the only true faith. Other faiths do claim that title, which discredits all other remaining faiths. By that logic, how does one decide which one is true—all faiths or none of them?

The social media works both ways. However, in the Indian context, social media may be adding more 'fuel to the fire' by exacerbating the already deep social divisions. The divisive forces aggressively circulate messages and videos around to polarise minds. Such forwards have the potential to influence people.

On a daily basis, the author receives numerous such videos from many people belonging to one section of the community. It would not be unreasonable to expect the author receiving similar videos and messages from other sections of the community if he belonged to those faiths. Maintaining a responsible, independent and balanced head is not very easy in this day and age when one is flooded on a daily basis by numerous messages, videos, news and fake-news; one can easily get swayed, influenced, brainwashed and opinionated— even people with high educational background.

Characteristically, peaceful people can carry out uncharacteristic and sometimes communal acts when they feel they are being marginalised, disadvantaged and taken for a ride. People must not be taken for granted; they will react. India must watch out to ensure national integration and peace in the land.

Many Indians are still ruing the Partition of India in 1947. They apprehend further fragmentation of the country if things are allowed to drift along, as they seemingly are, unless the divisive forces are prevented from causing any further harm.

The current political infrastructure and mood in the Indian democracy is conducive to flourishing of all such divisive forces. The only way to stop them from being successful is to stitch and bind the country together with a cocktail of strong internal glues and a strong external binding rope.

In the author's reasonable opinion, only a benevolent dictator, without any toxic and disruptive political interference from the country's internal enemies, can keep the country intact and integrated.

The Kashmir issue–A Myth

History revisited

The Kashmir issue is not what it is made out to be. It is more or less a myth. In a nineties Bollywood movie, *Mission Kashmir*, Kashmir has been portrayed as a 'company', which fills deep pockets of numerous individuals, groups and powers on either sides of the Line of Control (LoC). In such a case, it is hard to imagine if those individuals and parties, who have been milking the 'company' for so long, will ever like to see a normal progressive and peaceful Kashmir.

The problem, whatever it is, is not very deep or complicated either. The superficial complication is deliberate, as it serves the interests of many parties and stakeholders. The perceived and projected complication is a diversion to camouflage its script writers sitting across the LoC and mask its roots that are bedded in the idea of the Partition of India in August 1947 and the subsequent birth of the Islamic Republic of Pakistan on 23 March 1956.

The Kashmir problem is NOT associated with any religious suppression of the local Kashmiri Muslims. There is no religious suppression of the Muslims in Kashmir by anyone—within Kashmir or elsewhere in India—as is falsely claimed by the secessionist leaders and Islamists, a claim which is parroted in the international forum by Pakistan, but without any credibility. Some pseudo-intellectuals in India, including some established journalists and writers, who seemingly are paid attractive dole by the secessionists and their handlers across the LoC, also parrot this. It is basically a power tussle between the local Kashmiri Muslim politicians—Islamists versus the secular-minded ones—all of whom want to have a bite at the cheese. Law and order problems are dealt with by the local police.

The Kashmir problem is NOT an indigenous movement by Kashmiri Muslims against India. If that were the case, the local Kashmiri Muslims and their leaders would not have sided with India during the Partition of 1947 and, subsequently, during Pakistan's Operation Gibraltar in 1965. It is well-known that the local Kashmiri Muslims have a predominant representation in the local administration, State bureaucracy and all successive State governments, as well as in the State police. They also have decent representation in the Indian armed forces (eg, Jammu & Kashmir Light Infantry—JAKLI) and the Indian bureaucracy. In addition, they always have had a good representation in successive Central governments.

Since 1990, and even before that, thousands of Kashmiri Muslim policemen and hundreds of Kashmiri Muslim soldiers of Indian Army have been fighting against the armed militancy in Kashmir and elsewhere in India, created by India's enemies. Unfortunately, hundreds of them have been martyred. On 10 February 2018, in a terrorist attack on the army camp at Sunjwan, Jammu, five Indian soldiers were killed, which included four Kashmiri Muslim soldiers. A visiting father of a martyred Kashmiri Muslim solider was also killed in the unfortunate incident. In the words of a just retired Indian Army Colonel, who also happens to be a Kashmiri Pandit: *'JAK LI mostly comprises Kashmiri Muslims...some intruder might have double crossed them merely by visiting one of them as a relative... Having seen JAK LI operating in Nagaland, I have absolutely no doubt in their integrity.'*

In the June 2018 Ramadan ceasefire period, many Kashmiri Muslim policemen and soldiers of the Indian army were killed by the terrorists. In one such heartrending case, the body of a soldier, Aurangzeb, reached his home on the day of Eid festival. Thousands attended his funeral. His father is a retired Indian solider. The martyred soldier's brother, who is also in the army, swore to continue their fight against the militants.

The Sharda temple has been an important historical place of pilgrimage for Kashmiri Pandits. Unfortunately, as it falls in PoK, they are not able to visit it. A committee, led by Mr Ravinder Pandita, has been tirelessly campaigning over many years with both Indian and Pakistani governments to allow Kashmiri Pandits make their annual pilgrimage to the temple, similar to the Sikhs visiting the Nankana Sahib temple in Pakistan. Despite receiving significant support from many prominent Kashmiri Muslims from both sides of the Line of Control, and the media of both sides, the campaign is yet to see its fruition. The issue seems to be a deadlocked political affair between the governments of India and Pakistan.

Kashmir is indeed seeing a proxy war waged by Pakistan against India. It has always been fighting India—overtly through wars (1947, 1965, 1971 and 1999) and covertly through numerous terrorist activities since 1984. Pakistan's ISI has exploited the internal political power struggle in Kashmir to its advantage in its proxy war, with Jamat-e-Islami being the brain behind all this. Common people in Pakistan are also suffering due to the toxic influence of Jamat-e-Islami on Pakistan's political and military infrastructure since 23 March 1956, when Pakistan declared itself as Islamic Republic of Pakistan.

Jamat-e-Islami had not historically succeeded in growing their tentacles in Kashmir till 1983. In fact, in early 1986, during unrest in south Kashmir, many of them were targeted, along with many Kashmiri Pandits, supposedly by the activists of 'secular-minded' political parties. Many Islamists were physically beaten and the houses of many were burnt, which obviously had a backlash. Islamic Student League (ISL) and the Muslim United Front (MUF) were born and driven by fundamental Islamic ideology. Despite being routed in the March 1987 elections, albeit unfairly, the Islamists grew their tentacles across the valley, in the name of the religion, and brought in an alien culture and a fundamental Islamic mindset in the valley.

The author recalls, prior to 1990, not many Muslim youth and men would sport an Islamic style of beard in Kashmir (i.e. long flowing beard but without a moustache). However, during the last 28 years now, sporting such a beard has become a common practice and a standard facial feature in Kashmir, perhaps as mark of newly found religious identity. Educated people and their children generally prefer to speak in Urdu, and not Kashmiri. The traditional women's outfit has also changed drastically over time into a more Arabic look, with head and large parts of face fully covered.

The Islamists and radical Kashmiri Muslim fanatics may be crying foul about an (imaginary) religious suppression and calling for *azaadi*. Little do they realise that, with their newly acquired habits, alien culture and appearance, they have done no justice to the preservation of their traditional Kashmiri cultural identity and ethos. Their new Arabic names, common usage of the Urdu language and newly acquired stereotypical Islamic appearances don't support their claim for Kashmir as they don't look Kashmiris at all.

Genuine and benevolent leaders solve issues and not create issues. The Kashmiri secessionist leaders are definitely not genuine well-wishers of Kashmiri Muslims. No sane and sincere leader will ever incite the public or even think of exhorting them to rise violently against a progressive, fast developing country like India, which is also a secular democratic republic, and has the third largest Muslims population in the world. It is nothing but madness to ask people to fight in the name of Islam and join with an unsafe neighbouring country, Pakistan, which is almost a failed state, ridden with strife due to politic-religious issues of its own and battling a much weaker economy. A benevolent leader always thinks first about the safety, security and well-being of the people and does not incite violence.

Mahatma Gandhi is a fine example of such a leader. But a Gandhi comes once in a millennium.

An independent Kashmir on the other hand is inconceivable due to Pakistan's hawkish intentions, as well as the general inability of the Kashmiris to survive on their own. It needs a strong national character and immense hard work by the people to maintain the sovereignty and economy of an independent country, and both of these requirements are questionable in so far as the Kashmiri Muslims are concerned. They have shown a tendency to suffer from their identity crisis.

Interestingly, most of the veteran Kashmiri secessionist leaders have not lost any member of their family in the unrest. If they want to live in Pakistan, they can always migrate. There is no need to incite masses and get young people killed. They don't even have the mandate by the people. Many years ago, a Muslim woman advised the author, 'Son, please don't tell other people (referring to Kashmiri Muslims) that you are acquainted with that leader (referring to a particular veteran secessionist leader in Kashmir). Not many people like or support him; he has been responsible for much of this unrest and the loss of many young lives. So, if you tell them, many Kashmiri Muslims may react to you, so be careful...'

The following sections provide a historical snapshot to better understand the subject matter.

The Partition & Pakistan

In August 1947, India and Pakistan won independence from the British, following a nationalist struggle that lasted for nearly three decades.

In early 1947, the British announced their intention

to grant India her independence by June 1948. Lord Louis Mountbatten, the last Viceroy of India, however, decided to advance the date of independence. In a meeting in June 1947, various political leaders—Nehru and Abul Kalam Azad representing the Congress; MA Jinnah representing the Muslim League; BR Ambedkar representing the Untouchable community; and Master Tara Singh representing the Sikhs, agreed to the Partition of India along religious lines.

On 14 August 1947, Pakistan came into existence after being carved out from erstwhile British India. The remaining portion, now called India, gained independence a day after on 15 August 1947. Punjab and Bengal were divided along religious lines by the Radcliffe Commission, which led to intense communal rioting in the Punjab and over one million people—Hindus, Muslims and Sikhs—lost their lives on both sides of the border. The Partition was accompanied by the largest mass migration in human history of some 10 million people.

The border between the two new states, which was not announced until 17 August 1947, was hurriedly drawn up by a British lawyer, Cyril Radcliffe. Not only did he have poor knowledge of the Indian conditions, out-of-date maps and census materials were used by him. Communities, families and farms were cut in two. By delaying the announcement of the border to 17 August 1947, the British managed to avoid responsibility for the worst fighting and mass migration that followed.

If Pakistan was created as a homeland for Muslims, one fails to understand why far more Muslims were left behind in India than were incorporated into newly created Pakistan—a state that was created in two halves, one on the western side of the subcontinent (formerly West Pakistan, now Pakistan) and the other 1,700 kilometres away in the east (formerly East Bengal, now Bangladesh).

It is widely known that the idea of Pakistan was not thought of until the late 1930s. The agreement to divide British India into two separate states is commonly seen as the outcome of conflict between the elites of the two nations. It is possible that MA Jinnah simply wished to use the demand for a separate state as a bargaining chip to win greater power for Muslims within a loosely federated India.

One explanation for the chaotic nature of the Partition is Britain's hurried withdrawal from the subcontinent after the British government, devastated by World War II, realised it could not afford its over-extended empire, which it announced soon after the victory of the Labour Party in the British general election of July 1945.

Why did the British and Indian leaders not delay the date of Independence until a better deal over borders could have been agreed? An explanation could be that in the months and years immediately following World War II, leaders on all sides were losing control and were keen to strike a deal before the country descended into chaos. The last months of British rule were marked by a naval mutiny, wage strikes and successful demonstrations in every major city. In all of these conflicts, the British colonial government remained aloof, as it concentrated on the business of negotiating a speedy transfer of power.

Immediately before the war, India was ravaged by the impact of the Great Depression, bringing mass unemployment. The resulting tensions due to inflation and food grain shortages were exacerbated during the war by food rationing in Indian cities and the Bengal Famine of 1942. Widespread violence accompanied the Indian National Congress party's *Quit India Movement* of 1942, following which its entire leadership was imprisoned and its infrastructure dismantled. On the contrary, the Muslim League co-operated with the British and rapidly increased its membership, albeit still having very limited grassroots level organisation.

On 16 August 1946, MA Jinnah called for a 'Direct Action Day' in support of the demand for Pakistan. The day witnessed random violence and civil disruption across north India with thousands of lives lost. The British interpreted the riots as evidence of the irreconcilable differences between Hindus and Muslims. However, in reality, the riots were evidence of a simple lack of military and political control, as they were of social discord.

Several large Muslim landowning families in the Punjab and Sindh showed a strong support for the idea of an independent Pakistan, as they saw it as an opportunity to prosper within a captive market free from competition. The poor peasantry of East Bengal also supported it, as they saw it as an opportunity to escape from the clutches of moneylenders—often Hindus. The economy of Pakistan remained chiefly agricultural, and controlled by feudal elites, whereas ninety per cent of the subcontinent's industry and the base for taxable income remained with India. Pakistan won a poor share of the British India government's financial reserves. Despite having about 23 per cent of the undivided land mass, it inherited only about 17.5 per cent of the former government's financial assets. After meeting its defence expenses, it did not have much left for economic development of the country.

Ironically, the heartland of support for Jinnah's Muslim League lay in Uttar Pradesh, which was not included within Pakistan. Muslims from this region had to flee westwards and compete with resident populations for access to land and employment, leading to ethnic conflict in Pakistan, especially in Sindh.

Other Partition issues

At the time of the Partition, the British had to deal with those 580 princely states that controlled 43% of British India's territory and contained almost 100 million people. Lord Louis Mountbatten stated in 1947 that the ruler of each princely state should decide whether to merge his state with India or Pakistan, taking into account the geography of the state and the wishes of the population. Most princely states made their decisions and acceded seamlessly but the accessions of Junagadh, Hyderabad, and Jammu-Kashmir were sources of conflict between India and Pakistan. India was successful in gaining control over Junagadh and Hyderabad, but could not prevent Pakistan from seizing large areas of Kashmir. As a result, the two nations continue to quarrel over Kashmir.

Junagadh, with a mostly Hindu population and located about 210 miles to the southeast of Pakistan, along the Arabian Sea coast, was ruled by a Muslim prince. On 15 September 1947, the prince signed a document of accession merging his kingdom with Pakistan. India objected and demanded that a plebiscite be held to determine the wishes of the population. India also amassed troops along the kingdom's borders. The prince fled to Pakistan, and the prime minister of Junagadh invited Indian troops to counter threats from Hindu nationalists. Later a plebiscite was held, and the people overwhelmingly approved joining India. Interestingly, Pakistan still claims that the document of accession was legally valid and takes precedence over the plebiscite. This makes an important observation in that Pakistan determines the accession by a Muslim prince takes precedence over a plebiscite that was held in Junagadh. Pakistan's stance is exactly opposite of what it has been crying over Kashmir, which only proves its hypocrisy, yet again.

Hyderabad, with a population of 17 million (majority Hindu) and located in southern India, was the largest of the princely states and ruled by the Nizam, a Muslim prince who tried to maintain the independence of his kingdom. With the Partition, various disturbances occurred within the kingdom and along its border with India; tensions rose between Muslims and Hindus. On 13 September 1948, following more than a year of frustrating negotiations with the Nizam, the Indian forces invaded the kingdom and quickly defeated his army. Pakistan protested the Indian action and took the matter to the UNSC, but India claimed the matter was internal to India and incorporated the kingdom as one of its states.

Demographics

Islam came to the region with the influx of Muslim Sufi preachers from Central Asia and Persia, in early 14th Century.

As per the 1901 Census[1] of the British Indian Empire, the population of Kashmir was about 2.9 million, which included

---

[1] https://en.wikipedia.org/wiki/History_of_Kashmir

about 2.1 million Muslims, about 0.69 million Hindus, about 26,000 Sikhs, and about 35,000 Buddhists. The Hindus were found mainly in Jammu, where they constituted a little less than 50 per cent of the population. In the Kashmir Valley, the Hindus represented only about 5.24 per cent of the population and about 0.94 per cent in Ladakh and Gilgit.

As per the Census of 1901, the total population in the Kashmir Valley was recorded as 1.15 million, of which the Muslim population was about 1.08 million (i.e. 93.6 per cent of the population). As per the 1941 Census of British India, Muslims constituted about 93.6 per cent and Hindus about 4 per cent of the population in the Kashmir Valley. These percentages seem to have remained stable between 1900 and 2000. In 2003, the percentage of Muslims in the Kashmir Valley was 95 per cent and those of Hindus 4 per cent. In the same year, the percentage of Hindus in Jammu was 67 per cent and those of Muslims 27 per cent.

As per the 2001 Census, the population in the Kashmir division was about 5.5 million and about 4.4 million in the Jammu division. In the next 10 years, as per the 2011 Census, the respective populations grew to about 6.9 million in the Kashmir division and 5.4 million in the Jammu division. This means in 10 years, between 2001 and 2011, the population in the Kashmir division increased by about 1.4 million (i.e. 25.4 per cent), which is more than 1.0 million increase (i.e. 22.7 per cent) in the Jammu division.

Islamic Republic of Pakistan—23 March 1956

After coming into existence, Pakistan whole-heartedly pursued strong diplomatic relations with other Muslim countries and, based on its large population and military strength, tried to make a strong bid for the leadership of the Muslim world. A top ranking Muslim League leader of the time, Khaliquzzaman, declared that Pakistan would bring together all Muslim countries into *Islamistan*, a pan-Islamic entity. Some Arab countries saw the *Islamistan* project as Pakistan's attempt for domination over other Muslim states and, therefore, did not feel attracted to the project.

Being a self-appointed leader of the Muslims, Pakistan championed the right of self-determination for Muslims around the world. It played an active role in the independence movements in a number of countries, such as Algeria, Indonesia, Morocco, Tunisia and Eritrea, which led to close ties between Pakistan and these countries at that time.

Pakistan's founding father, MA Jinnah died of tuberculosis in 1948. A Deoband Islamic scholar, Maulana Shabbir Ahmad Usmani, who occupied the position of Shaykh al-Islam in Pakistan in 1949, described the founding father as the greatest Muslim after the Mughal Emperor Aurangzeb, while also comparing his death to the Prophet's passing. Usmani exhorted Pakistanis to remember Jinnah's message of Unity, Faith and Discipline and work to fulfil his dream: to create a solid bloc of all Muslim states from Karachi to Ankara, from Pakistan to Morocco...to see the Muslims of the world united under the banner of Islam as an effective check against the aggressive designs of their enemies.

Based on a movement led by Usmani and Maulana Mawdudi of Jamaat-i-Islami, the country's first Prime Minister, Liaquat Ali Khan, introduced the Objectives Resolution in the Constituent Assembly in March 1949, which declared that sovereignty over the entire universe belongs to God Almighty, with a core objective to transform Pakistan into an Islamic state. An Islamic republic is the name given to a state that is officially ruled by Islamic laws. In a vote of confidence in state parliament, Pakistan declared itself an Islamic Republic on 23 March 1956. This date changed the history of Pakistan, the life in Kashmir, and the wars that followed.

Two years later, in 1958, the military took control of the nation. The first military era remained for 14 years, from 1958 to 1971, the second military era for 12 years, from 1977 to 1988; and the third military era for nine years, from 1999 to 2007.

Pakistan has been the first country in the world to adopt the adjective 'Islamic' to modify its republican status. However, the country did not have a state religion until 1973, when a new constitution, more democratic and less secular was adopted. The Constitution of Pakistan, part IX, article 227 says: *'All existing laws shall be brought in conformity with the Injunctions of Islam as laid down in the Quran and Sunnah, in this Part referred to as the Injunctions of Islam, and no law shall be enacted which is repugnant to such Injunctions.'*

Indo–Pak wars & conflicts

The Partition came about in the aftermath of World War II, when both Great Britain and British India were dealing with the economic stresses caused by the war.

Since the Partition, Pakistan and India have been involved in four wars, including one undeclared war, and frequent and numerous border skirmishes and military stand-offs. The Kashmir issue has been the main cause, whether direct or indirect, of all major conflicts between the two countries, excepting the Indo-Pakistani War of 1971, which was born out of turmoil in the present day Bangladesh (erstwhile East Pakistan).

At the time of the Partition, the rulers of princely states, Janagadh, Kashmir and Hyderabad, had the choice of joining India or Pakistan or to remain independent.

The princely state of Jammu & Kashmir had a predominantly Muslim population but was ruled by Maharaja Hari Singh Bahadur, a Hindu.

The Indo-Pak War of 1947, also known as the First Kashmir War, started on 21 October 1947. When Pakistan feared that Maharaja Hari Singh Bahadur would accede to India, it sent tribal forces (Pashtun tribes—*kabailees*), supported by the Pakistan army, across the border to attack and occupy the state, which forced Maharaja Hari Singh Bahadur to turn towards India for help. At the time of Partition, both India and Pakistan laid claim to J&K. In return for Indian military aid, the Maharaja signed the Instrument of Accession to India on 26 October 1947; however, the nature of that accession has long been the subject of debate.

Following the Accession, Indian troops landed in Kashmir and started pushing the Pakistani army and infiltrators back, suffering heavy casualties initially but making significant gains over next few months in the process of the pushback.

- On 1 January 1948, India took the matter to the United Nations Security Council (UNSC) under Article 35 of the UN Charter, and complained that Pakistani nationals and tribesmen had attacked J&K, which was an Indian territory after its accession to India in

Oct 1947, India requested the UNSC to pressurise Pakistan to stop the attacks. Interestingly, India also announced that, despite the state's legal accession to India, it was prepared to conduct a plebiscite in the state to confirm the people's wishes, and would abide by the results of the plebiscite. Pakistan vehemently denied any involvement in the conflict; on the contrary, it made counter-accusations that India had managed to obtain the Accession by *'fraud and violence'* and was conducting *'genocide'* against the Muslims.

- On 20 January 1948, the UNSC passed Resolution 39 and established a three-member Commission to look into the complaints from both sides. The Commission, however, did not come into fruition until May 1948. In the meanwhile, the UNSC continued its deliberations but the war continued.

- On 21 April 1948, the UNSC passed Resolution 47 and increased the size of the Commission, established earlier by UNSC Resolution 39, to five members—Argentina, Belgium, Columbia, Czechoslovakia and the US. The UNSC instructed the Commission to: (a) restore peace and order to the region by active engagement of the governments of India and Pakistan; and (b) prepare for a plebiscite to decide the fate of Kashmir. Importantly, the UNSC Resolution 47 recommended a three-step process before the plebiscite could be undertaken.

(1) Pakistan was asked to withdraw all its nationals from Kashmir.

(2) India was asked to progressively reduce its forces to the

minimum level required for law and order.

(3) India was asked to appoint a plebiscite administrator, as nominated by the UN, who would conduct a free and impartial plebiscite.

Interestingly, the Resolution was adopted only paragraph by paragraph and no vote on the Resolution as a whole was ever taken.

India and Pakistan welcomed the mediation by the UNSC but raised objections to the Resolution. Following UNSC's mediation, the Commission amended the initial Resolution and adopted two resolutions of its own, which were both accepted by India and Pakistan. Subsequently, a formal ceasefire was achieved by the end of December 1948 and declared by the Commission on the night of 1 January 1949. The undeclared war, thus, came to an end, but the conflict remained.

Following the ceasefire, a ceasefire line was established, called the Line of Control (LoC), where the two countries stopped fighting and a UN peacekeeping force was established. India took back the control of about two-thirds of the state— the Kashmir valley, Jammu and Ladakh. Pakistan occupied the remaining roughly one-third of the state—Pak occupied Kashmir (PoK) and Gilgit–Baltistan.

As a condition of the ceasefire, the UN recommended that both India and Pakistan should adhere to their commitment to hold a referendum in the state. The referendum, however, has never been held.

A truce was never achieved due to disagreements over the process of demilitarisation in the war zone. Despite its considerable efforts, the Commission finally acknowledged its failure to resolve the conflict in December 1949.

- In 1954, J&K's constituent assembly ratified the state's Accession to India.

- In 1957, J&K approved its own constitution and modelled it along the Indian Constitution.

Since 1957, India has regarded the part of J&K state that it controls as an integral part of the Indian union. To the west of the LoC, Pakistan has been controlling roughly one third of the state. A small area, which Pakistan calls *Azad Kashmir* (Free Kashmir) and India calls Pakistani-occupied Kashmir (PoK), is semi-autonomous. The larger area, called the northern areas, which includes the former kingdoms of Hunza and Nagar, are directly administered by Pakistan.

J&K is the only Indian state permitted to fly its own state flag along with the national flag. J&K also has a separate constitution, which works under Article 370 of the Constitution of India. This is due to the state's special status under the Indian Constitution.

In 1955, a warlike situation had developed at the Indo-Pak border due to aggressive posturing from both countries but, thankfully, it did not materialise into a full-scale war.

The 17-day Indo-Pak War of 1965 (6 September-23 September 1965) was a culmination of numerous skirmishes that took place between the two countries, initially in the Rann of Kutch (Gujarat) and later in Kashmir, between 8 April 1965 and September 1965. In response to Pakistan's Operation Gibraltar, aimed to infiltrate Pakistan forces into J&K to precipitate an insurgency against India, the Indian forces finally launched a full-scale military attack on Pakistan on 6 September 1965.

Historically, since the Partition, the two countries remained in contention over several issues, the Kashmir conflict being the predominant one. Amongst other issues was the dispute over the Rann of Kutch, which arose initially in 1956 but ended with India regaining control over the area. Subsequently, in January 1965, Pakistani forces began patrolling in the Indian controlled territory.

On 8 April 1965, the armed forces of the two countries attacked each other's posts in the disputed area. In the following weeks and months, numerous intermittent skirmishes took place in the area between the armed forces of the two countries, which attracted the attention of the international community. Finally, British Prime Minister Harold Wilson successfully persuaded the two countries to end hostilities and set up a tribunal to resolve the dispute. (In 1968, as per the verdict of that tribunal, Pakistan was awarded 350 square miles of the Rann of Kutch, as against its original claim of 3,500 square miles.)

Emboldened by its performance in the Rann of Kutch, Pakistan thought it could capture Kashmir if it waged a quick military campaign across the LoC, believing the Indian Army was too weak to defend itself after suffering heavy losses in the Sino-Indian War of 1962. To ensure its military success, Pakistan also planned a resistance movement in Kashmir by the Kashmiri people against India, which was based on a (mis) belief that the Kashmiri people were discontented with the Indian rule.

On 5 August 1965, under Operation Gibraltar, aimed to infiltrate Pakistan forces into Kashmir to precipitate insurgency against India, around 30,000 Pakistani soldiers, dressed as Kashmiri locals, crossed the LoC and headed for various areas within Kashmir. However, to their surprise and dismay, the Pakistani infiltrators were soon discovered and the local Muslim populace tipped off the Indian forces about their presence.

On 15 August 1965, the Indian forces crossed the LoC. Initially, they met with considerable success, capturing three important mountain positions after a prolonged artillery barrage. By the end of August, however, both sides had relative progress; Pakistan had made progress in areas such as Tithwal, Uri and Poonch and India had captured the Haji Pir pass, 8 km into PoK.

On 1 September 1965, the aerial phase of the war began when, in retaliation to Pakistan's Operation Grand Slam, the Indian Air Force (IAF) made urgent air strikes against the Pakistani Army.

On 6 September 1965, the 15th Infantry Division of the Indian Army, under World War II veteran Major General Prasad, crossed the International Border on the Western front overcoming heavy resistance from the Pakistan forces. When he was close to Lahore International Airport, the US requested a temporary ceasefire to allow evacuation of its citizens from Lahore, which changed everything.

On 23 September 1965, a ceasefire was declared following diplomatic intervention by the USSR and the USA, and the subsequent Tashkent Declaration. The war witnessed the largest engagement of armoured vehicles and the largest tank battles since World War II. It caused thousands of casualties on both sides.

The ceasefire rendered the conflict militarily inconclusive. Despite both India and Pakistan claiming victory, most neutral assessments agree that India had the upper hand over Pakistan at the time of the ceasefire. The conflict is widely seen as a strategic and political defeat for Pakistan. Pakistan had neither succeeded in fomenting insurrection in Kashmir, which was its core objective, nor was it able to gain any support at the international level against India in relation to the Kashmir conflict.

The Indo-Pak War of 1971 (3 December-16 December 1971) did not involve the Kashmir issue. It was precipitated by the crisis created by the political battle in erstwhile East Pakistan (now Bangladesh) between the leaders of East Pakistan (Sheikh Mujibur Rahman) and West Pakistan (Yahya Khan and Zulfikar Ali Bhutto). The war culminated in the declaration of Independence of Bangladesh from Pakistan. Following Operation Searchlight and the atrocities on Bengalis in 1971, about 10 million Bengalis in East Pakistan took refuge in India. India intervened in the Bangladesh liberation movement.

Pakistan (West) pre-emptively attacked India at several places along its eastern border. The Indian Army responded immediately and decisively, and beat Pakistan back. Within two weeks, Pakistani forces in East Pakistan surrendered to a joint command of Indian and Bangladeshi forces. The war effectively came to an end after the Pakistani army in East Pakistan signed the Instrument of Surrender in Dhaka, on 16 December 1971, which marked the liberation of the new nation of Bangladesh. This war saw the highest number of casualties in any of the Indo-Pak conflicts. More than 90,000 Pakistani military and civilians were taken as the Prisoners of war (POW), the largest number since the World War II. It is said Pakistan lost half its navy, a quarter of its air force and a third of its army during the war. India also captured around 15,010 square km of Pakistan territory—in Pakistan Kashmir, Pakistan Punjab and Sindh sectors, which it gifted back to Pakistan, along with the release of over 90,000 POWs, as a goodwill gesture following the Shimla Agreement of 1972.

The Indo-Pak War of 1999 (May to July 1999) is known as the Kargil War. During early 1999, Pakistani troops infiltrated across the LoC and occupied Indian territory mostly in the Kargil district. India responded by launching a major military and diplomatic offensive to drive out the Pakistani infiltrators. It took Indian troops about two months to retake most of the ridges that were encroached by the infiltrators, which comprised about 75 to 80 per cent of the intruded area. The already fragile Pakistani economy weakened further. Many Pakistani army units suffered heavy casualties and the morale of the Pakistani forces dwindled after the withdrawal. The Pakistani government refused to accept the dead bodies of many army officers, which provoked outrage and protests in Pakistan.

Pakistan initially did not acknowledge many of its casualties, but Prime Minister Nawaz Sharif later accepted that over 4,000 Pakistani troops were killed in the operation and the country had lost the conflict. By the end of July 1999, Pakistan's hostilities in the Kargil district ceased.

Apart from the aforementioned wars, there have been skirmishes between the two nations from time to time, with some bordering on all-out war.

President General Mohammed Zia-ul-Haq

On 1 March 1976, the then Prime Minister of Pakistan, Zulfikar Ali Bhutto, promoted Lieutenant General Zia-ul-Haq, a 3-star general, to four-star rank and appointed him as the Chief of

Army Staff, which was a highly controversial move. General Zia was promoted ahead of a number of more senior officers. The promotion had political motives for Bhutto, as he saw Zia as firmly religious and an apolitical military figure, with distaste for politics. (With a similar mindset, a similar move was made subsequently by Prime Minister Nawaz Sharif, who promoted Pervez Musharraf, but only to be toppled by him in 1999.)

On 5 July 1977, General Zia deposed Prime Minster Bhutto in a military coup, following a civil disorder, and declared martial law. But, after being released shortly afterwards, Bhutto travelled the country amid adulatory crowds of Pakistan People's Party supporters. On 3 September 1977, he was rearrested by the army on charges of authorising the murder of a political opponent in March 1974. The trial proceedings began on 24 October 1977 and lasted for five months.

On 18 March 1978, the Lahore High Court declared Bhutto guilty of murder and gave him the death sentence on charges of the murder of the father of Ahmed Raza Kasuri, a dissident PPP politician.

On 16 September 1978, General Zia assumed the presidency of Pakistan. Bhutto was tried controversially by the Supreme Court of Pakistan which upheld the death sentence as passed by the Lahore High Court. Many appeals of clemency from various foreign leaders to commute Bhutto's death sentence were dismissed by President Zia.

On 4 April 1979, Prime Minister Bhutto was hanged.

President Zia was assassinated in a plane crash on 17 August 1988. He remains a polarising figure in the history of Pakistan. He is credited for preventing wider Soviet incursions into the region as well as promoting economic prosperity. But he is also decried for weakening democratic institutions within Pakistan and for passing laws that encourage religious intolerance.

Operation TUPAC

Following the failure of Pakistan's Operation Gibraltar in 1965, President Zia authorised Operation Tupac in 1988, which is an ongoing cold war military intelligence programme run by Pakistan's Inter-Services Intelligence (ISI) aimed to provide covert support of militancy and terrorism in Kashmir. The code name is derived from Tupac Amaru II, the 18th-century revolutionary who led the war of liberation in Peru against the Spanish rule.

Operation Tupac's three part action plan is to:

- Disintegrate India;
- Use the spy network to act as an instrument of sabotage; and
- Exploit porous borders between India with her neighbours—Nepal and Bangladesh—and set up bases in those neighbouring countries and conduct operations in India from across those porous borders.

Under Operation Tupac, ISI is believed to have spent a considerable amount of money in creating and sponsoring various militant groups operating in Kashmir, including Lashkar-e-Taiba.

Zia—From a villain to a hero

Kashmir had indeed changed in nine years between 4 April 1979—the day Prime Minister Bhutto was hanged—and 17 August 1988, the day President Zia died in a plane crash.

The author distinctly recalls 4 April 1979 when the Kashmir valley got paralysed after the news of Bhutto's hanging spread like wildfire after it was broadcast on Radio Pakistan and announced by the world media. Srinagar city saw many tense days leading to the day of hanging. People were apprehensive; they hoped the world leaders would prevail on the Pakistan government and prayed for clemency by President Zia, but that never came. Zia was seen as a villain and Bhutto became people's hero after he had earlier cleverly secured the release of those 90,000 plus Pakistani PoWs from India, offering nothing in return. Shimla Agreement had actually been a personal triumph for Bhutto and a diplomatic victory for Pakistan. Many major towns in Kashmir and Srinagar city were placed under curfew for about a week after Bhutto's hanging.

Widespread protests and slogans were shouted across the Kashmir valley in support of Bhutto and against Zia. As a 16-year-old engineering student then, the author recalls walking as a part of a miles long procession of students, under obligation to be with the majority Muslim students from Regional Engineering College and Kashmir University, which marched from Hazratbal to Srinagar, a distance of more than six km, shouting, '*Zia-Kod hai hai*'. Perhaps the term '*Zia-Kod*' meant '*Zia with a whip*' or a '*tyrant Zia*'.

One wonders what really happened and how did the peoples' hearts change in the next nine years when the news of President Zia's death, on 17 August 1988, in an air crash spread like wildfire across the subcontinent. The author recalls how he and his family had to suddenly abort their much-awaited three day excursion at Verinag on the very first night of their arrival, on pleas of their driver, Mohammad Shafi, who looked very nervous and pale, as he feared a massive law and order problem in the valley following the news. He was right. The family started from Verinag in the wee hours of the morning.

On 18 August, it took them more than fifteen tense hours, with risk to their life and vehicle, to cover a distance of about 88 km to reach their home in Srinagar, a distance which should not have normally taken more than 2.5 hours. On that day, the valley saw widespread violence on the roads and damage to numerous vehicles and government property. General life came to a standstill, with violent mobs shouting slogans against India, as there was a rumour based on a conspiracy theory that India had a hand in the air crash. President Zia was hailed as a martyr, a hero. It was the same Zia who was denounced and condemned just nine years ago as '*Zia-Kod*'. Can this change of heart be attributed to the characteristic whimsical nature of Kashmiris? Or could the change be attributed to President Zia's rigorous ground work in Kashmir in the name of Islam. The answer could be somewhere between the two.

Before launching Operation Tupac, President Zia must have undertaken a thorough desktop study and preliminary preparations in terms of a blueprint and readiness of the necessary armed training and logistical infrastructure across the LoC. After all, he had the resources—funds, weapons and the manpower at his ready disposal—supplied chiefly by the US and other countries—which he could easily siphon out from his country's western border with Afghanistan to the eastern border with India.

It was not long after Zia launched Operation Tupac that he was killed. In any case, before his death, as the events followed, it was evident that he had successfully managed to brainwash many Kashmiri Muslims against India and sow deep seeds of instability and unrest in the region. An uprising in Kashmir had indeed started brewing long before he died and he must have been happy about it. In 1988, there was a lot of murmuring in the valley about something unprecedented looming; a strange kind of excitement in some people about some forthcoming events which they could not hide from the general public. It only needed a keen observant eye and a sensitive mind to see that excitement.

Political instability 1984–1985

The Kashmir saga will not receive justice unless that period and the seeds of the start of the actual instability in the valley are discussed in this book.

In October 1983, a group of Islamists booed the Indian cricket team in Srinagar stadium; they supported the visiting West Indian team, waving Pakistani flags. The following year, 1984 saw the advent of violence in the valley in the form of several terrorist incidents:

- In February 1984, Mohammad Maqbool Bhat, the founder of Jammu Kashmir Liberation Front (JKLF) was hanged.

- In March 1984, there was a bomb explosion at a tourist resort in Nagbal.

- In April 1984, Kashmir University library saw a similar bomb explosion. Judge Neelkanth Ganjoo, who had sentenced Maqbool Butt to death, was attacked a few days later. A bus stand in Sopore was also attacked by militants in the same month.

- On 29 May 1984, Indian army vehicles were attacked in Srinagar, injuring five soldiers.

The perception was that Dr Farooq Abdullah, the Chief Minister of Jammu & Kashmir, had lost control over the civil administration and the general law and order condition in the state.

On 2 July 1984, Dr Farooq was dismissed by the then Governor of Jammu & Kashmir, Mr Jagmohan Malhotra. During the following months in 1984 and in 1985, the political environment in Kashmir remained unpredictable and general life was rather unstable, with curfews imposed on many days by Ghulam Mohammad Shah (of ANC), Dr Farooq's brother-in-law, who was appointed as the Chief Minister of Jammu & Kashmir on Dr Farooq's dismissal on 2 July 1984. Following communal riots in south Kashmir in February–March 1986, he was dismissed by Governor Jagmohan on 12 March 1986. Dr Farooq was reappointed by the Governor as the Chief Minister of Jammu & Kashmir.

Kashmir was witnessing an internal power struggle— between NC and ANC, as well as between Dr Farooq and Mr Jagmohan. The fallout of this struggle and family bickering was a growing dissatisfaction amongst the public. Islamists saw this growing unrest as an opportunity to exploit the situation to their advantage—undoubtedly, for gaining their own share of power and control in the valley. They were supported, encouraged and indoctrinated by hard-core Islamists—mainly Jamat-e-Islami players sitting across the LoC (facilitated and backed by the ISI) and numerous Deobandi Islamists on the ground, who had started living and working in the valley, as *halwais* and mullahs, and marrying into the local Kashmiri Muslim community.

Birth of MUF & Anantnag violence—Feb 1986

The developments in the year 1986 were a precursor to the developments in years 1989–1990.

Anantnag communal riots

Kashmir's Anantnag district saw the first ugly scenes of the armed communal violence in February and March 1986, which can be seen as the precursor to the 1990 violence. Many Kashmiri Pandits in Anantnag district were specifically targeted and attacked by the Muslim militants, instigated by Muslim United Front (MUF), a newly created group that was believed to have been created by some thinking Kashmiri individuals—academicians and so-called intellectuals—who had been fired from their work on reports of their indulgence in anti-India activities. Many Hindu temples were desecrated and ransacked.

Around the same time, hundreds of Muslims came out on the streets in downtown Srinagar, defying curfew and shoot-on-sight orders, and shouted slogans demanding *azadi* from India.

The readers must note that, the word 'Kashmir' means only the Kashmir valley, and not the Jammu district or Ladakh.

The First wave of exodus of Pandits

Alarmed by the Anantnag communal attacks and the Srinagar public demonstrations, Kashmiri Pandits lived in fear and bewilderment, wondering if and when they too would be attacked like their Anantnag brethren. This triggered the first wave of exodus of the Pandits from the valley, mostly from the Anantnag district.

Most of those Pandits immediately bought small residential plots at Udhampur and elsewhere in the Jammu township and constructed a small, basic dwelling in a timely manner.

Later, in 1990, at the time of the major wave of exodus, these visionary Pandits must have thanked their wisdom and timely actions of 1986.

State Elections 1987

Elections in Jammu and Kashmir were held on 23 March 1987, which was incidentally the Pakistan Day also. The elections are widely believed to have been rigged—by both the National Conference government in the state, supported to the hilt by the Congress government in New Delhi. Farooq Abdullah was reappointed as the Chief Minister. In the months leading up to the elections, a number of anti-establishment groups, including Jamat-e-Islami, aligned to form Muslim United Front (MUF), which actively aroused Muslim sentiments along communal lines. Communal riots in Anantnag seemingly supported that view, although some experts believe the violence was orchestrated by the so-called secular parties, and not the Islamists, in order to malign the image of the Islamists. The election manifesto of MUF called for a solution to all outstanding issues related to Kashmir according to Shimla Agreement; work for Islamic unity and against any political interference from the Centre. Their slogan asked for Islam law in the Assembly.

The leaders of MUF, who largely comprised the current Hurriyat Conference, strongly believed that they would win the elections. They liaised with the then BJP leaders in Jammu to form a coalition government in Srinagar. The election saw a very high turnout of the voters. Some estimates indicate about eighty per cent of the people in the valley voted. But, the elections were alleged to have been heavily rigged. The NC-Congress alliance won 66 seats, the MUF four seats and the BJP two seats. Syed Ali Shah Geelani won his Sopore seat.

Commentators believe that, in the absence of rigging, the MUF could have won 15 to 20 seats, a contention admitted by Dr Farooq Abdullah.

Allegations of corruption in the state administration and rigging in the election led to the disillusionment of Kashmiris, which was fully exploited by those handful of secessionist and subversive players, who claimed the people had been denied their democratic rights and, thereby, questioned the validity of the Indian democracy itself. Pakistan openly encouraged the Kashmiri youth to cross the LoC and receive arms training to begin an armed secessionist movement in the state. However, before proceeding ahead, it is important to revisit what exactly happened in the valley earlier in 1986.

The author considers it is most appropriate to make reference to an insightful article written by Daanish Bin Nabi, dated 5 August 2015, in *Raising Kashmir*, titled, *The 23rd March 1987, The Day That Changed Kashmir as Never Before*.[2]

This article provides the basis of the following sections, and the author's commentary. Excerpts are reproduced herein, some in the same verbatim in bullet points:

- Three professors—Abdul Gani Bhat, Abdul Rahim and Sharief-ud-Din—were instrumental behind MUF's creation. Prof Abdul Gani Bhat, a professor of Persian language at Sopore Degree College was dismissed from services in February 1986 along with two other professors for their 'anti-India' activities.

'I along with two other professors, Abdul Rahim of Geology

---

[2] http://www.jammukashmir.com/archives/archives2015/kashmir20150805d.html

Department and Sharief-ud-Din of Arabic Department was dismissed on 27 February 1986. Our services were terminated on the ground that we constituted a threat to the security of Indian state,' recalls Prof Bhat.

After their dismissal, the trio formed Muslim Employees Front (MEF) in March 1986, a prelude to MUF.

Author's Comment: How could the academicians have been fired without any rhyme or reason? Who made the complaints —Hindus or Muslims? The likelihood is that complaints against a handful of such academicians, who would have been observed to be networking to act against the country's security, would have been made by their own fellow Muslim colleagues only, as Muslims had the highest representation in the state in not only academics but in every state government department. The complaints are akin to how the local Muslims had tipped off the state police about the presence of the Pakistan infiltrators in 1965. Were all Muslim academicians in the valley fired in the valley? No, obviously not! It was just a problem of a few.

It goes on to prove that only a few disgruntled, disillusioned, restless, power hungry, mis-adventurous, so-called intellectuals were corrupted through money or persuasion or indoctrination by the script writers across the LoC.

- Prof Bhat: 'First, we organised ourselves as Muslim Employees Front (MEF). Ghulam Rasool Bach and Mohammad Ashraf Saraf were instrumental in doing that. MEF was formed at Prof Ghulam Rasool Bach's Sopore home. MEF took care of Muslim Employees and MUF dealt with political issues of Muslims. The constitution of MUF was adopted on 13 July 1986 at Botengo, Sopore. Molvi Abbas Ansari, Dr Qazi

Nissar, Khaja Mohammad Bhat (then Amir-e-Jamat-e-Islami, JeI), Dr Ghulam Qadir Wani, Hakeem Ghulam Rasool Wani were its founding members...There were financial, transportation and communication constraints. We were absolutely dependent on the JeI. The Jamat too had only one vehicle. With time not at our disposal, we still managed to mobilise the masses...then chief minister, Dr Farooq Abdullah, got jittery about the peoples' movement and in panic went to meet Rajiv Gandhi, then PM of India, and decided to rig the elections. For me, it was the moment when India changed Kashmir forever...'

Author's Comments: The violence against the Pandits in the Anantnag district was clearly linked with the birth of MUF. Reportedly, Dr Qazi Nissar and JeI were the main perpetrators of the attacks—arson and desecration of Pandit temples and houses in the Anantnag district. Also, why was the movement so urgent? What was the hurry? Was it all linked with the timing of the start of withdrawal of the Soviet forces from Afghanistan, and the preparation of grounds for Mujahideen to enter and operate in the valley?

The following bullet points go on to prove that it has been mainly about the power struggle between National Conference and the Islamists, represented by the MUF. Since the days of the historical alliance between Nehru and Sheikh Abdullah, an interesting kind of love and hate relationship had developed over time between the Congress party, which ruled the Centre for over 60 years, and NC that ruled the State in parallel for a similar duration. Some commonalties in the two political parties brought them together time and again. Both parties practiced similar tactics, divide and rule, to stay in power. Both parties practiced nepotism. Both parties used people's emotions, hailing their secular values and the past sacrifices of their forefathers in the freedom struggle of the subcontinent, to attract the votes of millions of the masses, which mainly comprised an overwhelming, uneducated and simple-minded, section of the population.

The NC party had somehow convinced the Congress leaders in Delhi that, without the self-professed 'secular' NC party in power in Srinagar, Kashmir would be lost to the Islamists and, as such, they were the only hope for Delhi to have Kashmir attached to India. It was definitely a political blackmail, which made the ruling Congress party in Delhi give the NC a free rope to do 'anything' to secure elections—at any cost—using any method, including the alleged rigging of the elections, which eventually backfired on both NC and the Congress. Both MUF and NC made counter claims about the rigging. Although the allegedly 'doctored' outcome of the 1987 elections decimated the MUF, its remnants reproduced a new alliance, called Hurriyat Conference, in the later years.

- As noted in the previous section, Islamists saw the growing unrest in 1984–86 as an opportunity to exploit the situation to their advantage—undoubtedly for gaining their own share of power and control in the valley. They were supported, encouraged and indoctrinated by hard-core Islamists—mainly Jamat-e-Islami players sitting across the LoC (facilitated and backed by the ISI) and numerous Deobandi Islamists on the ground who had started living and working in the valley as *halwais* and mullahs and marrying into the local Kashmiri Muslim community. Prem Shankar Jha, a leading journalist, had said to *Rising Kashmir*: 'If New Delhi had not rigged the elections, then people like Yasin Malik and Salahuddin (Yusuf Shah) would obviously have joined any other mainstream Indian political party and situation in Kashmir would have obviously been different.'

- The Islamic Students League (ISL), one of the constituents of MUF, was an influential organisations formed in 1984. Initially, it was known to people as 'Tala' party. It was renamed as the ISL in 1986. The ISL was instrumental in building sympathy and support for MUF in the Kashmir Valley and also supported it from outside. The main objective, according to MUF, behind contesting elections, was to address Kashmir's political question. Altaf Ahmad Shah, son-in-law of Kashmir's inarguably most popular resistance leader, Syed Ali Geelani, was also an active MUF activist.

- 'The 1987 elections were fought to control the assembly, not for governing J&K but to find a constitutional way out for creating international pressure on India so that it respected the aspirations of Kashmiris. Whether we would have passed the resolution or not is debatable, but the important thing about MUF was that all the constituent parties were pro-independence or pro-right to self-determination. Our primary objective was to pass a resolution favouring Kashmir's independence. That way we could have demonstrated to the world what Kashmiris wanted,' recollects Altaf Shah.

Author's comment: Mr Jha's above claim loses validity in the light of Altaf Shah's statement. The MUF had contested the elections, with strong support from the ISL, with seemingly a sinister motive—to declare independence from India or alliance with Pakistan—once they would have been in the State Assembly, which would have been detrimental to Kashmir's position within the Union of India.

One can reasonably assume that Dr Farooq's National Conference had a 'good sniff' of such sinister motives and accordingly, perhaps with good intentions, persuaded Delhi and obtained (a wrongful) consent from Delhi to do 'whatever' was necessary to prevent the MUF from entering the State Assembly.

Furthermore, as the two bomb blasts in March and April 1984, at Nagbal and the Kashmir University library, could be traced back to the ISL—the *Tala* party, the MUF had indeed a militant wing operating alongside and supporting from outside. It was a two-pronged approach to achieve the objectives.

Did the name *Tala* originate from Afghanistan's *Taliban*? There is a reason to believe so.

The earlier developments in Afghanistan were possibly a major factor and inspiration in the developments in Kashmir. There seems to have been a strong connection between the two—both ideology and armed militancy.

- Mohammad Yusuf Hakeem, then member of MUF's governing body is quoted as: 'I was one of the members from *Shia Rabita* Committee. Pakistan had no hand in creating MUF. This amalgam was totally indigenous. The root cause of militancy in Kashmir is the rigging in 1987 elections.'

Author's Comment: The above claim by Mr Hakeem does

not hold good. Jamat-e-Islami was at the core of the MUF, which had active support from across the LoC (facilitated and driven by the ISI), and Deobandi Islamists who had settled in Kashmir and mingled with the local Muslim community. The rigged elections can't be said to be the root cause of the militancy post 1987 elections. Militancy had already started in 1984, presumably by ISL.

- The build-up to the 1987 elections was euphoric. MUF's public rallies would mostly reverberate with religious slogans. Islam was invoked to mobilise the masses and attract the potential voters. Songs like *'Aei Mard-e-Mujahid Jaag Zara, Ab Waqt Shahadat Hae Aaya'* (O brave warriors wake up, the moment to achieve martyrdom has come), became popular in MUF's election rallies. Their election rallies and campaign songs became a major attraction for Kashmiri youth, who enthusiastically participated in them and went crazy while dancing.

- 'We introduced MUF candidates for legislative assembly in Iqbal Park because we had pledged that we will try our best to achieve our goal and would neither abandon our struggle nor give up on our principled stand,' says Sehrai.

- 'In my speech, I said let there be no mistake about it, I love Pakistan but it does not mean we hate India…,' says Prof Bhat.

Author's comment: It is normally expected in democratic elections that songs of martyrdom are played in election rallies to make people euphoric. Such activities are meant to sow the seeds of a planned armed resistance, leading to the potential loss of peoples' lives, other than the lives of the leaders themselves or the lives of their immediate family members.

Undoubtedly, the MUF, with support from the ISL, was not innocently preparing for the elections; they must have been up to something violent and they knew that very well. In such a volatile situation, if NC knew what the MUF was up to, was NC being a genuine friend of the then Indian government? If yes, was rigging the one 'fair' recourse to avert a potential disaster in the state Assembly? Couldn't the elections have been postponed, and the state put under the President's (Governor's) rule for a suitable time, during which all suspected anti-nationals would have been interrogated and cross-examined, and the proven anti-nationals put in jail as per law of the land? Obviously both the Central and State governments showed immaturity, and a clear lack of forbearance and vision.

Rigged elections undermine democracy and the faith of the people in the whole system. If indulging in anti-national activities is a serious crime (treason), rigging of elections is also a serious crime. Two wrongs don't make one right.

Similarly, if the rigged elections were a serious crime, armed militancy—also interpreted as 'terrorism'—is also a serious crime. Once again, two wrongs don't make one right.

The end does not always justify the means. It was all wrong.

- 23 March 1987 was chosen as the day for the elections in Jammu and Kashmir. It is a mere coincidence that 23 March is also the Pakistan Day...In words of Altaf Ahmed Shah, 23 March was an anti-India day in Kashmir.

- 'Farooq Abdullah and the NC government were

responsible for rigging. They feared that MUF might win it big. Since 1947, NC has had a formula of winning...Dulat, in his book has categorically said, that we would structure the elections in Kashmir, which says it all,' says Dr Javid Iqbal, a local commentator.

- Former chief of the JeI, Khwaja Mohammad is reported to have said, 'Elections were always rigged in Kashmir. That's why MUF jumped into the election fray to provide genuine democracy to people...Ali Mohammad Watali, the then DIG Police, was at the forefront in this *tamasha*. The army supported him in every possible way. Rajiv Gandhi, then India's Prime Minister, also gave it (rigging) a go ahead. On the counting day, our (MUF) fate was sealed.'

- Altaf Ahmad Shah says: 'The statecraft of Delhi always foresees things in Kashmir. New Delhi had all the data and profiles of MUF candidates and knew if MUF came to power it would not remain silent on the disputed nature of Kashmir. Delhi conspired against us and rigged the election through agencies.'

- NC's General Secretary, Ali Mohammad Sagar, is reported have said: 'All the allegations of rigging are a myth created by Mufti Mohammad Sayeed. Had we rigged the elections, how come the MUF won four seats? If there is any rigging in any assembly segment, there has to be some evidence to support it. Was there any complaint registered in the court of law? How was Syed Ali Geelani able to win his assembly seat? The allegations of rigging are totally baseless and misleading.'

- The rigging and subsequent arrests pushed the dissenters to start an armed struggle against India's rule in Kashmir in 1988. Non-violent separatist politics in Kashmir would take a backseat until the emergence of the All Parties Hurriyat Conference (APHC) in 1993, a conglomerate comprising of more than 23 religious, social and political groups committed to striving for Kashmir's resolution through peaceful means.

- Dr Javid Iqbal says, 'The people got disillusioned with Indian democracy and thought that democracy might not be a solution to their problems. In despair, people lost all hope in the democratic process.'

Author's comment: If there was one cause, one would not need 23 groups to come under an umbrella. Obviously there were 23 different types of groups, with their own interests and issues. One should also question how many people, in terms of percentage of the population, did these 23 groups represent? In the author's opinion, it may not more than one per cent of the population at the most. Most importantly, it is noteworthy that the secessionist leaders believe that the Indian 'democracy' has failed them and may not proved any solution to Kashmir. The last three decades have also provided that an armed movement will not provide any solution, except the loss of young lives from all sides—militants, normal citizens and the forces. So what do they want to see in India— a 'benevolent' dictatorship?

The Kashmir uprising

The script of the uprising was written across the LoC in the offices of ISI. However, the rigged election of 1987 was used as an excuse to mask Pakistan's deep involvement in the uprising at the grass root level and General Zia's Operation Tupac to avenge Pakistan's successive defeats in the previous Indo-Pak wars, in particular, the loss of East Pakistan. But, yes, the rigged elections of 1987 were used as a catalyst for a movement which was under cover till then.

Considering the history, as noted in the aforementioned sections, it is not surprising that a politico-religious uprising finally took off in Kashmir. It seemed Pakistan's ISI had truly understood the message from King Bruce of Scotland. '*If at first you don't succeed, try, try and try again*', Robert Bruce, King of Scotland, is known to have told his troops before walloping the English at Bannockburn in 1314. The idiom, said to have been inspired by a humble spider stoically weaving his web which King Bruce witnessed as he hid from his English pursuers in a cave, is particularly appropriate for the architects of the Kashmir uprising too.

The failure of Operation Gibraltar in 1965 must have left Pakistan heartbroken and demoralised, especially considering the local Kashmiri Muslim populace had tipped off the Indian forces about the presence and hideouts of the Pakistani infiltrators. Pakistan had, thus, not succeeded in fomenting trouble in Kashmir and winning the locals. But Pakistan being Pakistan, it would not give up on Kashmir. The dream of annexing Kashmir and victory in cricket matches unifies the ethnically diverse country against India. In its own words, Kashmir is Pakistan's jugular vein.

Operation Cyclone[3] brought the opportunity back to the doorstep of Pakistan in the mid-seventies. Operation Cyclone was the codename for CIA's programme to arm and finance

---

[3] https://en.wikipedia.org/wiki/Operation_Cyclone

the militant Islamic groups (mujahideen) in Afghanistan, from 1979 to 1989, prior to and during the military intervention by the Soviet Union in support of the (Marxist-oriented) Democratic Republic of Afghanistan. The CIA programme leaned heavily towards supporting the mujahideen that were favoured by the regime of President Zia-ul-Haq of Pakistan, rather than other, less ideological, Afghan resistance groups that had also been fighting the Afghanistan regime since before the Soviet intervention.

In the mid-1970s, Pakistani intelligence officials began lobbying the US and its allies to send material assistance to the mujahideen. Pakistani President Zia-ul-Haq's ties with the US had been strained during Jimmy Carter's presidency due to Pakistan's nuclear programme and the execution of Zulfikar Ali Bhutto in April 1979. But in January 1979, President Carter is understood to have said that it was vital to 'repair our relationships with Pakistan' in light of the unrest in Iran. In May 1979, the US officials secretly began meeting with mujahideen leaders through Pakistani government contacts.

As part of the Reagan Doctrine, President Reagan expanded the programme of aiding anti-Soviet resistance movements abroad and deployed CIA Special Activities Division paramilitary officers to equip the mujahideen forces against the Soviet Army. The CIA strategy comprised using a broad mix of weapons (including anti-aircraft Stinger missiles), tactics, logistics, and training programs to enhance the mujahideen ability to fight a guerrilla war against the Soviets. Reportedly, civilian personnel from the US Department of State and the CIA frequently visited the Afghanistan-Pakistan border area. It is also said the then CIA director, William Casey, secretly visited Pakistan numerous times to meet with the ISI officers managing the mujahideen, and personally observed the mujahideen training on at least one occasion.

The programme relied heavily on a close relationship between Pakistan's President Zia ul-Haq, and Charlie Wilson, a Texas Congressman. Pakistan's ISI was an intermediary for funds distribution, logistics of passing of weapons, military training and financial support to the mujahideen. Between 1978 and 1992, ISI armed and trained over 100,000 mujahideen, based on funding received from the CIA, as well as funding from other similar programs from Britain's MI6 and SAS, Saudi Arabia, and the People's Republic of China. ISI also encouraged the volunteers from the Arab states to join the Afghan resistance. Given American-Iranian tensions during the period, the US government aided the Sunni mujahideen, which was funnelled through the government of Pakistan.

Reagan's programme assisted in ending the Soviet occupation of Afghanistan. On 20 July 1987, the withdrawal of Soviet troops from Afghanistan was announced pursuant to the negotiations that led to the Geneva Accords of 1988. The last Soviets left the country on 15 February 1989. Soviet forces suffered over 14,000 killed and missing, and over 50,000 wounded.

Operation Cyclone was one of the longest and most expensive covert CIA operations ever undertaken; funding began with $20–$30 million per year in 1980 and rose to $630 million per year in 1987. Funding continued after 1989 as the mujahideen battled the forces of Afghan Mohammad Najibullah during the civil war in Afghanistan (1989–1992).

After the withdrawal of Soviet Union from Afghanistan, between July 1987 and February 1989, many unemployed mujahideen, sitting in Afghanistan and Pakistan, were systematically diverted towards Kashmir, in accordance with Operation Tupac, to train many disgruntled and brainwashed Kashmiri youth in camps across the LoC, under the watchful eye of the ISI and the Pakistan army, and send them back to the valley to start an uprising against India.

Elections in the state of Jammu and Kashmir were held on 23 March 1987. Farooq Abdullah was reappointed as the Chief Minister. The election is widely believed to be rigged.

ISI's job was made much easier by many so-called, power hungry and opportunistic leaders in Kashmir who had been (wrongfully) declared losers in the controversial state elections of 1988 and unfortunately/unfairly physically beaten by the state police—mostly Muslims—which acted on behalf of the then National Conference government, which was headed by a Muslim and mostly comprised Muslim MLAs and bureaucrats. Blinded by their personal indignation, these Kashmiri leaders were now ready and willing to sacrifice many Kashmiri Muslim youth in an uprising against the State government and India, in the name of religion, in the process blaming the Indian government for 'imaginary' religious atrocities on Muslims that never took place and spread the cock and bull stories about the lack of freedom to practice the religion in the valley. If there was any community that was suffocating in terms of religious freedom or feeling harassed on a daily basis—socially, politically and professionally—that was the minority Kashmiri Pandit community, which comprised just about 4% of the population.

The claims of the so-called Kashmiri Muslim leaders that Kashmiri Muslims had been suffering at the hands of the Indian authorities and forces is simply laughable, considering these very leaders have been feeding on Indian dole, and the free personal security and the VIP healthcare provided by India. They are even blind to the fact that India had more Muslims than Pakistan at the time of the Partition and even now has the world's third largest Muslim population. Pakistan is riddled with numerous ethnic problems—Muhajirs, Sindhis, NW Frontier, Pakistan Taliban etc. Unlike India, Pakistan has not made any substantial progress since its birth. Kashmiri Muslim leaders know very well what would be their fate in Pakistan and how much freedom they would have in that country or how much power they will wield in that country. They know it serves their interest to stay only with India, because the kind of lifestyle they have been living within the Union of India will only be a dream for them if they go with Pakistan. As a cunning ploy, they just use the Kashmir issue as a bargaining chip with both India and Pakistan to attract more funding from both sides. It is well known that Kashmir is the only place in India where most people eat meat and rice as their staple diet, generally don't pay taxes, are laidback and lead a relatively very easy and comfortable life in comparison to the rest of the people in the subcontinent. How can Kashmiri Muslims explain the ownership of their properties, not only in the valley, but also in the Jammu district, Pune, Bangalore and Delhi? They know Pakistan will not allow them such an easy lifestyle once they are Pakistani citizens. They also know if Kashmir achieves an independent status, Pakistan will not waste a minute in annexing it.

Someone was asked in the seventies, 'How many Kashmiris are with Pakistan?' He replied, 'Hundred per cent.' And when asked how many were with India, he said, 'Hundred per cent.' Another Kashmiri phrase from the seventies comes to mind: *Zuvjaanvandayo Hindustanus, Dil chum Pakistanus* (I give my life to India but my heart is with Pakistan). Can one blame them? If the Partition was created on the basis of religion, it should not be surprising that Kashmiri Muslim's heart could be with Pakistan in the same way as a Kashmiri Pandit's heart could be with India. Any Kashmiri Pandit, who was born and brought up in Kashmir, can say, 'Kashmiri Muslims are generally very warm and good individually, much better than many other people in the rest of the subcontinent; but in a mob they change, the mob mentally changes them.' It is also true that, generally, most Kashmiri Muslims were quite respectful towards their Pandit counterparts. But there was always a small number amongst the Muslims who had some kind of deep hatred and resentment towards the Pandits.

Hateful curses and taunting slogans, such as '*Battan hun byol, Khodayan gol* (May God destroy the seed of the Pandits!)' and '*Battnee battnee dodhyey muss, yeh keh kortham dal-e-gadvas* (Hey Pandit lady, what have you done to the sissy Pandit? May your hair burn!)' were commonly heard across the valley. The reasons underlying such hate could have been (a) the religion and Pandits' historical resistance to convert to Islam and (b) historical land-lordship (pre-1965) of a small section of the Pandit community.

Fatal flaws in the uprising

The politico-religious uprising in 1989-1990 (actually dating back to 1985-1986) was riddled with a number of fatal flaws in the planning.

Targeting Kashmiri Pandits and scaring them away from the valley was the biggest fatal flaw in the blueprint of the uprising. Had they been taken into confidence and assured of security to life, honour and property, Pandits would have proved to be invaluable assets to the Muslim leaders. It appears Kashmiri Pandits were targeted and scared away only for grabbing their jobs and properties in Kashmir—a movement driven by a handful of power-hungry political players.

Undertaking a violent resistance and targeting Indian forces was potentially ridden with significant risks in terms of loss of life, especially of the youth, which ought to have been prevented at all costs. Obviously, as the senior game players did not have their own sons fighting against the Indian forces, they did not mind sacrificing the lives of other people; they thought the youth deaths, which they termed as martyrdom in the name of Islam, would attract reaction from the Islamic world, within India and outside. And that was their folly. The whole world knew that, as of 1990, India had the second largest Muslim population in the world, which coexisted peacefully with others, as normal citizens of the country. Soldiers join the army to serve the country and defend the country and her citizens against the enemy; they have nothing personal against the citizens whom they are sworn to defend. It is a no brainer that the police and the army will retaliate in equal measure once they are attacked.

The uprising saw too many militant groups—some pro-Pakistan and some pro-independence—and numerous leaders of the movement, which diluted its effect. Existence and creation of numerous leaders indicated numerous interests and ideologies, some contradictory to one another. It actually reflected a struggle for power amongst those so-called leaders. If there was actually one cause, such as a rebellion against an 'imaginative' religious repression (eg in Iran) or a political movement (eg in Russia), there would have been one supreme leader, which was not the case. For example:

- Sayyid Ruhollah Mūsavi Khomeini (known as 'Ayatollah Khomeini')—a Shia Muslim religious leader and politician, led the 1979 Iranian Revolution that overthrew Mohammad Reza Pahlavi, the last Shah of Iran and routed out the 2,500 years of Persian monarchy. He was the founder of Islamic Republic of Iran. Following the Revolution, he became the country's first Supreme Leader, which is the highest-ranking political and religious authority of the country.

- Vladimir Ilyich Ulyanov (known as 'Lenin')—a Russian communist revolutionary, politician and political theorist, led the 1917 Bolshevik Revolution, spending the years leading up to the revolution in exile, within Russia and abroad. He was the founder of the Russian Communist Party, and the architect, builder, and first head of the Soviet Union. He served as head of government of Soviet Russia from 1917 to 1924 and the head of the Soviet Union from 1922 to 1924.

In 1990, if it was a genuine people's movement, at least 50% of the population in the valley, i.e. about 2.5 million people, would have peacefully marched towards the LoC. No army in the world could have killed them at the border. Had that happened, the UN and the rest of world would have immediately mediated and possibly Kashmir would have gained freedom. Instead, the uprising was defined by a very small percentage of demonstrators, say, cumulatively at the most 25,000 across the valley, which comprised about 0.5% of its population (assumed as 4.5 million in 1990). In any case, the demonstrators would not have comprised more than 1% of the population. In such a case, how could it be said that whole of Kashmir was involved in the uprising? Numbers don't lie.

On 1 March 1990, 47 people lost their lives in a couple of police shootouts. Of those, 26 protestors while killed in the army shooting at a road blockade at Zakoora when about 2,000 to 2,500 protesters, clad in shrouds and shouting pro-freedom slogans, were marching towards the office of United Nations Military Observers Group on India and Pakistan (UNMOGIP). The local police and civil administration had little or no control over the affairs of the state at that time, depicting a law and order problem. The same evening, 21 more people were killed in army shooting at Batamaloo. Two buses, carrying people on their roof tops and chanting anti-India and pro-freedom slogans, were involved in the shooting.

According to some reports, up to about 60,000 precious lives have been lost in Kashmir since 1990, which comprise up to about 1.2 per cent of the population. These include Kashmiri Muslim militants, public and the forces. These include hundreds of Kashmiri Muslim policemen who also laid down their lives and were martyred while fighting the militants. All these deaths could have been prevented if a single genuine leadership, fighting a genuine single cause, could have managed to make at least half of the Kashmir population march towards the LoC in a one-off event. So several questions arise? How many Kashmiri Muslims are actually with the movement? Is it not actually a game being played by a few players with personal and political interests to grab power and keep accumulating wealth without making much effort but at the cost of precious lives of some brainwashed Kashmiri youth?

The Exodus of Kashmiri Pandits

The rise of ISL and bomb blasts in Kashmir in1984; the rise of the MUF and communal riots in south Kashmir in 1986; violent incidents and demonstrations in the valley in 1988 and 1989; the targeted killings of many prominent Kashmiri Pandits in 1989; and the coordinated announcements from the PA systems of most mosques in the valley on 19 January 1990, asking Kashmiri Pandits to run, perish or convert (*raliv, galiv ya chhaliv*), deeply eroded the trust that Pandits had in their fellow Kashmiri Muslims in regard to their personal safety and security, which led to exodus of nearly half a million Kashmiri Pandit community from the valley.

It is true that, prior to 19 Jan 1990, Pandits had always felt marginalised in Kashmir, being a minority in a Muslim majority state. Most Pandits were habitual of facing some degree of harassment on a regular basis. If there was truly any religious group that saw some kind of religious repression in the valley, it was the Kashmiri Pandit community. Despite being indigenous to Kashmir, most of the Pandits had become used to living as second-class citizens in the state. It was an accepted way of life. In fact, in the normal course of life, many Pandits would try to appease their Muslim friends, neighbours, colleagues and superiors and try to keep them happy—a kind of reflex action for survival. The following example provides an excellent illustration of the degree of the appeasement.

One day, in 1988, the author overheard a Pandit colleague (at Regional Engineering College, Srinagar), who complained to his Muslim colleagues: 'Hey, I did not like being served my lunch in a plate in Mr A's wedding reception yesterday. Next time, in Mr B's wedding reception, I'll demand to be served in a *traami* (a large copper plate, shared by four diners) and eat my lunch with you guys.'

In the Pandit community, a golden rule taught by most parents to their children was: 'Just ignore any provocation and any taunt from any Muslim, pretend you are deaf and move straight, quickly. Act silly, if required.' This evasive behaviour of Pandits indirectly encouraged more and more indignation and harassment of the Pandits. However, despite that, they would not leave their Kashmir, their ancestral home. It definitely needed a massive armed militancy, such as witnessed in the years and months leading up to 19 January 1990, to scare them and force them to flee.

It must be noted that the mass exodus of 1990 was not a collective community decision; every family seems to have taken its own decision if, when and how to leave. In many instances, even brothers did not consult or apprise one another despite living in the same traditional, multi-storey house in downtown Srinagar area or elsewhere.

Pandits' cry for justice

Kashmiri Pandits have been crying for justice for the last 28 years, and so have Kashmiri Muslims, albeit for entirely different reasons. But what does the word 'justice' mean?

To the Pandits, the word 'justice' may carry one or a combination of the following:

- Monetary compensation for the loss of life and property;
- Capital punishment to the perpetrators of violence against the Pandits;
- Capital punishment to several self-declared killers of many Pandits;
- Peaceful return to the valley; and
- A separate autonomous area for the Pandits within the valley.

An important question arises: 'Can justice be really meted to all? Is it humanly possible that all demands of all one crore Kashmiris be met?'

Any person of reason and rationale will say that it is not humanly possible to serve justice to all Kashmiris—the Pandits and the Muslims—especially if their respective definitions of justice are conflictive and contradictory. But, for a peaceful resolution and sustainable peace, all fair and reasonable demands of both communities, albeit within the framework of Indian Constitution, must be met.

And then, after that, what should they do? They should all move on. That is the only way that we can bring peace to the valley and all her people.

Identity threat to the Pandits

The Kashmiri Pandits don't have the numbers or any strong political backing in India to receive full justice for their sufferings. As in the past, they have no other option but to fend for themselves. Even after 28 years, many people in India and abroad are oblivious to their history and their mass exodus.

One reason could be that they did not become a nuisance or menace to the Indian or the world communities; they adjusted silently and blended themselves seamlessly with their new host communities, as they had done in the past wherever they had lived.

Alarmingly, many Indians, young and not-so-young, even some ex-defence personnel ask, 'Why did your Pandit community not defend itself by arming itself?'

The answer has been:

- 'How could a minority Pandit community, comprising about 4 to 5% of the population, defend itself against armed militancy, which seemed to have direct, indirect, overt, covert support of the majority Muslim community?'

- 'What is the security for? Did we have to assume that the BSF, the army and the local police were incompetent and incapable of defending the country and the unarmed citizens like us?'

After their mass exodus from Kashmir, Pandits have become global citizens. They don't only belong to Kashmir now; they also belong to India, as well as all countries where they have settled. But now, after these 28 years, it is the Pandit community that actually faces a potential existential threat in so far as their cultural identity is concerned. After their mass exodus from Kashmir, they scattered around the globe, worked hard and reclaimed their lives back. In that respect, they became global citizens. A significant number of their youth, both in India and outside, have shown a growing tendency to marry out of the community, which has further exacerbated the potential for the erosion of their traditional culture—language, food, thought etc.

Unless a deliberate global movement is undertaken by their elders, one can imagine how long it will be before the Pandits will completely lose their identity. Pandit elders and youth must, therefore, do everything possible to retain their original Kashmiri cultural identity. They must let their global Kashmiri Pandit umbrella unify them, transcending their nationalities. As for their safe and dignified return to the valley, the onus lies with both the State and Central governments. The final decision to return or not, undoubtedly, remains with the Pandits. It must be their free will and call; they are free humans and not slaves or prisoners or animals who can be herded back to the valley.

Pandits must remain eternally indebted to Guru Teg Bahadur for their past survival and, more recently, Balasaheb Thackeray, who played a significant role in their settlement and education of their children in Maharashtra.

Jammu & Kashmir—a pampered state

Historically, the state of Jammu & Kashmir has been a pampered state, receiving disproportionately much more funds than other states and delivering disproportionately far less tax revenue. *The Hindu* reported on 24 July 2016: *J&K gets 10% of Central funds with only 1% of population.*[4]

This news report by TCA Sharad Raghavan, illustrates the special status that the state of Jammu & Kashmir has

---

[4] http://www.thehindu.com/news/national/other-states/JampK-gets-10-of-Central-funds-with-only-1-of-population/article14506264.ece

been enjoying, albeit at the cost of other states of India. Some excerpts from the news report are reproduced below:

'Jammu and Kashmir has received 10 per cent of all Central grants given to states over the 2000-2016 period, despite having only one per cent of the country's population…In contrast, Uttar Pradesh makes up about 13 per cent of the country's population but received only 8.2 per cent of Central grants in 2000-16. That means J&K, with a population of 12.55 million according to the 2011 Census, received Rupees 91,300 per person over the last sixteen years while Uttar Pradesh only received Rupees 4,300 per person over the same period.

Even among the special category states, Jammu and Kashmir receives a disproportionate amount of Central assistance. The state received Rupees 1.14 lakh crore in grants over the sixteen years under review, according to the Union Finance Ministry's data, which is more than a quarter of the Central funds disbursed to the 11 special category states in that period…Experts on the subject also say that this larger share could work as an incentive to ensure that the state remains with India.

This seeming imbalance in Jammu and Kashmir's finances—with Central grants accounting for 54 per cent of the state's total revenue and 44 per cent of its expenditure in FY16—assumes significance in light of the fact that the Comptroller and Auditor General of India in 2015 castigated the Jammu and Kashmir government for the pendency of a large number of inspection reports and observations highlighting 'serious financial irregularities' in the state.

'There were persistent errors in budgeting, savings, excess expenditure and expenditure without provision,' the CAG report on the State's finances for the year ended March 31, 2014, said. 'Anticipated savings were either not surrendered or surrendered at the end of the year leaving no scope for utilising these funds for other development purposes.' The report has entire sub-heads titled 'errors in budgeting process', and 'unrealistic forecasting of resources'.

Apart from the political reasons, there are also some fiscal reasons for Jammu and Kashmir receiving a larger share of Central grants. 'Service Tax is not levied in Jammu and Kashmir and hence the state does not get a share of the same in the devolution of central taxes to states,' Ranen Banerjee, Leader—Public Finance and Economics at PwC India said. This has led to a ballooning of Jammu and Kashmir's share in the total non-plan revenue deficit of all states. Mr Banerjee said the Centre has had to send it more money to finance this deficit.

Another reason lies in the Centre's treatment of the north-eastern and hilly states.

'Plan Grants were stopped by the Twelfth Finance Commission except for the north-east states and hilly states including Jammu and Kashmir,' Mr Banerjee said. 'Thus, Jammu and Kashmir and other hilly states continue to get the Plan grants while others do not get it.' However, this aspect does not explain Jammu and Kashmir's larger share of grants even when compared to other hilly states. According to the CAG report, 32,625 audit observations containing 8,518 inspection reports pertaining to the period 1998-2014 were outstanding as of 31 March 2014.

'Even though there might be legitimate reasons for Jammu and Kashmir receiving more Central grants, there is no call for such a large number of audit observations and questions lying unanswered with the state government,' another professor from NIPFP said. 'Ignoring CAG's warnings is a sure sign of trouble.'

As per Wikipedia[5], *List of states and union territories of India by tax revenues*, in 2015, Jammu & Kashmir figured at 18th place, amongst 28 states, with a tax revenue of Rupees 346 billion, with Maharashtra topping the list at Rupees 4,517 billion, and Uttar Pradesh (at 7th place) with Rupees 1,699 billion. The total tax revenue of India in 2015 is indicated as Rupees 30,330 billion. This means, Jammu & Kashmir's contribution was just 1.1 per cent of India's total tax revenue, and about one-fifth of Uttar Pradesh. From these figures, it is not difficult to see how unfairly the people of Uttar Pradesh and most other states of India are treated by Government of India in comparison to Jammu & Kashmir. Would it be unfair to call Jammu & Kashmir a pampered state, which takes much more than others and delivers far less in return? How do Kashmiri separatists justify this unfairness? How do we stop it?

Historically, a huge amount of money has been poured by India into the state, which has not been accounted for. This excludes numerous concessions, compensations, subsidies, incentives and cash doles which the state has received. The question is, '*Where has all the money gone or where does it go even at present?*' The answer to this question will provide a clue to underlying unrest in the valley and possibly a solution to the unrest. A common view is that the bulk of the money has possibly been pocketed by a few powerful and influential members of the Kashmiri community.

---

[5] https://en.wikipedia.org/wiki/List_of_states_and_union_territories_of_India_by_tax_revenues

Kashmir in 2018

An article by Syed Junaid Hashmi '*When will we accept, J&K Muslims are just pawns on the strategic chessboard of Pakistan?*', dated 18 March 2018, published in *Jammu Kashmir Newspoint*, provides a fresh snapshot on the current situation in Kashmir, and how Pakistan has been exploiting the Kashmiri youth in the name of religion in order to fulfil its own strategic but unfulfilled ambitions. The author of this article, a Musl raises numerous serious but fundamental questions about the modus operandi of Pakistan. Syed Junaid Hashmi clearly asserts that Islam does not allow anything that is being used by the militants in Kashmir and, thereby, demolishes all justification for using terror in the name of Islam. It also exposes the so-called Kashmiri leaders, who either genuinely misread the teachings of Islam themselves or deliberately mislead the youth by exploiting any ambiguities in the teachings and tweak them for their selfish, power-centric or nefarious ambitions.[6]

The following excerpts from the article are noteworthy. They support the author's point that the Kashmir issue, if at all, is not indigenous. It is just a play written and directed by Pakistan and played by its paid actors in Kashmir; unfortunately, religion is being used as a tool, and many young precious lives are sacrificed. This claim is substantiated by the fact that none of these so-called Kashmiri leaders have lost any of their children or next of kin in their struggle for whatever it is.

'When we are enemy of a nation which was created in the name of 'Islam', why Mr Syed…and his ilk support terror

---

[6] http://jknewspoint.com/when-will-we-accept-jk-muslims-are-just-pawns-on-the-strategic-chessboard-of-pakistan/)

and militant outfits seeking the merger of Kashmir with Pakistan, is a question which baffles you when homes of poor Gujjar and Bakkarwal Muslims are shelled along the line of control (LOC). Five members of a family were killed in heavy shelling by Pakistani forces on Sunday morning near the Line of Control in Jammu and Kashmir's Poonch district.

Choudhary Mohammad Ramzan, his wife and three minor sons were killed as shells hit their house in Devta Dhar village in Balakote sector. His two daughters are injured. A family has been wiped out. We wept profusely when family of a militant was wiped out in Anantnag district of South Kashmir and we are narrating the tale of this family during the religious sermons delivered by highly learned religious scholars in our mosques across Kashmir valley.'

The following comments and observations from the article raise a number of serious questions about Pakistan's hidden evil designs, its two-faced policies and dual practices:

- People repeatedly cry against oppression, but curiously fall silent when the killing bullet is Pakistani.

- Ramzan's two orphan daughters ask us: Why was our home shelled by the army of a nation that was created in the name of Islam? Without our father, how do we protect ourselves in these times when the beasts of humanity do not hesitate in raping even one-year-old baby girls?

- One gets perplexed why the army of the 'Mumlikat-e-Khudadad (State Given by Allah) does not hesitate in killing even those who profess the same faith?

- Pakistan has always had aversion towards all other faiths, the state of Pakistani Hindus and Christians is a fitting example. But when it guns down poor Gujjars and Bakkarwals living along the line of control, it shows that it employs religion as a tool to achieve strategic ambitions in Jammu and Kashmir. Pakistan follows a policy of a thousand cuts against India.

- Kashmiri youngsters are only just tools to achieve Pakistan's strategic goals. They are influenced by YouTube Jihadis from Pakistan and the Middle East to pick up guns against Indian security and get killed in the process.

With a sense of deep frustration and helplessness, the author raises a number of fundamental questions against the use of violence used by the Kashmiri youth, on behest of Pakistan:

- The Kashmiri youth 'should explain what in Islam justifies collateral damage? What in Islam justifies killing innocents and unarmed civilians?'

- 'What in Islam justifies killing of security forces when they are unarmed and when they cannot retaliate in equal measure? What in Islam allows killing a holidaying BSF Jawan? What in Islam allows planting an IED with intent to kill soldiers either returning home or on routine patrol?'

- 'What in Islam justifies killing young and old, women and men, children and even new born babies to achieve strategic aims? What in Islam allows a Maulana to deliver emotive and provocative lectures, which is equivalent to blackmail? What in Islam justifies keeping youngsters miles away from reality?'

- 'Where in Islam is picking up guns to liberate a piece of land justified? Where in Islam is space for celebrating the killings, be it of the commoners or the security forces? And how can Pakistan, which is not even an Islamic state per se, claim to being sole custodian of a religion, which established permanent peace in a state where even cock fights would lead to human causalities?

The author angrily makes some very important conclusions about Pakistan's evil designs:

- 'Pakistan has nothing do with Kashmiris and, if required, it won't mind dropping a nuclear bomb over Kashmir if that would be of any strategic help. The sooner those who call Kashmir the jugular vein of Pakistan realise this, the better it would be.

- A state where Sunnis kill Shias for their faith, Barelvis are after Deobandis and vice-versa, Salafis call all others non-believers and deviants; and killings are a matter of routine should not be the one we wish to be part of. An Indian state, with all its communal and caste issues, is a far better option on any given day.

- Killing of Mohammed Ramzan's family bears testimony to the fact that Pakistan views every individual living on Indian side as an enemy and every youngster picking up a gun a pawn on its strategic chessboard.

The author does not even spare the Indian government and concludes his article with a hint of despair and frustration:

'Indian state is more about winning an election and less about calling my faith better than yours and killing innocents. It will for centuries continue to be a battle between secularism and communism, right-wing and left-wing but it will never be allowed to boil down to a war between religions, fought with automatic weapons, bombs and rocket-launchers. Indian state bows to electorate, which is wise enough to understand who should be given the chance to rule and who should be condemned. Though he was hanged, it took Indian state eleven years to hang a member of the minority community allegedly involved Parliament attack. In Pakistan, the so-called Islamic state, none knows who is hanged, where and why? Poonch killing should open our eyes. And if it does not, none can save us from doom.'

Another significant article by Syed Junaid Hashmi, '*If Sajjad Lone, why not we? Kashmir's moderate separatists likely to plunge into electoral politics?*', dated 20 March 2018, published in *Jammu Kashmir Newspoint*, is equally interesting and important from the point of view of working out a mechanism to deal with the issue.[7]

The article provides a snapshot of a changing paradigm in Kashmir's political scenario, which justifies the author's viewpoint that, for opportunistic Kashmiri politicians, it is and has always been a power struggle. Their inherent weakness for power has been exploited by Pakistan, who mentored them, funded them, armed their followers and supported them remotely or not-so-remotely. One way or the other, all they want is to gain attention, keep receiving money from both sides, and wield power at the cost of peace in the valley and lives of young men. Most importantly, in the article, a separatist leader has been quoted as admitting the so-called Kashmir issue has a big (global) economic dimension to it, which will negate all

---

[7] http://jknewspoint.com/if-sajjad-lone-why-not-we-kashmirs-moderate-separatists-likely-to-plunge-into-electoral-politics/

efforts for restoring peace to the valley. What does that prove? It has become a business, a business for achieving and exerting power, which is conducted maliciously through exploitation of the youth and their religion.

The following excerpts of the article are noteworthy:

'In what could be easily termed as significant change in the political landscape of Kashmir valley, some moderate Kashmir-based separatist leaders are mulling the option of changing track and taking-up the electoral route to further their agenda of seeking resolution of the Kashmir issue, according to the aspirations of the people of Jammu and Kashmir. "If staunch supporter of plebiscite and merger with Pakistan, Syed Ali Shah Geelani, once considered elections an option, why should we refrain from entering the political battlefield? We must contest elections. What is the harm? If people support us and we are their real representatives, why should we desist from taking on these mainstream politicians?" is what a Hurriyat leader told *Jammu Kashmir Newspoint* on the condition of anonymity.'

The pragmatist 'separatist leader' is also understood to have expressed his following realisations, which reflects his vision and care for Kashmir and its people:

'Times have changed. Pakistan is not in a position to convince the world on Kashmir. We have to accept that terror charge has destroyed the credibility of Pakistan world over. And with India assuming an important role in the world economics, we have no option but to change track and save our younger generation from death and destruction. It is madness to continue with a hard-line approach when you know it is not yielding much.'

The now-realised separatist leader is quoted to have provided the following advice to the separatist political party to save the precious lives of Kashmiri youth and move forward:

'Hurriyat should join electoral politics and by winning seats from all over the state, put a complete stop to the propaganda that Hurriyat is not the real representative of the people of Jammu and Kashmir. We have to come out and speak in one voice. It doesn't make sense if we continue on a beaten track. We are losing young men on a daily basis and there is no one in the world to listen to why they are getting killed. We must change track.'

The separatist leader, feared that people may call him an Indian agent, but asserted such potential allegations will not stop him from telling the bitter truth.

- 'Important thing is message should be conveyed to the top leadership and not who is the one conveying the same.'

- 'When the organisation whose leaders always promoted the idea of merger with Pakistan extended support to a mainstream political party during the 2014 assembly elections, we have no reason to sit silent for fear of getting killed. We have to call a spade a spade. The sooner we do it, better it would be.'

- 'This is my opinion and it is not binding on anyone. I have a right to have my opinion...I live in a pathetic state yet I am of the opinion that changing track has become need of the hour. Otherwise, we would be left with no option but to sit back and watch our young kids getting killed.'

- 'Business of separatism and separatist ideology is feeding several thousand homes in Kashmir valley, then why would someone want permanent peace in Jammu and Kashmir? If peace returns, thousands of shops across the world would be shut and people would be rendered jobless.'

The author of this article also claims that there are several Hurriyat party leaders who share similar views with the above leader but the fear of gun and the influence of hard-line Hurriyat leaders prevents them from opening taking a stand. They hold secretive and close-door meetings with low-profile, but well-connected, leaders of both National Conference (NC) and People Democratic Party (PDP).

The author concludes this article with:

- 'Though direct participation of separatists in elections is seemingly impossible, given their stand over Kashmir, they are likely to field proxy candidates and then, extend all possible support to them to ensure their victory. Most of these moderate leaders who are holding these parleys have for most part of their political career in a separatist amalgam opposed the ideology and stand of firebrand Hurriyat leader, Syed Ali Shah Geelani.'

- 'They have also been too vocal in differentiating between participation in electoral politics for *Bijli, Pani, Sadak* issues and being the proponents of *Azadi* at the same time. Sources said that these separatist leaders are also likely to contest assembly elections.'

An article published in *The Times of India*, dated 21 March 2018, *Sikh youth being trained at ISI facilities in Pakistan, says Indian government*, substantiates a claim that Pakistan is deeply involved not only in causing disturbance in Kashmir but in other parts of India. As such, Pakistan is heavily bent upon undermining India's integrity by arming and abetting all anti-national elements in India, be it in Kashmir or in Punjab or in the North-East, via several traditional routes that pass through Kashmir, Nepal, Bangladesh or Sri Lanka.

The following excerpts of the article are reproduced herein for completeness of this claim:

'The Home Ministry has conveyed to a parliamentary panel that Sikh youth are being trained at ISI facilities in Pakistan to carry out terror activities in India, and members of the community who are settled in Canada and other places are also being instigated against the country with false and malicious propaganda. Top officials of the home ministry, led by the Union Home Secretary told the Committee on Estimates…that radicalisation of youth by terrorist groups through the misuse of internet and social media has emerged as a big challenge.

According to the report of the committee…there have been some developments on the Sikh militancy front. The "commanders" of terror groups based in Pakistan are under pressure from ISI to further the Pakistani spy agency's terror plans not only in Punjab but also in other parts of the country, it said.

"Sikh youth are being trained at ISI facilities in Pakistan. Interdictions and interrogations have revealed use of jailed cadres, unemployed youth, criminals and smugglers by Pakistan-based Sikh terror groups for facilitating terror attacks," the report said.

Sikh youth based or settled in Europe, the US and Canada are also being misguided and instigated against India with false and malicious propaganda, but the situation is being watched closely by the central and state agencies and they are taking lawful action as and when required…'

Kashmir Violence–April 2018

The start of the month of April 2018 witnessed violence in the Kashmir valley, yet again, which claimed twenty lives, including thirteen suspected militants, three security personnel and four civilians. What a waste! The same question arises, 'Why? Every life is so previous! Why do humans kill other humans, for their thoughts and due to the differences in their belief sets?'

The author does not believe the killed suspected militants could have been the likes of the youth that he had met and interacted with a month ago. During his short, five-day, personal visit to the valley, in early March 2018, the author was deeply impressed with many young Kashmiri youth, many of them born after the Kashmiri Pandit exodus of 1990. Their deportment, body language, mannerism, conduct, speech and tone were quite friendly and reminiscent of a distant past; their hugs and handshakes felt warm. Obviously, their parents seem to have done a good job of their upbringing. The author does not even believe the killed militants were even Kashmiris. But that is his 'belief', which may not be the truth. Can he verify the truth? No, he can't, because he was not there when the killings happened. Kashmiris say one thing, Pakistan says another thing and India reports another thing, with different perspectives of the same incident, depending upon their belief sets and interests. Which one is believable? The international media report the news as they see it, which may not also present the true picture on the ground.

Al Jazeera's Paul Chaderjian wrote on 2 April 2018: *Kashmir violence: At least 20 killed in clashes-Security forces in Indian-administered Kashmir opened fire on villagers trying to stop the arrest of suspected armed separatists.*[8]

Paul reported: 'At least 20 civilians, rebels and soldiers have been killed in Indian-administered Kashmir during the deadliest anti-government protests and fighting so far this year. The violence broke out simultaneously in several villages in the Shopian Hill District.'

Time's Eli Meixler also wrote on 2 April 2018: *20 Dead After a Weekend of Violence in India-Controlled Kashmir*[9]

Some excerpts from Eli's news clip are as follows:

Authorities said 20 people died during clashes in India-administered Kashmir…Three Indian soldiers and 13 suspected militants were killed in a series of clashes near the city of Srinagar, Agence France-Presse reports. Police said hostilities broke out while security forces were conducting anti-militant operations. Four civilians were also killed when police reportedly opened fire on thousands of demonstrators, some throwing stones and demanding an end to Indian rule…The turmoil brought much of the city to a standstill, the Associated Press reports, as authorities closed schools and imposed a curfew in some areas…

Soon after the 1st April killings, the Kashmir valley witnessed another round of attacks. This time, however, tourists were the targets.

On Tuesday, 3 April 2018, *The Times of India* (TOI) published a report: *'Stone-pelters attack tourists in J&K, 4 hurt'*. The local police initially denied the incidents.

---

8 https://www.aljazeera.com/news/2018/04/kashmir-violence-20-killed-clash-es-180402054211213.html

9 http://time.com/5224341/kashmir-india-pakistan-srinagar/

On 4 April 2018, the report was updated in the TOI as: *Tourists attacked in Kashmir at multiple locations.*[10]

Some interesting excerpts of M Saleem Pandit's report are reproduced herein as:

'The Jammu and Kashmir police on Tuesday denied a TOI report that tourists had been attacked by stone pelters on Sunday, but acknowledged that *"two tourists got minor injuries on April 1...because the vehicles came in the middle of an area where pelting was going on"*.'

Another tourist bus (no. UP17AT505) of Sehgal Tours, carrying 42 tourists from Mandya district, Karnataka, was attacked by stone-pelters in Kangan on Tuesday. Driver Ramesh told TOI the bus was on its way from Sonmarg to Srinagar. Two tourists suffered injuries from the shards of the glass windows that were smashed by stone-pelters.

Sources confirmed to TOI that stone-pelters did attack tourists on Sunday evening causing injuries to two women— Sandhya Kumari (25), wife of Manish Kumar, and Mandana Jaswal (35), wife of Ajay Jaswal, both from Uttar Pradesh.

The incident, according to officials, occurred around 8 pm at Awantipora on the Jammu-Srinagar national highway when a mob of around 100 pelted stones on the vehicle in which tourists were travelling towards Srinagar. "The vehicle was partially damaged and two persons sustained injuries. The doctors at the hospital discharged the injured tourists after investigation," officials said.

---

[10] https://timesofindia.indiatimes.com/india/tourists-were-attacked-in-kashmir-on-multiple-locations/articleshow/63597571.cms

Awantipora SP Zahid Ahmad confirmed the incident but not the location. 'It is ok (sic), but it didn't take place in Awantipora police district. It happened somewhere near Khanabal in Anantnag,' he said.

In another incident, two women sustained head injuries when the cab they were travelling in was hit by stones at Humhama on the airport road on Sunday afternoon. The NRI tourists were staying at Taj Vivanta and remained confined to the hotel on Monday owing to a shutdown in the valley following a strike called by separatists. Taj Vivanta refused access to the tourists. However, Muzaffar Baba, owner of Alka Salka restaurant, where the tourists had stopped for lunch after escaping stone-pelting, confirmed the incident to TOI. The tourists had narrated the incident to Baba.

In another incident, two buses carrying a group of tourists from Indonesia were attacked with stones near Dalgate at the Dal Lake bank on Sunday evening. However, houseboat owners at the lake chased away the mob, eyewitnesses said. A senior district officer, who did not want to be named, confirmed the incident, and said, 'Some rowdies threw stones on the bus but they were chased away.'

Vikram Kumar, general secretary of a local hotel association, told TOI 'a group of youths threatened tourists in Royal Velvet hotel at Nai Sadak and asked them to leave Srinagar. The youths had an altercation with the hotel owner who tried to stop them, following which they smashed the glass of dining tables in the hotel. A few youths have been identified and detained in Kral Khud police station.'

The above report is quite significant in the context of Kashmir issue. Some so-called leaders have been fighting for freedom of Kashmir from India. A freedom fighter is supposed to be the one that strives for the freedom of one's country. A simple question arises: 'Freedom from whom and why?' A simple answer could be: 'From the enemies of the country and for the well-being of the people.'

Who does not know that the bulk of economy of Jammu & Kashmir runs mainly based on tourism and exports of various items, such as seasonal fruit, nuts, handicrafts—shawls, carpets, papier-mâché, walnut furniture etc.? Who does not know that livelihood of millions of Kashmiris depends on the tourists? Who does not know that Kashmir has traditionally been enjoying the status of one of the world's most famous tourist destinations?

Which freedom fighter will incite the youth to attack tourists? No freedom fighter!

Does that person deserve to be called a freedom fighter? No!

Does a person who exhorts youth to pelt stones at Indian or international tourists deserve to be called a leader? No!

Does a human being who pays youth to injure or kill unarmed civilians deserve to live a free life? No!

Will a well-meaning Kashmiri try to adversely affect the livelihood of fellow Kashmiris? No!

If the answer to all above questions is 'no', who are these people who undertake such reprehensible and heinous acts of violence?

A simple but bold answer is: 'They are not Kashmiris at all. These miscreants are infiltrators into Kashmir; they are aliens. They are enemies of Kashmir who are bent upon or paid to disrupt the traditional peace and quiet of Kashmir.

Does Kashmir need mediation?

If two quarrelling parties ask for help from a neutral third party and that third party agrees to help both of them, without any bias or prejudice—with the sole aim to effect reconciliation, settlement, or compromise it is a case of mediation. As per Law Dictionary on Merriam Webster, the definition of mediation is: '*one that works to effect reconciliation, settlement, or compromise between parties at variance....*'[11]

However, if one party gets a third party involved on its own, without the consent of the second party—with the sole aim of gaining support from that third party —and that third party involves itself in the matter but without seeking the consent of the second party—it will be termed as a case of meddling. It is not unusual to see meddlers claiming innocence when challenged or when they realise they have messed up. As per Merriam Webster, the definition of meddling is: '*to interest oneself in what is not one's concern: interfere without right or propriety...*'[12]

Pakistan has been meddling in Kashmir and internal affairs of India. India points its fingers towards Pakistan and accuses it of arming and abetting the militancy in Kashmir in all imaginable ways, which Pakistan denies. India claims Pakistan, provides arms and arms training, cash and other necessary logistical support, and fire cover to the militants when they cross from the Pakistani territory into the Indian territory.

Pakistan claims innocence and says the Kashmir struggle is indigenous. Pakistan says it only provides moral support

---

[11] https://www.merriam-webster.com/dictionary/mediator
[12] https://www.merriam-webster.com/dictionary/meddle

to Kashmiris in their struggle against India, which is nothing but meddling. It also refused to accept the evidence produced by India, which nailed Pakistan's role in the Mumbai terrorist attack and the Pathankot Airbase attack.

India calls the Kashmir issue its internal matter. Pakistan wants the world community to mediate. The world knows Pakistan champions the cause of Kashmiris around the world— at the UN, and with the OPEC and Islamic countries, with the sole aim to put political pressure on India. Pakistan has spoken numerous times at the UN and other internal forums against India's occupation and 'terrorism' in Kashmir. There is a video clip making rounds on the social media which shows a young Pakistani lady, in visible pain and distress, speaking on the recent killings in Kashmir. She has exhorted Pakistani people to come out on the streets to protest against the Indian 'terrorism' in Kashmir. She has also appealed to the Pakistani government to take the issue to the UN and other international bodies, and 'liberate' Kashmir from India's terror. Is she believable? This lady's cry for justice for Kashmiri Muslims is nothing new.

Pakistan has been crying for liberation of Kashmir from India and justice for Kashmiri Muslims since its birth seventy years ago. The world has to independently decide the veracity of the truth and judge who is lying and who is telling the truth; who is the victim and who is the aggressor. Just because a party claims to be the victim does not make the other party an aggressor. The accusations must be verified independently by the judges before any conclusions are drawn.

Making allegations is not enough. Pakistan must approach the UN and the International Court of Justice (ICJ) with evidence to support its accusations against India. If ICJ has reasons to believe India is the aggressor in Kashmir, it must take action.

For that matter, even the UN does not have a clean track record in mediation. It has been found wanting on many occasions around the world in the past, as well as at present, when it has just witnessed and not done anything to stop wrong things from happening. It has a track record of succumbing to the pressures from the mighty donor countries that have had their own way and have got away with their irresponsible and immoral acts. So on moral grounds, the UN should not meddle in Kashmir and India's internal affairs without receiving an expressed invitation from India.

It is ironical, rather nonsensical and extremely unfair, that India, which is home to one-fifth of humanity, is not a member of the United Nations Security Council (UNSC). This only shows how the world politics is tilted and skewed. So how can India expect fairness from the UN or UNSC?

As for other countries—no country has the birthright or moral authority to dictate things to India or meddle in India's internal affairs. It only takes one to open the history books to read what most powerful countries have done in the past and how (unfairly) they have mistreated not only other countries but even their own. All these powerful countries have their own agenda and axe to grind in the subcontinent, so they all face a massive conflict of interest.

In an ideal situation, a mediator must be wise and not reactive. He must listen to both parties, and not only one party, tread carefully and show forbearance. Any deliberate or inadvertent bias by the mediator will exacerbate the strife and potentially worsen the situation. The mediator must remember that it is not his fight; his role is only to achieve reconciliation, make the two sides see common perspectives and try to bring back harmony between the two. Those mediators who listen to only one party and believe that party and make opinions based on what that party tells them, without verifying the facts, run a huge risk of getting blinded to the truth. They become a party to the strife, and contribute to the mess. As an analogy, when a plane gains altitude, one can see much more than one can see on the ground. One can see far and wide. One can see what lies across those walls at the airport and then the hills and the mountains; the whole perspective changes. That does not mean that when one is on the ground, one's perspective is wrong; it only means that one's perspective on the ground is limited.

Let us now look at the ground situation. Militancy in Kashmir is limited to a small percentage of people; not every Kashmiri Muslim supports militancy. People are sick and tired of strife; they want to live a peaceful and progressive life. But, as the Kashmir issue has been hijacked by several internal and external agencies which have their own vested interests in the Kashmir issue, the valley is not going to see peace in a long time, unless such agencies stop exploiting the situation or are made to stop their interference.

Do all Pakistanis support their country and the militancy in Kashmir? No!

Do all Indians see the Kashmiri militancy as indigenous? No!

Do all Indians support India's role in Kashmir? No!

It is a complex issue. Not everyone can verify the veracity of the truth on the ground. There are no black and white answers to the Kashmir issue.

In conclusion, Kashmir needs no mediation or meddling by any country. Kashmir irreversibly acceded to India in 1947 and, thus, is an integral part of India. Any issue—political, social, financial, natural, cultural, environmental—in Kashmir is an internal matter for India and India alone unless, of course, India asks for help.

India is a sovereign republic, a responsible nuclear power, a fast growing economy, and a progressive and young country. She can't be bullied by anyone.

Possible social & political solutions

Relationships are all about heart. When hearts are hurt, patience and healing balms are needed to heal them. But it takes time. Any force used by one or both parties is counterproductive; force can never bring hearts together. Mutual respect and trust are the foundation of any relationship, like steel and concrete in the foundation of a building. A relationship can survive any upheaval provided mutual respect and trust remain intact. Once these are gone, the relationship is dead and buried.

To move forward, one must focus on the present and not on the past. Kashmir, being the geographical head of India and an ancient seat of spirituality and education, with a unique tapestry of Sufi-Shaivite thoughts and lifestyle, needs a healing balm and a positive direction. Kashmiris have the right to live and thrive in peace.

Reconciliation and mutual trust-building between the two Kashmiri communities is paramount, by reminding them of their common ancestry, culture, language, food and numerous other commonalties. Focus must be on the common and not on the differences to bring the two communities together.

Religion must not be allowed to be exploited any further to divide the two related communities.

Importantly, to face the truth and lessen the deep hurt suffered by the Pandits, all lies and myths spread by some mischievous elements in the valley, about why Kashmiri Pandits were forced to leave their home, must be quashed.

Arguing about the reasons of old (chronic) disputes gives birth to new conflicts. Instead, one must show forbearance, look ahead and attempt to resolve the issue in good faith. One would only wish that historians and so-called political and religious experts could solve the current Kashmir conflict!

Revisiting history is important but never at the cost of losing the objectives of restoring long-term sustainable peace to the valley. On a positive note, what does history teach us? It teaches that all chronic disputes and conflicts eventually found some kind of peaceful resolution. For example, the (bloody) history of Europe eventually gave way to a peaceful powerful wealthy Europe. The Berlin Wall also came down in time. Similarly, American War of Independence and the civil war paved the way for a powerful America.

Kashmiri Muslims must be immunised against any further exploitation from across India's borders. Kashmiri Pandits must be urgently helped to preserve their identity and culture; their grievances must be heard and addressed.

Every land belongs to its youth and their future generations. To move forward, it is a waste of time and effort to focus on the old and aged members of any community, as they always carry huge debilitating baggage with them to settle their old scores, which plunges the issues back in a Catch-22 situation. For the Kashmiri Muslim community, it is essential that their youth are Indianised. That means the Kashmiri Muslim youth:

- must be instilled with hope; and their fears and apprehensions about India, in particular, are addressed carefully;

- are exposed to the richness of a multi-cultural, multi-ethnic, multi-faith India;

- are made to believe that not only Kashmir belongs to them but India as a whole also belongs to them;

- are made to understand that India is home to the world's third largest number of Muslims;

- are helped to develop a sense of belonging to India;

- are exposed to their Pandit cousins to discover their common roots and bonds; and

- are provided with ample opportunities within the valley and outside to develop into responsible citizens of the country, to thrive and prosper.

People's Mindset & Psychology

To work out a solution, one must understand the root of the problem. In case of Kashmir, one must understand the interesting history of Kashmir and the typical mindset and psychology of the Kashmiri people.

For a range of reasons, in this landlocked valley of Kashmir with its long and harsh winters, people are laidback and lazy. Historically, the area has seen all kinds of people, from west Asia, Asia and south Asia, from Alexander the Great and his multi-ethnic army, the Chinese, the Turks and the Persians and other immigrants from the Indian peninsula.

To survive, Kashmiris have naturally acquired good acting skills; some of their political leaders are good actors. In general, people are melodramatic and love hatching conspiracies against others for their own benefit or just for pure fun. With time, they have learnt the art of achieving maximum with minimum effort by pitting people against one another. The tough living conditions and religious conservatism in Pakistan and PoK, in general, are not unknown to most Kashmiri politicians and the people. One has to be a fool to leave the Indian democracy and a relatively more liberal, developed and richer society in India and a far easier lifestyle in Kashmir, and go with Pakistan. Kashmir politicians are not fools. They are clever and conniving. They are opportunists. They know how to cry foul, spread rumours to arouse people's sentiments, and blackmail governments.

It is no secret that India has been pumping lots of money into Kashmir; it is another thing that the money has not gone to the grass roots but instead into the pockets of many influential political families in Kashmir, leaving a majority of population disgruntled and open for exploitation—in this case religious exploitation. Pakistan and other countries have also pumped lots of money—both genuine and fake currency to train and arm the misguided youth, entice people and buy their loyalty, incite violence—stone throwing, reward families of dead militants, logistics etc. So, when money is pouring from all sides—from one side to make peace and from the other side to break peace—why should the players kill the hen that lays the golden eggs? That hen is the so called 'Kashmir Issue'. It helps many veteran players from all sides to keep the issue alive, so that they can keep milking the cow. In the words of a Pakistani friend, a barrister with a PhD, 'Every year, for higher defence budget allocation, Pakistani army starts shelling Indian posts to provoke the Indian fire in retaliation in the weeks leading to Pakistan's budget announcement.'

History has it that whenever life in the valley looks to be relatively normalised and settled, the veteran political players in Kashmir (not the common man in the street), and their coaches in Pakistan, become anxious and worried. Money starts pouring in from across the LoC through a range of mechanisms, including the *hawala*. Most of this money is pocketed by these players; some is spent in rumour mongering and inciting violence, with provision for rewarding the families of the dead, hoping some excited youth are killed in the police firing. Similarly, when violence escalates beyond a certain level, Indian administration starts pumping money, through incentives, compensation for loss of lives and 'bribe' to the game players to get things under control. So, money pours in from both ways—to 'light a fire' and to 'put out that fire'. So 'lighting fire' works! To understand the issue, one has to understand the creation of Pakistan itself. The concept of Pakistan was supported by a few rich and influential opportunistic Sindhi and Punjabi families who wanted to have good control on the governance of the new country and further their prosperity. Otherwise, Muslim League was born in the heartland of India (UP), which remained with India.

Note that most of the policemen in Kashmir are Muslims and thousands of Muslim policemen have become martyrs, laying down their lives while doing their job when they have been killed by the Muslim militants. If it were a case of religious suffering of the people, why would the Muslim policemen fight the Muslim militants? It is, therefore, not a religious war as it is shown to be. It is a power game played by many corrupt, mischievous, opportunistic, so-called leaders and politicians.

The following supports the argument that Kashmir is just a power game of a few, supported at the behest of Pakistan for political gains and water, and not an indigenous religious struggle, as is wrongly portrayed to mask Pakistan's nefarious designs:

- Sheikh Mohammad Abdullah, a Muslim, also popularly known as Sher-e-Kashmir (the Lion of Kashmir), did not join Pakistan after the Maharaja left the valley in October 1947 and Kashmir was left to its people. Historically, at that time, Sheikh Mohammad Abdullah was the people's leader in the Muslim majority state. As per *The Hindustan Times*[13], dated 8 Feb 2017, Sheikh Abdullah's note to Nehru, on 26 October 2017, saved Kashmir from falling into the hands of Pakistan. The story has been told by the then Jammu & Kashmir PM, Mehar Chand Mahajan. The meeting had taken place at Nehru's residence. Mahajan's recollections come from his autobiography, *Looking Back,* that was first published in 1963. Mahajan was succeeded by Sheikh Abdullah as the PM of Jammu & Kashmir.

- Maqbool Sherwani, a handsome young Muslim man, aged about 19, was martyred by the *kabailees* (tribal invaders from the NW Frontier Province in Pakistan)

---

[13] https://www.hindustantimes.com/india-news/how-sheikh-abdullah-s-note-to-nehru-saved-kashmir-from-falling-into-the-hands-of-pakistan/story-ob6o1p3BTQl9ZjUO-jjJJoM.html

on 7 November 1947, at Baramulla. 'They tied him to two pillars of Khan Hotel, near Regina Cinema, and put 14 bullets in him,' says Khaliq Parvaiz, a writer from Baramulla.

According to one version, Maqbool Sherwani misled the *kabailees* that he would show them the way to Srinagar; instead, he led them astray, slowing them down for days and, in the process, allowing the Indian army time to land at the Srinagar airport on 27 October 1947. In another version, Maqbool Sherwani rode around on a bike after the *kabailees* invaded Baramulla on 22 October 1947, urging them not to move towards Srinagar, lying that the army had already landed. His tactics stalled their advance towards Srinagar. The invaders were intercepted by the Indian forces, (who had by then landed in Kashmir), and routed at Shalteng, a few kilometres outside Srinagar, on 7 November 1947. When the *kabailees* realised that they had been tricked by Sherwani's ruse, they returned and hunted him down at Sumbal, about 35 km from Baramulla. They brought him back to Baramulla and killed him. His body was not allowed to be touched by anyone and stayed nailed up on the two posts for many days, a grim reminder to other people. If not for Sherwani's supreme sacrifice, the *kabailees* would have reached Srinagar and history would have been different.

Pakistan's Operation Gibraltar of 1965 failed when the locals Kashmiri Muslims tipped off the police and the Indian army about the presence of Pakistani infiltrators, who were actually Pakistani army soldiers in civil dress.

What now?

The solution for Kashmir lies in the solution for India. *'Fix India to fix Kashmir'*—not in isolation. In addition to what has been discussed above, the Government of India must call the bluff. As noted previously, Kashmiri Muslim leaders don't want to an independent Kashmir or go with Pakistan, they are just milking the cash cow.

The so-called Kashmiri Muslim leaders know that, in an independent Kashmir, they will have to work very hard for nation-building and sustain their independence, which they cannot. They are not used to working hard. They have been pampered by India over decades and have been enjoying free facilities and money from India, Pakistan, Saudi Arabia and other countries, albeit at the cost of the Kashmiri Muslim masses, who have been exploited by them in the name of religion. They know, if they become independent, Pakistan will sooner or later annex them and take away their sovereignty, if any.

The so-called leaders also know that, in a scenario where Kashmir joins Pakistan, that country will reduce their status to anonymity. Pakistan wants the territory to address its potential water problem, and not for any love for the people. The world knows how Pakistan has treated the people in the PoK since 1947 and what kind of sovereignty or development—infrastructural and educational—the PoK has.

All corrupt individuals and organisations within the country, Kashmir included, who have been acting against the integrity and progress of India and the greater well-being of the people, must be dealt with sternly in one massive countrywide operation (Operation Clean-up) after the imposition of

Emergency in the country or when a benevolent dictator takes over, as discussed in the next chapter.

All proven mischievous individuals and enemies of the country and the J&K state, who misuse their rights provided by the Constitution of India and the current Indian democracy, and incite violence by provoking the citizens of the country under the garb of freedom of speech, must be rounded up and transported to the Andaman and Nicobar islands on a one-way ticket and settled there for life. The imposition of Emergency for a certain period will take care of the country's law and order. As part of the Operation Clean-up, the Executive Council will need to engage the international community and get the important international players on board, with assurance of fair and proportionate treatment of those rotten eggs and preservation of basic human rights of all other citizens of the country.

Alternative Systems of Governance

To a new system

India needs a total change in its system of governance, as argued by the author in the preceding chapters. The traditional values of the country from the past times—patience, mutual respect, tolerance, spirituality etc. (when the subcontinent was ruled by hundreds of kings and princes, some brutal)—have fast eroded after 1947, with the erosion process exacerbated by a rapidly increasing population. As a consequence, people in 2018 are much more materialistic and dissatisfied; angrier and unhappier, more selfish and insensitive, and more brutal than their ancestors a hundred years ago.

The new system must rein in the unaccountable and disproportionate power, authority and wealth enjoyed by numerous individuals and organisations in the country who have been flourishing by mainly exploiting the poverty, ignorance and illiteracy of the unprivileged masses, which form the bulk of the Indian community as a whole. Wealth and power must be spread out to close the gap between the privileged and underprivileged sections of the society so that the net happiness and the well-being of the whole community increases. Societies where such gaps are wide live within an environment of unhappiness. The reason being the people who are privileged and own disproportionate wealth constantly live with a feeling of threat and potential loss. They keep striving for more and more of what they already have, whilst constantly suffering from a fear of losing it to those who don't have or potentially getting killed by their rivals or by the poor people in need. That is why the very rich and influential are always surrounded by their personal security personnel. The common man is not allowed to come near them.

It is paradoxical that the so-called powerful people are not actually powerful at all; they are weak and timid and, therefore, need bodyguards, as they feel insecure. Their houses are equipped with the state-of-the-art security systems. Their constant worries cost them their sleep and good health. The best lawyers in the country are on their payroll. On the other hand, people who don't have wealth or power keep striving to get them. If they don't succeed, they become unhappier and if they do, they want more and more of what others have; they compete in a rat race and the cycle continues. In the end, no one is happy.

Materialism thrills and brings short-term happiness but no internal peace, contentment and sustainable joy. Likewise, capitalism kills the net happiness of the country. Some militarily powerful democracies in the world where capitalism is practiced are not amongst the happiest nations in the world. For example, the capitalistic US, which ranks low on Happiness Index and where it is hard to take away the gun from the community despite public shootings on a regular basis.

Democracy, as is known and practised, is based on populism and populism is indirectly based on majoritarianism. A vital question arises; 'Is it possible that majoritarianism will serve the interests of all the people in a democratic system?' An obvious and logical answer would be, 'No!' Then is it ethical and moral to disregard the interests of the minority, whose interest tends to be overlooked in a democratic system?

John Stuart Mill & India 2018

John Stuart Mill[1] (May 1806–May 1873) wrote many books. Many of his books have direct relevance to India in 2018.

Mill, arguably the most influential English language philosopher of the nineteenth century, was also a naturalist, a utilitarian and a liberal. His famous works include: *System of Logic* (1843), *Principles of Political Economy*(1848), *On Liberty* (1859), *Utilitarianism*[2] (1861) and *An Examination of Sir William Hamilton's Philosophy* (1865). Towards the end of his life, he provided a vivid and moving description of his own life in *Autobiography* (1873).

Mill's works have significance in terms of the time he lived in and wrote his books. The world had just seen the American

---

[1] https://plato.stanford.edu/entries/mill/
[2] https://www.utilitarianism.com/jsmill.htm

war of Independence (1775–1783) and the French Revolution (1789–1799), which saw uprising against King Louis XVI (1754–1793) after two decades of unrest among peasants and the urban poor, mainly due to poor cereal harvests, drought, cattle disease and skyrocketing bread prices. In reaction to the taxes imposed by the regime, people violently expressed their desperation and resentment by rioting, looting and striking.

Mill was an administrator in the East India Company; he retired soon after the Mutiny of 1857. He was educated by his father. By the age of twelve, he was a competent logician and a well-trained economist by sixteen. His nervous breakdown, when he was twenty, made him to believe that more was needed in life than devotion to the public good and an analytically sharp intellect. Thereafter, till he died, he persuaded the British public about the necessity to adopt a scientific approach to understand social, political and economic changes, whilst not ignoring the poetic imaginations and insights of writers.

In his book, *System of Logic* (1843), Mill does not only discuss the importance of logic, but also of a scientific approach to deal with both social and natural phenomena. Besides formal logic, which he termed as '*the logic of consistency*', he believed that there was a *logic of proof*— a logic that shows how evidence proved or tended to prove the conclusions that one draws from the evidence. That led him to the analysis of causation and to inductive reasoning.

In his book, *Principles of Political Economy* (1848), Mill reflected on the difference between what economics measured and what humans really valued. Most importantly, he argued that '*we should sacrifice economic growth for the sake of the environment,* and should limit population as much to give *ourselves breathing space in order to fend off the risk of starvation for the overburdened poor'*. This philosophy is most pertinent to the modern day India—its issues and their solution. It is also noteworthy that Mill believed that *'conventional economic analysis could not prove that socialism was unworkable'*, whilst suggesting his preference for an economy of worker-owned cooperatives. This book has the most relevance to India in 2018.

Mill's book, *Utilitarianism* (1861), remains the classic defence of the view that *'we ought to aim at maximising the welfare of all sentient creatures, and that welfare consists of their happiness.'* Mill's defence of the view that we ought to pursue happiness has been the object of savage attack by others. He insisted happiness was to be assessed not merely by quantity but by quality. His doctrine *'a dissatisfied Socrates is not only better than a satisfied fool, but somehow happier, too'*, has puzzled generations.

Mill's book, *On Liberty* (1859), aroused great controversy in his lifetime. Mill and his wife, Harriet Taylor, constantly expressed in their letters to one another that they lived in a society where bold and adventurous individuals were becoming all too rare. Some critics have thought that Mill was frightened by the prospect of a mass democracy in which working-class opinion would be oppressive and perhaps violent. It was a fear he had picked up from reading Alexis de Tocqueville's *Democracy in America*. At that time, America was a prosperous middle-class society, and Mill feared that it was also a society that cared nothing for individual liberty.

Mill lays down "one very simple principle" to govern the use of coercion in society; by coercion he means both legal penalties and the operation of public opinion; it is that we may only coerce others in self-defence—either to defend ourselves, or to defend others from harm. Crucially, this rules out paternalistic interventions to save people from themselves, and ideal interventions to make people behave "better". It has long puzzled critics to explain how a utilitarian can subscribe to such a principle of self-restraint. In essence, Mill argues that, only by adopting the self-restraint principle, can we seek out the truth, experience the truth as "our own", and fully develop individual selves.

Mill's book, *The Subjection of Women* (1869), advocates equality for women and the liberal feminism. It makes a case that, 'if freedom is a good for men, it is for women...If women have different natures, the only way to discover what they are is by experiment, and that requires that women should have access to everything to which men have access. Only after as many centuries of freedom as there have been centuries of oppression will we really know what our natures are.

Mill's book, *Three Essays on Religion* (1874) was deliberately not published until after his death. He argued that 'it is impossible that the universe is governed by an omnipotent and loving God, but not unlikely that a less omnipotent benign force is at work in the world.'

The early 1800s was the time of change, called the Romantic era, which was characterised by intense political, social, and cultural upheavals. The Romantic era is conventionally believed to have begun in 1789 with the French Revolution and ended in 1832 with the passing of the Great Reform Bill. External events (eg the French Revolution) were internalised by English writers and poets in Romantic literature as a part of the debates on issues in English politics (American Revolution and the Irish Uprising of 1798).

Famous poets of the Romantic period, such as William Wordsworth, Samuel Taylor Coleridge, and Robert Southey, sympathised with the French Revolution. Wordsworth used satiric poetry to deal with the trauma of the Revolution's bloody transformation. Later, Byron and Shelley also sympathised with the principles of individuality and equality embodied by the Revolution and adopted these principles to criticise the English government of the time. Their poetry also turned towards other European conflicts of that time. Byron's opening lines (On Freedom), '*When a man hath no freedom to fight for at home, let him combat for that of his neighbours,*' suggest his involvement in the European conflicts offered him a substitute for a lack of efficacy in the British political reform.

The age of Romanticism was also a move away from industrialisation. People wanted to just live a good life, a free and just life, with liberty and equality for all.

As India is currently witnessing times similar to what Mill and the other poets witnessed in England about 200 years ago, in early to mid-1800s, in terms of effects of industrialisation, environmental issues, population, gender inequality, the concerns of these writers is very much relevant to India.

Indians are not yet evolved to respect the ethos and spirit of democracy, which was thrust upon them in 1947 by some English-educated politicians, who are long gone. The country is still backward and poor. The masses are illiterate; what do they know about 'democracy'? All they do is work to survive somehow and breed.

In 2018, India lives neither with Western refinement, nor

with Eastern traditions. The last seven decades have produced a mongrel society, which is both chaotic and lost, just consuming everything that comes its way, with scant care for the future generations. The country needs God to mind it, but God can't come down on the earth as a human being. So the country needs a human being who will think and work as God, so he or she has to be a dictator. As one knows, 'absolute power corrupts absolutely', so all necessary checks and balances will need be identified and introduced at every level of governance. Therefore, the dictator must be both benevolent and visionary, and stay in the chair for at least one generation (25 years) to first decelerate her rapid descent, stabilise her and to finally make her cruise with good health.

What after dictatorship? Return of Indian democracy? No!

Sociocracy, which aims to satisfy the core objectives of democracy, is a much more suitable alternative to dictatorship in the long-term. But, as sociocracy cannot be implemented overnight, a transitional system will be required to move from one system to the other. A benevolent dictatorship in the country will provide the transition.

Sociocracy

The term 'sociocracy' was coined in 1851 by Auguste Comte, a French philosopher, as a parallel term to 'sociology'. He believed that a government led by sociologists would use scientific methods to meet the needs of ALL people, and not just the people from the ruling class. Later, in 1881, Lester Frank Ward, an American sociologist, also advocated for sociocracy to replace the political competition created by the majority vote.

Sociocracy[3] is a governing system that aims to promote a harmonious working and social environment within an organisation via the introduction of a decision-making process within that organisation that is driven only by consent between the responsible members which, in turn, results in increase in the overall productivity of the organisation.

As per wikipedia: *'Sociocracy is a governance method that makes collaboration, self-organisation, and distributed authority practical and effective. A deeper democracy uses the methods of sociocracy to achieve the values of democracy—transparency, inclusiveness, and accountability.'*[4]

The website adds: 'Sociocracy has specific methods and practices for ensuring that decision-making and power are linked and shared. Democracy was originally revolutionary by allowing the common citizen to make decisions using majority vote. But it has no structure for ensuring that those decisions are implemented. A sociocratic system of communications and control would ensure better decision-making and give more power to democratic values.'

In simple terms, in a sociocratic system, therefore, people who know one other and are entrusted to take decisions, don't use a majority vote but instead carry out the decision-making process by consent and consensus, unlike democracy.

The Boeke Sociocratic Model

Kees Boeke (Cornelius Boeke, 25 September 1884–3 July 1966) was a Dutch reformist, educator, Quaker missionary

---

[3]   https://en.wikipedia.org/wiki/Sociocracy
[4]   http://www.sociocracy.info/category/history-theory/decisions-power/

and pacifist. He was married to Beatrice 'Betty' Cadbury, an English educator. Being a pacifist, Boeke spoke against war with Germany, for which he and Betty were expelled from England when the war started.

He returned to the Netherlands, where the couple settled in his hometown, Bilthoven and continued their peace work. Boeke was arrested by the Germans during the occupation. He continued to write about the abuses of power that were becoming evident in democracies during his time. His most well-known essay is: *Sociocracy: Democracy as It Might Be.*

In 1926, Boeke and Betty Cadbury founded the first sociocratic organisation when they started a school called Children's Community Workshop, which was run as a workshop based on the egalitarian principles of the Quakers. Reportedly, the school still exists and functions according to its founding principles.

At the school, the students, the staff and the teachers were regarded as equals and equally participated in the running of the school and the educational programme. Students, instead of being dictated to, were allowed and encouraged to contribute their ideas, through educational reforms, a process that he termed 'sociocracy'. Boeke regarded schools as workshops, with students and teachers as co-workers. Decision making was conducted by consensus, whereby no action was taken until everyone involved in the decision-making agreed.

At the school, approximately 400 students and teachers would make the decisions together, in weekly talk-overs, and find mutually acceptable solutions. The individuals in each group would then agree to abide by the decision.

Boeke defined the following three fundamental rules:

- That the interests of all members must be considered and the individual must respect the interests of the whole;

- No action should be taken without a solution that everyone could accept; and

- All members must accept these decisions when unanimously made.

For functionality, some important features of the model were:

- If a group could not make a decision, the decision would be made by a *higher level* of representatives chosen by each group.

- The size of a decision-making group should be limited to forty, with smaller committees of five to six members making *detailed decisions*. For larger groups, a structure of representatives would be chosen by these groups to make the decisions.

For the sociocratic process to be effective, this Boeke model emphasises the role of the trust factor between all decision-making members. It pre-supposes that mutual trust will be built over time as long as this method of decision-making is used. As an extrapolation, when the model is applied to civic governance, citizens *'would be forced to take an interest in those who live close by.'* Only when people learn to trust one another in their neighbourhood, the next higher level of sociocratic governance can be established.

Boeke said: "Everything depends on a new spirit breaking through among men. May it be that, after the many centuries of fear, suspicion and hate, more and more a spirit of reconciliation and mutual trust will spread abroad. The constant practice of the art of sociocracy and of the education necessary for it seem to be the best way in which to further this spirit, upon which the real solution of all world problems depends.'

The Enderberg model

In the mid-60s, Gerard Endenburg, a Dutch electrical engineer and entrepreneur, a former student of Boeke and influenced by him, started testing and modifying his application of Boeke's principles. By the mid 70s, he had started using the sociocratic method to run his own company.

In 1978, Endenburg and his colleague, Annewiek Reijmer, founded the *Sociocratisch Centrum* (Sociocratic Centre) in Rotterdam, and began working with other organisations in the Netherlands in adopting the sociocratic system of organisation. In 1992, Endenburg obtained a doctoral degree from the University of Twente, based on his dissertation, *Sociocratieals Sociaal Ontwerp*, which was later translated and published in English as 'Sociocracy as Social Design'.

Endenburg aimed to introduce an environment of cooperation and harmony in his business that he had earlier experienced as a student in Boeke's school. He recognised that, with a diverse and changing workforce in his company, he couldn't wait for his workers to trust one other before they could make decisions, as required by a sociocratic organisational system. As a solution, he used his understanding of physics, cybernetics, and systems to further develop the social, political, and educational theories put forth by Auguste Comte, Lester Frank Ward and Kees Boeke. In essence, he applied his knowledge of mechanical and electrical systems to human systems.

Endenburg developed a formal organisational method called *Sociocratische Kringorganisatie Methode* (Sociocratic Circle Organizing Method) after years of experimentation and application. The method was based on the circular feedback process then called the '*circular causal feedback process*', which is now commonly referred to as the '*circular process and feedback loops*'.

The method uses a hierarchy of circles corresponding to units or departments of an organisation. The basic philosophy underlying the working of Endenburg's sociocratic organisation is summarised as follows:

- Being a circular hierarchy, the links between each circle join to form feedback loops up and down an organisation.

- Policy decisions that pertain to the allocation of resources and constrain operational decisions, require the consent of all members of a circle.

- Day-to-day operational decisions are made by the operations leader within the policies established in circle meetings.

- Policy decisions affecting more than one circle's domain are made by a higher circle formed by representatives from each circle.

- The structure of linked circles that make decisions by consent aims the efficiency of a hierarchy while preserving the equivalence of the circles and their members.

Essential principles of Sociocracy

There are four principles underlying sociocracy. However, it must be noted that, in his original formulations of the Sociocratic Circle Organizing Method, Endenburg proposed only three principles and regarded the fourth principle (elections by consent) not as a separate principle but as a method for making decisions by consent when there are several choices. However, many people misunderstood that elections of people to roles and responsibilities are allocations of resources and, thus, policy decisions. To emphasise the importance of making these decisions also by consent in the circle meetings, Endenburg separated it and proposed it as the fourth to convey its importance.

Principle 1: Consent governs all policy decision-making

All policy decisions are made by consent and consent alone; decisions are made when there are no remaining 'paramount objections'.

Objections are encouraged to give vent to every stakeholder's concern, a process that is called 'objection harvesting'. A decision-making process that focusses first on the objections leads to a more efficient decision making. Objections must, however, be reasoned and argued, and must be based on the ability of the objector to work productively toward the goals of the organisation

Principle 2: Organisation in circles

A sociocratic organisation comprises a hierarchy of semi-autonomous circles which, unlike autocratic hierarchies, does not constitute a power structure.

Each circle governs a specific area of responsibility within the broader policies of the larger organisation. As such, it has the responsibility to execute, measure, and control its own processes in order to achieve its allocated goals. It is also responsible for its own development and the development of its members. As 'integral education', a circle and its members are expected to determine what they need to know to remain competitive in their field and to meet the allocated objectives of their circle.

Principle 3: Double-linking

Individuals that act as links function as members of their own circles and also the next higher circle. These links form a feedback loop between circles. The logical links are a circle's elected operational leader, who represents the circles' interests in the next higher circle.

At the highest level of the organisation, there is a 'top circle', similar to a Board of Directors, the difference being the 'top circle' does not rule, but works within the policies of the circle structure.

The 'top circle' includes the Chief Executive Officer, at least one representative of the general management circle and external experts in law, government, finance, community etc. who connect the organisation with the community and the country. All members have full knowledge of the organisation's mission. In a corporation, it could also include a representative of the shareholders.

Each of these circle members participates fully in decision-making in the top circle.

Principle 4: Elections by consent

This principle is an extension of the first principle.

Individuals are elected to their roles and entrusted with their individual responsibilities by consensus and in open discussion.

Members of a circle can nominate themselves or any other member of the circle, presenting reasons for their choice. After discussion, people can change their nominations, and the discussion leader will announce the election of a person who has received the strongest support for that role. Some circle members may object, which will lead to a further discussion. For a role that many people may be interested in, the discussion may continue over several rounds. The circle may also decide to choose someone who is not a current member of the circle.

Important notes

- The sociocratic principles are interdependent and the application of all four of them is essential for an organisation to function sociocratically. Each principle supports the successful application of the others.

- The principles require transparency in an organisation. All members of the organisation must have access to information because decision-making is distributed throughout the organisation; the only exceptions being the proprietary knowledge and any information that would jeopardise the security of the organisation or its clients. All financial transactions and policy decisions are transparent to members of the organisation and its clients.

- Sociocratic organisations apply the circular feedback process of directing-doing-measuring to the design of work processes. In business organisations, as compensation is based on a market rate salary, plus long-term and short-term payments, based on the performance and success of a circle, the operational practices of sociocratic organisations are compatible with the best practices of contemporary management theory.

- Sociocracy clearly differentiates between 'consent' and 'consensus' in order to emphasise that circle decisions are not expected to produce 'a consensus'. It doesn't mean agreement or solidarity. Understanding this distinction is paramount for successful working of a truly sociocratic organisation.

In sociocracy, consent is defined as 'no objections,' and objections are based on one's ability to work toward the aims and objectives of the organisation. Members discussing an idea in consent-based governance commonly ask themselves if it is 'good enough for now, safe enough to try'. If not, then there is an objection, which leads to a search for an acceptable adaptation of the original proposal to gain consent.

To exemplify and illustrate the difference between the two, *Sociocratisch Centrum* co-founder, Reijmer, has said: 'By consensus, I must convince you that I am in the right; by consent, you ask whether you can live with the decision.'

Democracy versus Sociocracy

For the benefit of readers, the difference between democracy and sociocracy is illustrated by a simple example as follows:

- A decision-making group comprises eleven members, nos. 1-11.

- The group has to decide the venue of a group holiday in summer.

- The sub-group A, comprising five members (nos. 1 to 5), propose Shimla as the holiday destination; the sub-group B, comprising four members (nos. 6 to 9), propose Kashmir; the remaining two members (nos. 10 and 11) are independent and both are undecided.

If the Indian democratic system was used to decide the final venue, the decision process would possibly follow the sequence:

- Democracy follows majority vote. In the current situation, a party that wins more than fifty per cent votes (ie six votes) should be able to decide the holiday destination.

- The sub-group A, with five votes, is short of just one vote to attain the majority vote. The group members look towards the two independent members for support.

- The sub-group B, with four votes, is short of two votes to attain the majority vote. Similar to sub-group A members, the sub-group B members also look to the two independent members for support.

- The two independent members, nos. 10 and 11, see this situation an opportunity to feel important and bag some incentives.

- Following an aggressive, behind-the-curtain, lobbying process involving offering of favours and some incentives (bribe), the sub-group A manages to secure the vote of no. 10 and the sub-group B manages to secure the vote of no. 11.

- Due to a majority vote, therefore, the sub-group A succeeds in getting Shimla chosen as the holiday destination for the entire group.

- The sub-group unwillingly accepts the decision. They wanted to go to Kashmir, but instead are forced to go to Shimla. They sulk with the outcome of the voting process and are left to feel as losers.

The above process illustrates that, due to the majority vote decision-making process, a democratic system does not take care of all voters. On the contrary, in a sociocratic system, the decision-making process will follow a consensus process and everyone is taken care of, as illustrated below:

- The system requires the members to take decision based on consensus.

- All members are required to provide reasons why they prefer their choice of holiday destination.

- An open discussion is undertaken by all members.

- The members of the sub-group A cite personal security and a relatively shorter travelling distance as their prime reasons behind their choice of Shimla, whereas the members of the sub-group B cite the variety of scenic destinations in Kashmir behind their choice.

- The sub-group A is able to convince the members of sub-group B and the two independent members with their reasoning and succeed in securing their consent to go to Shimla.

- The entire group, thus, agrees that due to security issues in Kashmir, Shimla offers a safer destination. All members of the group also agree that they could consider Kashmir as their next holiday destination subject to a review of security situation there.

The above sociocratic decision-making process follows a logical process, based on rationale, for the sake of overall well-being of the group. It leaves no one sulking or feeling like a loser.

Sociocracy, thus, truly serves the essence of democracy, as explained above. All people are served in sociocracy whereas only the majority are taken care of in democracy.

Transition to sociocracy

India is a young nation, a flawed democracy, vastly uneducated and backward in many respects. The country is heavily overpopulated, with an unsustainable population growth. It is a developing economy, with lopsided and skewed development.

The country lives in several ages at the same time, with more than seventy per cent people living in underdeveloped villages, with no or poor educational and civil infrastructure.

The country is ridden with numerous historical social divisions—religious and sub-religious; ethnic and sub-ethnic; castes, regions etc. which have been fully exploited by the corrupt politicians over past decades for their own gains. These divisions have resulted in differential degrees of inertia within the country, with different parts moving in different directions.

Many desperate people wonder how the country can move to any other system—sociocracy or dictatorship—especially after it has been corrupted by the Indian version of democracy during the last seven decades. They believe it is practically impossible to do so. The strong brotherhood within the bureaucracy and political fraternity will oppose tooth and nail even on a sniff of any conceptual change in the ideology or any actual change in the system of governance. One must note that seven decades is an extremely short period of time in the history of a country. If one wills, one can bring about any sea change, provided people want the change—a change for the better— before it is too late! Once the change has been brought about, it will not take much time for the country to notice a positive difference and adapt to the new system. Indian democracy will be a forgotten chapter as soon as the people notice positive changes in the social, political and ecological environments in the country.

Indian democracy has benefited many rich and powerful people, who will raise a hue and cry against any such change. The heavily corrupted social environment and political system have undoubtedly empowered them, with nothing beyond their reach. They love the system, whilst falsely claiming that they love their country. They will throw in their kitchen sink (colloquially Australian) to fight. Understandably, it will never be easy for the country to move into an alternative system of governance. A seamless change is difficult, if not impossible. No change will be without hiccups.

In engineering, like other human systems, a transitional system is used to facilitate a change. In the context of this book, a dictatorship (benevolent, of course), such as virtually seen during the state of Emergency in a country, is deemed to provide a suitable and effective transition. The length of the transition (i.e. term of the dictatorship) will depend upon how fast the transitional administration will be able to create a new sociocratic system for effective implementation in the country. It will not be unreasonable to allow at least 25 years for the dictatorship to do its work.

The readers must note that the following paragraphs provide only a brief conceptual outline and philosophy about how a change could be initiated, and not any nuts and bolts for the change, all of which will, however, be required in a detailed plan prior to initiating the change.

The initiator, i.e. the face of the change could be one of the following:

- The Prime Minister of the country: This change will be relatively seamless and least disruptive. Most people in the country, especially the villagers, who comprise about 70 per cent of the population, will not be overly alarmed, many will not even notice what has actually happened. Majority of Indians will quickly start reaping fruits of decisive governance and notice that they live in a more streamlined country. The opposition parties will panic and get disoriented. They will try desperately to realign and try to work out a common front. The telecommunication sector will see an unprecedented peak in national and international calls. India's neighbours will be on their highest alert.

  Multinational corporate companies operating in India will be worried initially, but will soon settle down and carry out their business as usual, after receiving reassurances from the new administration.

  The armed forces, who report to the President of India, who is the Commander-in-Chief of the Armed Forces, will welcome the change. They will support the change to the hilt. The change will result in least violence.

- The President: The President of the country dissolves the Parliament and acquires full control in his hands. The President may himself run the country or, alternatively, appoint the current Prime Minister or the Chief of the Armed Forces as the Chief Executive of the country's new administration. The new Chief Executive will possibly appoint a cabinet to assist in the administration. The response to the change and the behaviour from the people in India, and the reaction from the international community, will be similar to the previous scenario if the Prime Minister takes over.

- Chief of the Armed Forces: This change will put the entire world on notice. The coup will be a global event, like a tsunami of titanic proportions. The news will make headlines in all newspapers of the world. The change will be disruptive for a while but the situation will settle quickly. India's neighbours will immediately switch on to the highest alert level.

It will be like a warlike situation on the border. On the ground, the military coup will send waves of excitement in the poor, exploited and the suffering masses of India and the disillusioned individuals. Anti-national elements will immediately go into hiding. Politicians, as well as the wealthy and influential people will quickly try to establish contacts with the powerful individuals in the armed forces for continuing to enjoy their concessions.

The modern-day, self-aggrandising maharajahs will, undoubtedly and without restraint, use all their power and resources to keep their power and authority by corrupting all their contacts in the new military administration. It is another thing if the military will ever fall for their tactics. Soldiers are trained to defend the country against the country's enemies—all enemies, within and outside. It will be their time to truly serve their mother country and weed out the lurking monsters undermining the nation, and they will not mess up, they never have!

It is the author's opinion that, if one of the above three scenarios doesn't occur, the country may see a people's movement across the country similar to either the French Revolution of 1879 or the Bolshevik Revolution of 1917 in Russia. The revolution may possibly spread violently across the length and breadth of the country and may last for many months or years before coming to an end. Two scenarios may emerge: either the country comes out intact, integrated and strong, or it disintegrates along religious or regional lines.

This people's coup will be the most unfortunate event in context of India's stability and survival; the country does not deserve it and it must be prevented by all stakeholders from occurring at all costs.

The New Administrative structure

The Chief Executive will be supported by an Executive Council comprising professional experts with proven credentials from all areas of public life and administration—environmental health, public health, education, science & technology, civil infrastructure, natural resources, law and justice, defence, internal security, emergency services, commerce, economy, civil administration etc.

As a measure of checks and balances, the Executive Council will have veto power. The decision making will follow the sociocratic principles, i.e. the policy decisions will follow a process of consensus, and not majority vote.

In all, the country shall have 512 local governments.

- The country shall be divided into 8 Zones: Zone 1 (north-north), Zone 2 (north-central), Zone 3 (north-east), Zone 4 (north-west), Zone 5 (central-west), Zone 6 (central-east), Zone 7 (south-west) and Zone 8 (south-west). Each Zone shall have a Zonal Council of Executive and a Zonal Council of Lawmakers.

- Each Zone shall be divided into 4 Regions: Region 1 (north-east), Region 2 (north-west), Region 3 (south-east) and Region 4 (south-west). Each Region shall have a Regional Council of Executive and a Regional Council of Lawmakers.

- Each Region shall be divided into 16 Areas: Area 1 to Area 16.

- So, for identification purposes, an area, say, Area 3 in the south-west of Jammu & Kashmir can be defined as: Zone 1/Region 4/Area 3 or Z1/R4/A3.

Each member of the Executive Council will head a Zonal sub-council of professional expertise from all eight zones who, in turn, will head Regional sub-council for all four regions from their respective zones.

Voting process

For the implementation of sociocracy and the formation of a sociocratic administrative structure, voting of the lowest tier Administrative Council of representatives in each of the 16 areas, which will mirror the Executive Council in terms of the various areas of expertise, will be undertaken by the public based on the majority vote. Considering the mass population, it will not be practical to use a sociocratic election process at this level. But, since the current party system and party politics will not be existing, one can take a leap of faith that only deserving, well qualified and popular candidates will represent the people in that area. At least three candidates, all experts in their specific field of expertise, will contest the elections for each position at the ground level. The candidate who wins the majority vote will be elected to the Administrative Council as the people's representative in his field of expertise, eg public health, education etc.

The election process will then cascade upwards. The members of 16 Administrative Councils will vote upwards to elect the members of their respective four Regional Councils of representatives sitting above them, who in turn will elect the members of the eight Zonal Councils.

Finally, the members of eight Zonal Councils will elect the Executive Council.

The armed forces of the country will report to the Chief Executive Officer.

Compulsory National Services

To develop a national character, all youth will be required to serve in the National Services—the national army, paramilitary or police—and perform jobs befitting their capability and physical build—as part of their service to the nation, for at least two years, before entering any regular job or professional training, similar to Singapore.

The two-year National service period will begin immediately after the completion of Year 10 (Matriculation).

Right to Vote

Voting rights will be linked with the completion of basic school education, at least Year 10. The prospective voters will be compulsorily required to attend school from the age of 6 up to at least the age of 16 before they are provided with the voter's card. The reason being, as the people's representatives at the ground level will be chosen by the majority vote, it is important that the votes are cast by the people who are educated and informed enough to ascertain the background and integrity of the candidates representing them in the election process.

Currently, in the Indian democratic system, it is not uncommon to see many dim-witted politicians addressing large election rallies. From their appearance and facial expressions, one can easy imagine the poor educational background of the people sitting on the ground in those rallies. Such people can be easily deceived and exploited by many slimy sweet-talking politicians.

Holistic education

India's path into a healthy, liveable, happy, bright and prosperous future lies in education and education alone. Education will remove numerous veils of ignorance and darkness from the minds of millions. It will restore the gender equality. Education will help to bring harmony amongst its various communities by instilling inter-religious inter-ethnic inter-caste, tolerance. Education will help to inculcate environmental awareness and responsibility. Education will help in India's economic and spiritual progress.

Education is India's panacea but it must first and foremost help to make good and complete human beings. As their number grows in a confined land mass, a sickening competition between the humans, at all levels, takes a significant toll on their humanness. People become anxious, angry, impatient and individualistic, ready to do anything to survive and control others.

The current educational system in India is not designed for complete human development. The Indian students will need holistic education for turning out to be complete human beings as adults.

Currently, in India, as in most other developing countries and some developed countries, most parents send their children to school, school, college, university so that their children are employable after the completion of their 'education'. Currently, education is seen a means to earn money.

The educational curriculum should be balanced – for both personal development and professional development— one that encourages the students to think critically and independently.

In addition to the traditional curricula for employability, arts and literature; mathematics and sciences, engineering and technology, the curriculum must have equal provision whereby the students are made to develop the following, not in any particular order, during their school years:

- Respect for their immediate and wider environment and ecology;

- Respect for inherent human dignity;

- Respect for all fellow citizens and the citizens of the wider world, without prejudice or bias against people based on religion and creed; gender and sexual orientation; ethnicity and colour; language and level of education; profession etc.;

- Respect for the inherent dignity of work;
- High awareness for the importance of environmental sustainability;
- Environmental ethics and environmental responsibility;
- Social ethics and social responsibility; and
- Common morality.

Holistic education must make the students realise their essential relationship with the ecology and environment on the planet, their interdependence on flora and fauna, their dependence on the role and input of the wider mankind, all of which make their survival possible on the planet.

Education must make them unselfish and responsible towards all people around them. They must be made to truly understand that any selfish act on their part will potentially endanger all life forms on the planet, including theirs, as no human being can survive on his own without the input of billions of humans and life forms around them.

What does it take to impart holistic education to the students?

Top-down flow process

It would take a whole new system comprising a '*top-down*' educational process, implemented by the Central Government and directed right from the top, to holistically educate the whole country before the students are to be educated. Before young lives receive holistic education, it is essential their parents, older siblings, neighbours and entire communities are educated, via a well-coordinated and time-framed process that should flow from the top and reach the young lives at the bottom of the social chain. This process looks a mammoth and Herculean task, practically impossible to be implemented within a reasonable timeframe in the context of India's large size and population. Are there any alternatives to the '*top-down*' education process?

Bottom-up flow process

The education process could be a *bottom-up* process, where the process could start at the grass roots with the education of young lives in their early years. The young students would then be used to educate their older siblings and parents at home, and then their communities. The young children would, thus, be empowered to be a vital starting point of the whole educational process. This way education will percolate from the bottom to the top. The process will be analogous to how the groundwater normally seeps upwards in the soil by a process called 'capillary action', by surface tension and against gravity, by tens of metres. Thereafter, it flows through the roots of a tree and then the sap flows upwards through the main trunk of the tree and reaches each and every branch and finally every leaf of every branch of the tree. For this process, however, it is important that the groundwater is not too deep, and the tree gets enough sunshine to allow photosynthesis to occur, otherwise the tree needs adequate watering on a regular basis to thrive. The educators (teachers) must be holistically educated, efficient, committed and dedicated, and most importantly empowered by the Government to nurture the young minds and shape them holistically. The mantra thus becomes: '*Empower the teacher to empower the child student, who will then empower the community with holistic education.*'

Coming back to India's population and the urgency—does the nation have the time to allow only one of the above two processes? Given that time is of the essence, is there any other alternative?

Yes, there is!

Multi-directional flow process

This is the most aggressive process and capable of achieving a relatively much faster progress. It will be a hybrid process between the above two—*top-down* and *bottom-up* processes. In addition, it will also allow lateral educational process where required, at appropriate levels of education to speed up the process and fill up the voids that may be left by the vertical flows.

All above processes are possible in theory, but each one of these will be effective only if the following conditions are met:

- A blueprint for the whole process is prepared by experts and made ready for implementation.

- The administrative process is headed and overseen by a visionary leader.

- The educational process is implemented by a team of dedicated, committed and sincere administrators and educators, via a corruption free process.

- Every member of the team is deemed to be accountable for progress.

- All members of the team should be contracted through mutual agreement to meet clearly defined Key Performance Indicators (KPI).

- All teachers should be appraised regularly for their

performance. The reward should be keeping one's job and the punishment should be losing it.

- The process of implementation at the grass roots is undertaken by holistically well-trained, academically brilliant and well-paid, honest and committed educators and teachers.

- The Government continuously campaigns for holistic education.

- The education process is armed with a healthy budget, much more than what is currently allocated, and provided with adequate educational infrastructure and the state-of-the-art technology—audio-visual medium and the internet.

- All children up to Year 10 receive free but compulsory, top quality education as per their Right to Education.

Any sensible person in India will dismiss this whole project and deem it practically impossible considering the inertia and corruption in the country; thus, a need for a benevolent dictator. The need for a dictator magnifies due to corrupt practices followed by teachers and the entire community in the whole process, as illustrated by some realistic examples about the ground situation:

The first example is about the various environmental models that the curriculum requires the students to prepare in a classroom environment.

- In a few schools, only a few teachers are capable of making the models in the classroom environment and, due to lack of resources, the students cannot make the models at school. In most others schools, the teachers are not adequately trained and capable of making the models. Also, they lack the resources.

- In most cases, therefore, the teachers ask the students to get the models prepared from home.

- Most parents don't have the capability to make the models.

- Some private booksellers and tutors see this as a business opportunity. They prepare the models and sell them at the bookshops.

- The parents buy the models from the market and the students carry them happily to school.

- The teachers tick the boxes on a sheet of paper that the models have been prepared. All are happy.

A few questions arise:

- Was the objective of the curriculum met? No!

- What did the students learn? Not much!

- Who benefitted from the curriculum? The booksellers and private tutors.

- Did the exercise help the economy? Yes.

As per a common practice, many private schools direct their students to buy all stationery and text books from only their preferred vendors, a practice that reflects business alliances between the schools and the vendors.

So, what must be done?

- As an essential controlling measure, squeeze the population growth to a manageable level; over population and a high population growth rate are the root cause of most serious issues and social sicknesses in India.

- The government must launch an aggressive campaign for 'holistic' education.

- The education ministry must identify an army of dedicated and passionate students and teachers for the specialised 'holistic' training, but based purely on aptitude, merit and commitment, through open competition and interviews. At no cost must reservations or nepotism or corruption be allowed for the selection of trainee teachers.

- The selected trainee teachers must be provided the specialised in-house training through an intensive programme similar to the civil servants.

- To attract the best minds, the trainees must be provided with all required facilities and paid handsome stipend during the training and, thereafter, top-of-the-scale salaries upon graduation.

- All existing and new schools must be provided with the required civil infrastructure and the resources— financial, technological (reliable electric power supply, including generators; over-head projectors; computers and internet connectivity), and the necessary human resources to implement and run the holistic educational programme.

- Attendance of students must be compulsory. Defaulting parents must be penalised.

- It would be useful if parents also are involved as partners by the schools and the Government, as additional resources in overseeing and running the programme, which will speed up the pace of the education and educate the parents themselves. This will prove to be a multi-directional flow process—*top-down, bottom-up* and *lateral flows.*

The educational infrastructure

The Indian population at present is believed be in the order of 1.35 billion.

As per Wikipedia, as of June 2017, the country is believed to have a total of 696 universities, distributed in 32 states and territories.[5]

The oldest universities (established 1857) are the University of Mumbai, the University of Madras and the University of Calcutta. The break-up is as follows:

- Central universities: 47

- State universities: 367

- Private universities: 282

In addition, India also has 123 *deemed universities.* By definition, *deemed university* refers to a status of autonomy granted to an institution by the Department of Higher Education on the advice of the University Grants Commission (UGC).

In comparison, the state of Western Australia (WA) where the author lives, has five universities. The University of Western Australia (UWA) is the oldest university established in 1911. It is amongst the world's top 1 per cent of academic institutions

---

[5] https://en.wikipedia.org/wiki/List_of_universities_in_India

and one of the top 100 research-intensive universities in the world. The population of WA is about two million and it has five universities. Considering university education is seen as one of largest exports of Australia, all universities try to attract overseas students. Due to this, the universities in Australia are run as corporate companies and the students are seen as clients. If overseas students are taken out of equation in WA, the state would need just about two universities to accommodate local students; that would make it one university per million of the population.

Extrapolating the aforementioned 'demand to supply' equation, India will need at last 1,350 proper universities. Therefore, it appears India will need to double the number of universities to meet the demands of its current population. Of course, if the population is allowed to keep growing at the present rate, the demand will keep increasing.

As per Wikipedia, the 2011 Census data has indicated India has a total number of 649,481 villages.[6]

To establish a good educational infrastructure, India should ideally have the following educational infrastructure to meet the demands of its massive population:

- One primary school in every village, i.e. at least 650,000 primary schools
- One secondary school every 10 villages, i.e. at least 65,000 secondary schools
- One college (up to Bachelor's level) for every 50 villages, i.e. at least 13,000 colleges

---

[6] (https://en.wikipedia.org/wiki/List_of_villages_in_India)

- One proper university for every 500 villages (catering to 10 Bachelor's level colleges), i.e. at least 1,300 universities (note: this figures tallies with the number estimated earlier based on WA's example).

The priorities for the education system should be:

- Deliver at least one year's growth in learning for every student every year;

- Equip every child to be a creative, connected and engaged learner in the present rapidly changing world;

- Cultivate an adaptive, innovative and continuously improving education system.

The basic objectives for education infrastructure and policies must be to:

- Lay the foundations for learning;

- Equip every student to grow and succeed in a fast paced changing world;

- Create, support and value a profession of expert educators;

- Empower and support the schools—Principals, teachers, student representatives; and

- Raise and achieve aspirations through innovations and continuous improvement in the curriculum, the subject content, and the quality of teachers and the method of teaching.

Back to the start...

India needs a major overhaul to improve its liveability, educational infrastructure, and the environment. Population growth, Kashmir issue, pollution and corruption need to be sincerely addressed with urgency.

The present deteriorating conditions, especially in the urban areas which are fast turning into gas chambers warrant drastic and urgent measures, such as 'one-child' policy, immediate ban on immigration from rural to urban areas, crackdown on everything that pollutes air and drinking water, compulsory and free schooling of all children across the country, quick and harsh punitive measures to deal with all lawbreakers. But the existing political infrastructure will not allow any such measures to be undertaken. Therefore, India needs a new system of governance—a benevolent dictatorship—that can address all above issues in a timely manner and without many hurdles.

Both education and Kashmir need urgent and undivided attention, with fit-for-the-purpose approaches to deal with them. Without holistic education permeating through the length, breadth and depth of the country, India will continue to be home to a significant number of uneducated, unhealthy and unhappy people.

The political monster of Kashmir instability has the potential to destabilise the whole country if not controlled soon. Kashmir is the geographical head of India and, therefore, it must be at peace. Kashmir problem must be dealt with sincerity, firmness and pragmatism. Since its independence, India has been constantly embroiled with it and, as a result, a significant portion of the budget goes towards it every year, leaving lesser resources for health and education in the country. Sadly, the current budget allocations for health and education are only about 1.2 per cent and 3.8 per cent of GDP, respectively. These essential areas need much more than that; but that is only possible if unnecessary distractions like

Kashmir are addressed once and for all.

To conclude, the author reiterates that for survival, sustainability and health, India needs to implement the following on an urgent basis:

- *One-child Policy*: As a drastic control measure against the population growth, which must be driven and enforced by the state;

- *Holistic Educational Programme*: This must comprise a compulsory, but free, education of ALL children up to Year 10, via a reformed system that combines arts, humanities, environment, ethics, social and moral science with the STEM education—through top quality, well paid, well-qualified and well-trained teachers, with strong passion to teach effectively and make a positive difference in the country, and by the provision of all necessary educational infrastructure;

- *National Service Programme:* A two-year compulsory *National Service Programme* (NSP) is a must for the country for building national character and integration after the successful completion of Year 10 examination;

- *Right to Vote*: The country must implement the *Right to Vote*, which must be granted only after the successful completion of the NSP; and

- *Uniform Civil Law*: For national integration and national character, the country must introduce a *Uniform Civil Law* across all religions, castes and ethnicities.

A double-headed poisonous snake of corruption and politics, which has been thriving and flourishing in the Indian democratic system since 1947, will never allow implementation of any of the above. So, this makes a genuine and pressing case for someone from within the country, with vision, wisdom, fearlessness, benevolence and leadership qualities, taking over the country, as a benevolent dictator to implement all that is necessary to save the country from imploding and from a potential anarchy in the future; and instead lead it towards good health and sustainability through *sociocracy*, which is a much fairer and cleaner system of governance than democracy. Sociocracy does not allow much room for corrupted politics like what is seen in India nowadays.

Time to think fast, hard and deep, and act earnestly!

***

References

Aghion, P, Howitt P, Brant-Collett, M,& García-Peñalosa, C (1998). *Endogenous Growth Theory:* MIT press. https://mitpress.mit.edu/ books/endogenous-growth-theory.

Ali, A & Shubra, C (2010). *Efforts to reverse the trend of enrolment decline in computer science programs.* The Journal of Issues in Informing Science and Information Technology, 7, pp 209-224.http://iisit.org/ Vol7/IISIT-TOCwithTitleLink.pdf.

ATAL Tinkering Laboratories—Innovation Challenge (2017).http://niti. gov.in/content/atal-tinkering-laboratories-%E2%80%93-innovation-challenge.

Barber, M & Mourshed, M (2007). *How the world's best-performing school systems come out on top*: McKinsey & Company.https://www. mckinsey.com/industries/social-sector/our-insights/how-the-worlds-best-performing-school-systems-come-out-on-top.

Barro, R J (1991). *Economic growth in a cross section of countries.* The quarterly journal of economics, 106 (2), pp 407-443.https://www. econ.nyu.edu/user/debraj/Courses/Readings/BarroGrowth.pdf

Benhabib, J & Spiegel, M M (1994). *The role of human capital in economic development evidence from aggregate cross-country data.* Journal of monetary economics, 34(2), pp 143-173.https://ideas.repec.org/a/ eee/moneco/v34y1994i2p143-173.html

Burgess, B (2011). *The Educational Theory of Socrates.* http://www. newfoundations.com/GALLERY/Socrates.html

Chambliss, J J Aristotle BC (384 – 322) - *Education for a Common End.* http://education.stateuniversity.com/pages/1763/Aristotle-384-322-B-C-E.html

Dewey, J (1934). *Art as experience.* New York, NY: The Berkley Publishing Group

Dewey, J (1938). *Experience and education.* New York: Collier

Dillon, A (2004). *Education in Plato's Republic.* Santa Clara University. https://www.scu.edu/character/resources/education-in-platos-republic/

Duignan, B and Cranston, M *Jean-Jacques Rousseau. Encyclopaedia Britannica.*https://www.britannica.com/biography/Jean-Jacques-Rousseau

Doyle, M E and Smith, M K (2007) *Jean-Jacques Rousseau on nature, wholeness and education.*http://infed.org/mobi/jean-jacques-rousseau-on-nature-wholeness-and-education/

Elias, C (2009). *The decline of natural sciences*: confronting diminishing interest, fewer scientists and poorer working conditions in western countries. A comparative analysis between Spain and the United Kingdom. Papers: revista de sociologia (93), pp 69-79.

Finland: Teacher and Principal Quality (2017).http://ncee.org/what-we-do/center-on-international-education-benchmarking/top-performing-countries/finland-overview/finland-teacher-and-principal-quality.

GDP in Science Research. 27 November 2014

Hanushek, E A, Wößmann, L, Jamison, E A& Jamison, DT (2008): *Education and economic growth*, Education Next, (8(2).

Hare, R M (1989). *Plato on Education.* Oxford University Press. http://infed.org/mobi/plato-on-education/

Hattie, J (2008). *Visible learning: A synthesis of over 800 meta-analyses relating to achievement*: Routledge.

Indian School Education System An Overview (December 2014). https://www.britishcouncil.in/sites/default/files/indian_school_education_system_-_an_overview_1.pdf

Indian *Science & Engineering Fair.*(2017). http://sciencesociety.in/index.html.

Innovation in science Pursuit for Inspired Research (2017).http://www.online.inspire.gov.in/.

INSPIRE Awards – MANAK (2017). At a form http://nif.org.in/inspire_awards.

Jamie (2009).*Great Thinkers on Self-Education*: Socrates http://

selfmadescholar.com/b/2009/06/02/great-thinkers-on-self-education-socrates/

Lavergne, M, Doppelhofer, G & Miller, R I (2004). *Determinants of long-term growth*: A Bayesian averaging of classical estimates (BACE) approach. *The American economic review*, 94 (4), pp 813-835.

Lee H PD(1955). *Plato. The Republic. London*: Penguin.

Lee, M (1994). *Plato's philosophy of education*: Its implication for current education. https://epublications.marquette.edu/dissertations/AAI9517932/

Malti (2017). *Need and importance of STEM Education in Indian Schools*. Indian Journal of Research, 6(1), pp 852-853.

Mankiw, N G, Romer, D & Weil, D N (1992).*A contribution to the empirics of economic growth.*The quarterly journal of economics, 107 (2), pp. 407-437.

Mays, E (2014). *The Educational Theory of Aristotle.* http://www.newfoundations.com/GALLERY/Aristotle.html

Muirhead, JH (1904). *Wordsworth's Ideal of Early Education.* The University of Chicago Press International Journal of Ethics, Vol. 14, No. 3 (Apr., 1904), pp 339-352. https://www.jstor.org/stable/2375922?seq=3#page_scan_tab_contents

National Children Science Congress.(2017). http://www.ncsc.co.in/.

National Council of Educational Research and Training.(2018). http://ncert.nic.in/.

National Innovation and Science Agenda Report (2015). Sourced from Office of Chief Scientist, Australian Government website: https://www.innovation.gov.au/page/national-innovation-and-science-agenda-report.

National Policy on Education (2016). http://www.nuepa.org/New/download/NEP2016/ReportNEP.pdf.

National Policy on Skill Development and Entrepreneurship (2015). http://www.skilldevelopment.gov.in/National-Policy-2015.html.

Nelson, R R & Phelps, E S (1966). *Investment in humans, technological diffusion, and economic growth.* The American economic review, 56 (1/2), pp 69-75. http://federation.ens.fr/wheberg/parischoeco/formation/fcses/_boitdocu/0607s1_lect02_a.pdf.

Paul, Rand Elder, L (1997). *Foundation For Critical Thinking*.http://www.criticalthinking.org/pages/socratic-teaching/606

Piaget, J (1960). *The psychology of intelligence*. Totowa, NJ: Littlefield, Adams & Co.

Robb, F C (2009). *Aristotle and education*. https://www.tandfonline.com/doi/pdf/10.1080/01619564309535765

Reynolds, K (2014). *Perceptions of childhood*. https://www.bl.uk/romantics-and-victorians/articles/perceptions-of-childhood

Rothwell, J (2013). *The hidden STEM economy*: Metropolitan Policy Program at Brookings.https://www.brookings.edu/research/the-hidden-stem-economy/

Sarangapani, PM (2017). *Three Challenges Facing Indian Science Education*. http://www.esocialsciences.org/eSS_essay/Science_education/Three%20Challenges%20Facing%20India_Sarangapani.pdf.

Schon, D A (1992). *The Theory of Inquiry*: Dewey's Legacy to Education. Curriculum Inquiry, 22(2) 119-139.

School Education in India (2014-15). http://www.dise.in/Downloads/Publications/Documents/U-DISE-SchoolEducationInIndia-2014-15.pdf.

Science Exhibition (2017). http://www.ncert.nic.in/programmes/science_exibition/index_science.html.

Science Express (2017). http://www.sciencexpress.in/

Science, Technology and Innovation Policy (2013) http://www.dst.gov.in/st-system-india/science-and-technology-policy-2013.

Science, technology, innovation—keys to India's progress: Modi 19 July 2017). https://www.deccanchronicle.com/nation/current-affairs/190717/science-technology-innovation-keys-to-indias-progress-modi.html.

Scientist, A Ootc (2014). *Science, Technology, Engineering and Mathematics: Australia's Future*: Office of the Chief Scientist.

Singh, S P (2014) *AIYD Education Taskforce Report*: Expanding horizons of Education Transformation between Australia and India. Sourced from Australia India Youth Dialogue website: http://aiyd.org/publications/.

Sjøberg, S & Schriener, C (2005). *How do learners in different cultures relate to science and technology.* Asia-Pacific Forum on science learning and teaching. https://www.eduhk.hk/apfslt/download/v6_issue2_files/foreword.pdf

Stewart, V (2010). *Raising teacher quality.* Educational Leadership, 2011. http://www.ascd.org/publications/educational-leadership/dec10/vol68/num04/Raising-Teacher-Quality-Around-the-World.aspx.

Thomas, B & Watters, JJ (2017). *Perspectives on Australian, Indian and Malaysian approaches to STEM education.* International Journal of Educational Development, 45, pp 42-53. https://eprints.qut.edu.au/89486/

Tytler, R, Osborne, J, Williams, G, Tytler, K & Cripps Clark, J (2008). *Opening up pathways*: Engagement in STEM across the primary-secondary school transition. https://docs.education.gov.au/system/files/doc/other/openpathinscitechmathenginprimsecschtrans.pdf

UK Essays. (2018). *Impact of Aristotle on Education.* https://www.ukessays.com/essays/philosophy/aristotle-education-plato.php

WH Magazine. *Socrates and his philosophy of education.* http://wh-magazine.com/educational-philosophy/socrates-and-his-philosophy-of-education

World Bank, 2018: *World Development Report 2018*: Learning to Realize Education's Promise, Washington, DC. World Bank. Doi:10.1596/978-1-4648-1096-1. License: Creative Commons Attribution CC BY 3.0 IGO